RUSSIA
AND THE
WEST

Gorbachev and the Politics of Reform

JERRY HOUGH

SECOND EDITION

A TOUCHSTONE BOOK
Published by Simon & Schuster Inc.
New York   London   Toronto   Sydney   Tokyo   Singapore

Touchstone
Simon & Schuster Building
Rockefeller Center
1230 Avenue of the Americas
New York, New York 10020

First Touchstone Edition, 1990

TOUCHSTONE and colophon are registered trademarks
of Simon & Schuster Inc.

Designed by Irving Perkins Associates
Manufactured in the United States of America

10 9 8 7 6 5 4 3 2 1

10 9 8 7 6 5 4 3 2 1 Pbk.

Library of Congress Cataloging in Publication Data

Hough, Jerry F.,
    Russia and the West : Gorbachev and the politics of reform / Jerry
Hough.—1st Touchstone ed.

        p. cm.
    1. Soviet Union—Politics and government—1917–   2. Gorbachev.
Mikhail Sergeevich. 1931–   . 3. Soviet Union—Foreign relations—
United States.   4. United States—Foreign relations—Soviet Union.
5. Soviet Union—Foreign relations—1917–   I. Title.
DK266.H59   1990
947.085'4—dc20   89-26363
                                                              CIP

ISBN 0-671-61839-3
ISBN 0-671-67558-3 Pbk.

The author is grateful for permission to reprint from *Almost at the End* by
Yevgeny Yevtushenko, translated from the Russian by Antonia W. Bouis,
Albert C. Todd, and Yevgeny Yevtushenko. Copyright © 1987 by Yevgeny
Yevtushenko. Translation copyright © 1987 by Antonia W. Bouis, Albert C.
Todd, and Yevgeny Yevtushenko. Reprinted by permission of Henry Holt
and Company, Inc.

To Sheila Fitzpatrick,
from whom I learned much about Soviet history

Contents

Introduction

INFORMED Americans have lately been shocked by one event after another in the Soviet Union—the election of a pro-reform general secretary, the release of Andrei Sakharov, the withdrawal of Soviet troops from Afghanistan and their unilateral reduction in Europe, competitive elections to a new legislature, demands of the Baltic Communist leaders for sovereignty, strikes in Siberian coal mines, the toleration of free elections in Eastern Europe. Each of these events contradicts everything we have been told about the Soviet Union. With each surprise we assume that Gorbachev has made some mistake and is therefore closer to a coup d'etat and anarchy, but we have never stepped back and tried to rethink our assumptions. In fact, Gorbachev has been completing a classic consolidation of power, and the Soviet Union is nowhere near anarchy. It is we who have been wrong, not Gorbachev. Already, because of our lack of understanding, we have made serious miscalculations in policy, and even more crucial ones lie ahead.

The great paradox is that during the 1970s we unconsciously

changed our most basic assumptions about the Soviet Union and its evolution. Our new assumptions led us to incorrect predictions, while our old assumptions would have pointed us in the right direction—and, indeed, did so for those who continued to accept them.

We used to believe that the democratic revolution of March 1917 represented the natural line of development of Russian history, and that the Communist (Bolshevik) Revolution was an aberration made possible only by the accident of World War I. Now we see the Bolshevik Revolution and the Soviet regime that followed it as the natural continuation of an authoritarian, xenophobic, security-oriented Russian political culture.

We used to believe that the essence of Communist ideology was a drive to transform society, an obsession with increasing national power, and a willingness to sacrifice the present for the future. Now we see Communist ideology as a conservative force, dedicated to the preservation of a soft life for the workers, and a major obstacle to the transformation needed if Russia is to maintain national power.

We used to believe that the managerial class was the suppressed middle class—a potential force for change as its numbers increased over the decades. This, for example, was the position of the conservative French thinker Raymond Aron in the 1950s. Now we see the managerial class as "bureaucrats," a powerful force for maintaining the dictatorship. For some reason they want to preserve the restrictions on their travel, the dullness of their newspapers. They want the one- or two-bedroom apartments they had under Brezhnev—in order to ensure that the workers they manage will not be disciplined.

We used to believe that the Soviet political system had fatally weak controls over the power of a General Secretary. We saw as the central element of his authority his ability to build a political machine by appointing regional party secretaries from above. Now we see only the obstacles in front of him and the restraints upon him, and we see the party apparatus as his biggest enemy. His only hope, we say, is to end the appointment of regional party secretaries from above and their election from below.

Even when we haven't abandoned our old assumptions, we have refused to accept their implications for the Soviet Union. We still recognize that protectionism is harmful for innovation, efficiency, and quality, and we naturally would assume that 70 years of total protectionism would result in disaster. Yet, we do not interpret Soviet economic problems in these terms (although it would be accurate to do so). We do not draw the correct conclusion that any Soviet leadership committed to the restoration of national power absolutely must open the country and the economy to the outside world in order to attack the protectionism enjoyed by the country's monopolistic ministries.

The same confusion marks our understanding of international relations. Everyone who has thought seriously about the international situation knows two things. First, the Russians no longer face a threat from Europe; they have found relations with countries like Austria and Finland more advantageous than relations with Communist "satellites" like Poland and Romania. Second, China and India are countries with atomic weapons and a billion people on the Soviet border, and they will evolve into huge superpowers sometime in the 21st century. Yet, few draw the obvious conclusion that the natural consequence is the gravitation of the Soviet Union toward the Western countries in response to its evolving national interest. And a person who was told that a new Soviet leader was rejecting many aspects of the old ideology would be particularly likely to think that national interest would be decisive in Soviet foreign policy.

The tragedy is that our old assumptions were basically correct. Lenin *was* the great fanatical extremist of 1917, not the Swedish Social Democrat described in contemporary Soviet sources; and left-wing extremism and right-wing extremism *are* quite similar. Lenin's revolution *was* an unnatural break with Russian history. The most prominent recent example of right-wing extremism has been the Ayatollah Khomeini's revolution in Iran, and, strange as it may seem, the Bolshevik Revolution can be seen as the Khomeini revolution of Russian history in that it was anti-West (at least anti-*modern*-West) at its core.

Like Khomeini's program, Leninism appealed to the anxieties of the mass of villagers streaming into the city during a pell-mell industrialization program. Although the previous two Russian tsars had been politically reactionary, the great British historian B. H. Sumner was correct when he said, "During the half-century between emancipation and the First World War, the industrial revolution profoundly changed the economic structure of Russian life, and in so doing westernized it to a far greater extent than previously."[1] The half-peasants, half-workers of Russia reacted to this westernization and those promoting it much as their counterparts did in Iran. Lenin's program responded to these feelings.

Lenin charged that European economic institutions totally exploited both domestic workers and less developed foreign countries. (He spoke of colonies, but Russian workers knew Russia had great foreign investment.) He viciously denounced European democracy as fraudulent "parliamentarism," and he treated the culture and values of Western Europe as a "superstructure" that reflected the interests of the exploiting ruling class. Although Lenin presented socialism as a successor to Western European capitalism, his program really implied a different path of development—a path emphasizing old communal values and an absence of the insecurity of the market. In a real sense the same xenophobic emotions that produced the anti-Jewish pogroms then produced the Bolshevik Revolution but now were directed at the entire Europeanized part of the population.

And, in fact, the Soviet system delivered on its implicit promises to its main supporters. The Soviet system as it evolved under Lenin and especially under Stalin protected the new city dwellers against that which was disturbing them with two Iron Curtains—one against frightening market forces, especially Western ones, and the other against modern Western culture.

Now, however, a series of things has happened. First, the Westernized elite of Peter the Great has been recreated. Not only has a huge middle class been formed, but it has very different values from the peasants and workers who were its fathers and grandfathers. The Gorbachev generation took industrialization for granted and did not find urban life as unsettling as Stalin's and Brezhnev's generations did. Moreover, the xenophobia of Stalin led to an emphasis on Russian literature in the schools, and the students of the Gorbachev generation absorbed the Western values of the nineteenth-century elite that were reflected in this literature. Gorbachev himself has reported with warmth that he still knows many poems from school by heart.[2]

But whatever the reason, we have observed the youth of Russia since the mid-1950s and know much about it. Certainly, unlike the youth of Teheran in the 1970s and of Russia in 1917, most Soviet youth have not seen Western ideas and fashions as satanic. Instead, they have been fascinated by jazz and blue jeans and Western films and the thought of travel to the West. Now the twenty-year-olds of the 1950s are the fifty-year-olds of the 1980s. They no longer want blue jeans, but their basic orientation to the West has not changed. The members of the educated middle class—the much maligned bureaucrats and professionals—have become a powerful force for change.

Second, the protection of frightened people from unsettling market forces meant the creation of monopolistic ministries that totally protected the country's industrialists from foreign competition. Even when foreign goods were imported in the 1970s and 1980s, the industrialists lost no business and did not have to raise the quality of their goods to world levels. Instead of bringing the Soviet Union to a position of world leadership, autarchy and protectionism meant that the country began to fall further and further behind. Even countries such as South Korea acquired the ability to produce and export sophisticated goods that the Soviet Union could not match.

Westerners wrote that "we face a long-term situation where Soviet external expansion will accompany internal decline."[3] But Gorbachev knew better. Three months before assuming power, he stated flatly that "only an intensive economy which is developing on the most modern scientific-technical basis can . . . safeguard the strength of the country's position in the international arena and allow it deservedly to enter the twenty-first century a great and prospering power."[4] Three months after assuming power, he repeated that "foreign circumstances" demanded fundamental change. Without it, Russia could not serve as a model to the rest of the world, and without it even the ability of the country to defend itself was in doubt.[5]

Third, Russians sensed, perhaps unconsciously in part, the rise of India and—especially—China on their southern border. Imagine that the United States was in a period of deep stagnation, with something clearly wrong with its economic system. Imagine that Canada on its northern border had a population of one billion people, nuclear weapons, and was surging ahead. Imagine that at the same time Mexico, on its southern border, also had a billion people and nuclear weapons—not to mention a well-justified complaint that much of the southwestern United States had been taken illegally from them a century and a half ago. Imagine that Mexico had been growing 10 to 15 percent for a decade. And imagine that the United States was totally isolated from the powers in Asia and Europe. You will then get some idea of how the Russians feel—and their anxiety is compounded by the several centuries of Mongol rule that has left deep historical fears about the threat from the East.

Fourth, the creation of a huge administrative machinery did not strengthen the power of the party organs, but weakened it. Power was concentrated in Moscow, but that was not the same as in the hands of the party leadership. As the Soviet sociologist Tatiana Zaslavskaia put it, the central feature of the Soviet system was an overconcentration of power in the middle levels—in the ministries—at the expense both of the central organs above them and of the enterprises (and regional party organs) below them.[6] The leadership had to seek more effective instruments of control and direction if it wanted to succeed, and it knew from the experience of the West that the best instruments were indirect and economic ones.

In short, as the 1970s gave way to the 1980s, an extraordinary congruence of factors was working for transformation in the Soviet Union. The broad educated public—the bureaucrats and the professionals—were eager for a relaxation of the dictatorship and an opening to the West. They were able to say that the closed nature of Soviet society was a central cause of the country's backwardness and a major threat to long-term defense. They could convincingly urge that what they wanted for themselves personally was absolutely necessary for the achievement of the most basic national goals. And the party leadership, central and regional, had come to understand that it only had the semblance of power, that most decisions were being made in monopolistic ministries.

This combination could be expected to be explosive, and it was. Leonid Brezhnev, like Mao Tse-tung in China, was powerful enough to thwart the pressures for change, but behind the facade the generation coming to power scarcely bothered to conceal its intentions. Almost every reputable Soviet economist was arguing in print that integration into the world economy and a partial use of the internal market were far more conducive to economic growth in the Third World than the Soviet model. A group so policy-oriented would not have been so unanimous if it did not have a clear sense that the next generation of leaders was virtually unanimous about the need for change.[7]

Certainly the only Politburo member under the age of fifty-five at the time of Brezhnev's death, Mikhail Gorbachev, was convinced that modernity and receptivity to Western ways was the politically advantageous message to give to the regional party secretaries and governmental officials on the Central Committee who would be selecting a new leader. Gorbachev's office in the Central Committee building in 1981, as John Chrystal, an Iowa banker with a longtime interest in Soviet agriculture, discovered, did not have the standard stodgy and formal decor. Instead, Gorbachev had deliberately decided to furnish his office with Scandinavian furniture.

When Gorbachev gave a major speech just three months before his election, he could scarcely have been more explicit in his "campaign promise" of a "deep transformation in the economy and the whole system of social relationships":

> Life puts before us a task of enormous political significance—to lead the economy out onto a qualitatively new scientific-technical and organizational-economic level. It is impossible to permit any slowness in exposing the problems which have developed or in overcoming them.[8]

Serge Schmemann, *The New York Times* bureau chief in Moscow, wrote prior to Gorbachev's election that in this speech the future general secretary "seemed to be calling for a transformation of the nation as radical as the one wrought by Stalin in the brutal industrialization drive of the 1930s."[9]

The various factors that have produced change thus far will continue to work with great power. The political back of the conservative opposition has been broken. The ideology, the sense of national pride, the tradition of sacrifice—all of these not only drive the Soviet leaders, but they provide themes that can be used to appeal for support among the broader population and even the conservatives. To the extent that Gorbachev has an opposition or potential opposition that worries him, it is from the forces of change and the intellectuals who speak for them. The danger for Gorbachev is that these forces will want to push forward even faster and that they will get out of control as in Hungary, Czechoslovakia, and Poland. It is, however, a danger that he is likely to be able to handle, at least for the rest of this century.

Paradoxically, the ethnic demonstrations that have captured so much of our attention are the central stabilizing factor for Communist rule in the Soviet Union. If the Soviet Union were an all-Russian country (in the sense that Poland has only Poles), Russian students and workers would have been in the streets demanding real democracy. They would either have achieved it already, or would be on the verge of doing so. But the Soviet Union has twenty Quebecs—areas with enough people speaking their own language to be independent countries—and full democratization would mean separatist movements in all of them. Yegor Ligachev described the situation very accurately in July 1989:

> Recently there have been calls for a multiparty system. In conditions of a federative state such as the Soviet Union, this is simply fatal. A multiparty system would mean the disintegration of the Soviet federation. . . . The Communist Party is the only real political force that rallies and unites all the country's peoples into a united union of republics. And there is no other way.[10]

Perhaps in twenty years, as sovereignty takes on a different meaning even in Western Europe, Russians will feel differently about the question, but today Ligachev speaks not only for Gorbachev, but for the vast majority of Russians. As a consequence, Gorbachev faces a relatively comfortable situation.

It is vital that the United States begin to understand what is going on. We have been like a ship without rudder or ballast on a choppy sea, and the only constant has been our anxiety and our affinity for waiting to see how it all turns out. In fact, we do not have the time simply to wait. Already Gorbachev has turned around public opinion in Western Europe, especially in West Germany. Far more is still to come.

It is not the Cold War that is over, not even just the postwar period, but the abnormal "Khomeini period" of Russian history. At the beginning of the century, frightened half-urbanized Russians turned to a demagogic fanatic who promised the overthrow of the westernizing elite and who began the process of erecting iron curtains against modern Europe. Now at the end of the century the self-confident, educated Russians are returning home to Europe.

Gorbachev understands, as we do not, that Americans have a European culture and that we Europeans—from the Elbe to California—have created a common home of 600,000,000 persons. He does not want to divide Western Europe from the United States, but rather to move Russia gradually back into our European—we would say Atlantic—community. In the 21st century, when the superpowers will be China and India with a billion people apiece, Gorbachev is thinking of a billion "Europeans" as being a formidable force themselves.

Today the Soviet Union is the only military threat to the United States, but in ten to fifteen years, war between the Russians and other Europeans (including those in the United States) will be as unthinkable as war now is between Great Britain and Germany. It will not be easy to manage this transition, all the more so because a common European home cannot long have Germans divided against their will. We will be required to rethink many of our assumptions and to learn to operate in a new environment. But unless we try to negotiate a stable transition to a new world, we will continue to force Gorbachev to follow less stable paths.

Many may think that the future has just been described in colors that are too vivid and stark. Perhaps it has. But those who have accepted the assumptions—our own old assumptions—have not been surprised by the flow of events over the last five years. The time has come for others to explore the possibility that those assumptions also illuminate the future. At the very least, they should recognize that the situation is flexible enough to enable us to reshape the contours of international relations in a way that has not been possible for decades.

1

Gorbachev
and His Generation

ON March 10, 1985, at 7:20 P.M. Konstantin Chernenko
died, the third Soviet leader to do so in two and a half
years. The next day a plenary session of the Central Committee
of the Communist party was convened to elect fifty-four-year-old
Mikhail Gorbachev as his successor. Both events were reported in
the Soviet newspapers of March 12, and the format was identical
throughout the country. The front page featured a report of Gorbachev's election, his biography, and a large photograph; the second page reported the death of the old leader and printed his
obituary and a photograph. Never before had a new Soviet leader
been able to make such an immediate show of strength and so
clearly repudiate the policies of the past.

Gorbachev had worked for nearly a quarter of a century in the
grain province of Stavropol in southern Russia and had been
brought to Moscow as Central Committee secretary in charge of
agriculture only in 1978. He was not named a voting member of
the Politburo until October 1980. And now, scarcely four years

later, he was the top man in the Soviet political system, fifteen years younger than the average age of the other Politburo members.

Andrei Gromyko, the foreign minister, gave the nominating speech. Although it had all the standard glorification of the candidate common to such speeches around the world, one paragraph had a special meaning:

> We are living in a world in which, figuratively speaking, various telescopes are trained on the Soviet Union, and there are many of them—big and small, short-range, and perhaps more long-range than short-range ones. And people look to see if they can eventually find cracks of some kind in the Soviet leadership... The Politburo's unanimous opinion is that this time too we—the party Central Committee and Politburo—will not allow our political opponents any satisfaction on this score.[1]

The official purpose of this statement was to convince the Central Committee to support Gorbachev's nomination unanimously, but the leading member of the older generation on the Politburo was also pledging to carry out Gorbachev's foreign policy faithfully. Basically, though, the statement had an additional message: a plea to Gorbachev not to remove Politburo members such as Gromyko and give the West the satisfaction of proof of divisions in the leadership.

The Brezhnev Generation

That Gromyko would want to appeal to Gorbachev for unity is hardly surprising. The Brezhnev-Gromyko generation had been so unique, and the differences between its experiences and those of Gorbachev's generation so great, that the worry about real differences in attitude was legitimate. It is not only that Gromyko was seventy-six years of age in 1985 and Gorbachev fifty-four. The Great Purge of 1937–38 had thrust Gromyko and his colleagues into very high posts while they were still in their thirties. Born in 1909, Gromyko had a degree in agricultural economics and went to work in the Institute of Economics in Moscow in the 1930s. He had risen to a relatively minor administrative position (scholarly secretary) when, to his utter surprise, he was recruited into the diplomatic corps. At the age of thirty, he found himself head of the American desk of the foreign ministry in 1939.[2]

Gromyko was typical of his generation, except that Stalin wanted his young officials in the domestic sphere to have technical education and some experience along with their youth. In 1928–29 Stalin had transformed the educational system to emphasize engineering education and to recruit students with a working-class or peasant background—often persons who were already working. For example, Leonid Brezhnev was a twenty-five-year-old agricultural administrator when he went to engineering college in 1931. Aleksei Kosygin was a twenty-six-year-old trade official. Andrei Kirilenko was a twenty-five-year-old former worker who had just moved into low-level trade union work, while Dmitrii Ustinov was a twenty-year-old worker.[3]

These students graduated in the mid-1930s and then were promoted with dizzying speed in the wake of the purge. Kosygin was thirty-five when he became people's commissar (minister) of light industry in 1939. Ustinov was thirty-three when he was named people's commissar of armaments in 1941. In 1939 Mikhail Suslov and Nikolai Patolichev (the minister of foreign trade in the Brezhnev era) were thirty-seven and thirty-one respectively when they became party first secretaries in Stavropol and Yaroslavl provinces respectively.

So it was throughout the Soviet system. The only difference in the provinces was that many of the officials did not have a college degree. Yurii Andropov had only graduated from a trade school preparing sailors for river transport when he was named first secretary of the Yaroslavl Young Communist League committee in 1939, at the age of twenty-four. Konstantin Chernenko had no education beyond high school when he was named ideological party secretary, one of the six top officials, in a large Siberian province in 1941, at the age of thirty.

The memoirs of those who passed through this experience universally testify to a sense of shock, of unpreparedness for such enormous responsibilities. Many of those promoted during the purge were found wanting and were quietly demoted. (In fact, Chernenko was sent to a party school in the midst of the war and then given a somewhat lower job.) Yet those who did cope picked up vast amounts of experience very quickly and at a very young age. The postpurge generation occupied virtually all the important positions in the Soviet system during the war. Andrei Gromyko, for example, was soon sent to Washington as a counselor in the embassy, and in 1943 he was named ambassador—the Soviet representative to its most important ally.

Different observers have characterized the Brezhnev generation in quite different ways over the years. One authority in the 1940s referred to the young engineers of 1934 as "a restless element, inclined toward experimentation, record-breaking, speed-up, 'storming.' They brought élan into the plants, a sense that people somehow became embodied in the gigantic recovery of the new revolutionary country through work in which they submerged themselves completely."[4]

A student of Soviet middle-brow fiction in the postwar period suggested, however, that in addition to being immersed in its work, the Brezhnev generation also showed a deep yearning for middle-class respectability and stability.[5] By the late 1950s the most perceptive of the British observers, Edward Crankshaw, was describing this yearning in far more contemptuous terms:

> The Party functionaries born between roughly 1890 and 1920 [are] the lost generation... [They] survived either because they were too stupid to be considered dangerous, or because they brought sycophancy to a fine art, or because they were as cunning as the fox. Nothing in this world is more depressing to contemplate than the average Soviet official of high or low degree at present between the ages of forty and sixty... Those who started their rise in their thirties during the great purges of twenty years ago... are incomparably the worst.[6]

Crankshaw's picture may have been overdrawn, but the Brezhnev generation had been the "revolutionary guard" generation of the Civil War period, and most had no more desire for a market reform and a great influx of Western ideas than they had had in their youth.

TABLE 1   MEMBERS OF THE POLITBURO, JUNE 1980

Member	Year of Birth	Position
Leonid I. Brezhnev	1906	General Secretary of the Central Committee
Konstantin U. Chernenko	1911	Secretary of the Central Committee
Andrei P. Kirilenko	1906	Secretary of the Central Committee
Mikhail A. Suslov	1902	Secretary of the Central Committee
Arvid Y. Pelshe	1899	Chairman of the Party Control Committee
Aleksei N. Kosygin	1904	Chairman of the USSR Council of Ministers
Nikolai A. Tikhonov	1905	First Deputy Chairman of the USSR Council of Ministers
Andrei A. Gromyko	1909	Minister of Foreign Affairs
Dmitrii F. Ustinov	1908	Minister of Defense
Yurii V. Andropov	1914	Chairman of the KGB
Viktor V. Grishin	1914	First Secretary of the Moscow City Committee
Dinmukhamed A. Kunaev	1912	First Secretary of the Kazakhstan Central Committee
Vladimir V. Shcherbitsky	1918	First Secretary of the Ukrainian Central Committee
Grigorii V. Romanov	1923	First Secretary of the Leningrad Regional Committee

Gradually in the 1950s and the 1960s younger officials were moved into key posts in the middle levels of the system, but the Brezhnev generation continued to dominate its top reaches. As table 1 indicates, the membership of the Politburo in June 1980, just before Gorbachev was elected, had an incredible appearance. The members had been born in 1909 on the average, 1907 for the members working in Moscow, and they had all been in important posts for decades. The average governmental minister was only a little younger, sixty-six.

Hence when Mikhail Gorbachev, who was born in 1931, became a voting member of the Politburo in October 1980, he was over twenty years younger than the average Politburo member. Only two other members were within sixteen years of his age. But because of the precipitous promotion of most of his colleagues, the difference was even greater than age. In 1939 Gorbachev was in the second grade, but Gromyko was already head of the American desk of the foreign ministry. In 1957, Gorbachev was two years out of college, but Gromyko was already minister of foreign affairs.

Gorbachev's Youth

Mikhail S. Gorbachev was born on March 2, 1931, in a peasant family in the village of Privolnoe in Stavropol Province.[7] His grandfather had been a chairman of the village's collective farm, his father a party member.[8] By all reports, however, his mother was and remains a practicing member of the Russian Orthodox Church. Unlike Stalin, who was an ethnic Georgian; Khrushchev and Brezhnev, who were Russians raised in the Ukraine; Andropov, who had a Jewish grandparent; and Chernenko, who had a Ukrainian last name, Gorbachev was thoroughly Russian in his roots.

There were, however, different Russian traditions. Russia is associated with serfdom, and a large proportion of the peasants were serfs until 1861. Yet, serfdom had different forms, and in the early nineteenth century, just over half the Russian people were not serfs at all. Some of the latter group were city dwellers, some were members of some rural elite, but many lived in areas in which serfdom generally did not exist or had very shallow roots. One such area was Siberia, but another was the Kuban, of which Stavropol was a part. Rightly or wrongly, Soviet citizens often say that descendants of serfs today have a noticeably different psychology than those of a different background. Rightly or wrongly, it is often assumed that Gorbachev's energy, drive, and innovative ways are the product of a nonserf, cossack ancestry. "A real Kuban cossack," one admirer called him—a man riding through Russia with sword in hand and turning to Siberians with a similar nonserf background for his chief lieutenants.

Gorbachev was born shortly after the launching of the collectivization drive and just before the great famine of 1932–33, but by the time he became conscious of life outside his family, the rural scene had settled down. Gorbachev's father worked for forty years as a machine operator, and at thirteen Mikhail, like other peasant children, began to work in the fields. At fifteen he became an assistant to a combine driver at the local machine tractor station.

The first great event in the life of Gorbachev and his generation was World War II. Ten years of age when the war started, Gorbachev was too young to have fought in it, and some Americans have said that his generation is the first not to have known war. It is a fundamental mistake, for the youth of Russia—and all of Europe—knew war all too well.

Indeed, war can have a more decisive impact on a child than an adult. On the one hand it can be a particularly horrifying experience. A man who fights in a war remembers it as a heroic experience. As he ages, he may remember it as the great time of glory of his life. For a small child who sees his world shattered, the experience is something quite different. The Soviet poet Evgenii Evtushenko is two years younger than Gorbachev, and neither the Moscow in which he lived nor the native Siberian village to which he returned at the beginning of the war was ever occupied. Yet he has recorded his memories of the opening days of the war, when he was only eight years old:

When I came to [my village] Zima Junction, I witnessed what perhaps was the most terrible thing I have seen in my life—the weddings of 1941. Young boys called up to the front were handed their papers and given two or three days to get ready... Their girls chose to be their wives if only for a day.... These were the terrible weddings I saw, the weddings where the first night of married life was to be the last.[9]

Such weddings were also part of the ten-year-old Gorbachev's life, but, in addition, his village, like that of so many of his generation, was occupied by the Germans from the summer of 1942 through the early winter of 1943. There are a number of rumors that Gorbachev's family actually remained in the village during German occupation, but this would have been foolhardy. Gorbachev's mother was thirty-two years old and the daughter of a collective farm chairman. Normally the women and children fled before the advancing Germans, and a close friend in college, Zdenek Mlynar, suggests that the Gorbachev family did so as well.

At a minimum, Gorbachev returned to a village ravaged by war. He did not go to college until 1950, five years after the fighting stopped. As he reported in 1986, his trip to Moscow in 1950 created an awful impression: "I went to study at Moscow University and I traveled through Stalingrad which had been destroyed, through Voronezh which had been destroyed, Rostov was destroyed. Kharkov was destroyed. Nothing but ruins everywhere. I traveled as a student and saw it all. The whole country in ruins."[10]

War, however, can have other impacts. Ivan Frolov was also the son of a peasant who was to be an undergraduate and then graduate student at Moscow University from 1948 to 1956. He was named Gorbachev's personal assistant for ideology in 1987, and chief editor of the Central Committee newspaper, *Pravda*, in October 1989.[11] He was four years older than Evtushenko, and at twelve in 1942 he dropped out of school for a year and a half to work in a staging area that assembled supplies for the front. For Frolov and many others, war meant the onset of manhood at the very beginning of his teenage years—the development of a sense of independence and responsibility that he remembers as a real step toward rapid maturity and self-confidence.

The most obvious impact of the war upon the Gorbachev generation was upon its education. During the war, youth of his age were entering or passing through high school. Those who were not highly motivated found it very easy to drop out of school. Much of European Russia was occupied, and schools were destroyed and millions of people were being uprooted. As men were drafted into the army, high-school dropouts found all child labor laws relaxed in the desperate drive for victory. Moreover, much of Soviet secondary education has taken place in the evening schools after the normal high school graduation age of seventeen. The war disrupted this process for those born before 1928, and then the labor shortage after the war was so severe that the financial incentive to obtain secondary technical education was minimal.

The result is seen in table 2. Many like Frolov who dropped out for a short period, returned to school, but others did not. The Soviet period has seen a general rise in the percentage of each successive age group with higher and secondary education, but this process was essentially halted and even reversed for those born in the late 1920s and early 1930s. The 1959 census found that 23 percent of those born from 1919 to 1923 had received at least a high-school diploma, but that only 17 percent of those born from 1929 to 1933 had.

But if a student of the Gorbachev generation were properly motivated and talented, he or she got the benefit of a first-class education. At the time of the launching of the first Soviet *Sputnik* into space in 1957, Americans spoke in glowing terms of the rigor of Soviet schooling. They pointed to the college-oriented character of its curriculum, the amount of homework, and the large dose of mathematics, science, and literature within it. They wrote of the tough competition for college entrance, with the only important political factor being the influence of parents from the top administrative and professional stratum. No doubt, this image was somewhat exaggerated, but it was correct in suggesting that preference was no longer being given to those with worker and peasant origins and that the curriculum was making few concessions to the mediocre or to the student not aiming for college.[12]

TABLE 2 PERCENTAGE OF SOVIET POPULATION, TEN YEARS AND
OLDER, WITH HIGHER AND SECONDARY EDUCATION, 1959

Years of Birth	Higher Education	Incomplete Higher and Complete Secondary	Incomplete Secondary Education
1914–1918	3.6%	12.4%	16.5%
1919–1923	4.8	18.4	26.9
1924–1928	3.9	14.0	32.5
1929–1933	4.4	12.5	25.7
1934–1939	1.3*	26.5*	37.9

*The group born from 1934 to 1939 still had many of its members in college in 1959, and these people were listed with incomplete higher education at the time. In general, a number of Soviet citizens continue to obtain higher and secondary education while adults, and the figures for all the groups are higher in the 1970 census.

This fact is crucial to keep in mind when we consider Gorbachev's biography. The central media indicate that he worked from 1946 to 1950 as a combine harvester driver on the collective farm of his village, or really on the machine-tractor station that did the mechanized work for the farm. Some Westerners have concluded that his peasant background and his excellent work record (he received a very high award—the Order of the Red Banner of Labor) made his admission to Moscow University a simple matter and that he may not even have had a full-time high-school education. It is a serious misreading of the period.

Gorbachev's letters of recommendation may have helped, but lower-class origin was just not useful for college admission after the war. Gorbachev had to pass the highly competitive entrance exams or, more likely, to have been a medal winner at school (somewhat the equivalent to a class valedictorian or salutatorian in the United States). In fact, a local Stavropol newspaper said that Gorbachev's work as a combine operator was simply summer work, although it may have gone on a bit longer, for village schools were often closed during the harvest.[13]

De-Stalinization and Xenophobia

De-Stalinization was as great an event for the Gorbachev generation as the war. During their youth, Stalin was the great wartime leader, and they usually accepted the Godlike image of the Soviet dictator that was being propagated. Certainly few parents could have dared to contradict it and risk their child blurting out an anti-Stalin statement in school. The death of Stalin, even for those who were to become intellectual innovators, is often described as a shock and personal blow.

Then it turned out to be a lie. The period from 1953 to 1955 featured a gradual increase in the criticism of the practices and policies of the Stalin period. Restrictions on the flow of ideas were significantly reduced, and the dogmatism of the Stalin era began to be attacked in field after field. At first, the police abuses were blamed on the secret police chief, Lavrentii Beriia, who was arrested in June 1953 and later executed. In February 1956, however, Nikita S. Khrushchev gave a secret speech at the conclusion of the Twentieth Party Congress, denouncing Stalin himself as a murderous monster.[14]

The last years of Stalin's life had been marked by a grotesque xenophobic campaign that not only lowered an Iron Curtain between Russia and the West, but also treated praise of Western ideas—even of technical ideas—as unpatriotic "cosmopolitanism." Stalin prevented all access to contemporary Western ideas and culture—even the art of Communists such as Picasso or the novels of an opponent of Franco in Spain such as Ernest Hemingway. The United States in particular was treated as a totally dominating country and its ideology as repulsive and subversive. Roald Z. Sagdeev, a future director of the Space Research Institute, who graduated from Moscow University in 1955 (the same year as Gorbachev), later recalled that when he met American scientists for the first time at a conference shortly after graduation, "I was looking at them as extraterrestrials."[15]

Some Westerners have looked at the late 1940s and early 1950s and have concluded that the intellectual background of the Gorbachev generation is thoroughly Stalinist. In reality, the situation was much more complex. The Gorbachev generation first became aware of the outside world at a time when Hitler was a deadly enemy and the United States was a crucial ally. During the war the United States was described in very different terms, and even today members of the generation recall the Lend-Lease of the time, and especially the Studebakers that were widely used inside the Soviet Union not only during the war, but also afterward. During the war they saw American films that showed America in a favorable light and even an America friendly to the Soviet Union.[16] Perhaps as a consequence, a man such as Sagdeev seems typical in the ease in which he overcame his initial feeling of estrangement. "Throughout my career I felt very close to my American colleagues."

In addition, Stalin's xenophobia, coupled with his commitment to high-quality education in the postwar years, had one paradoxical result. Gorbachev's generation received a heavy dose of science and mathematics in school, but the denunciation of Western ideas and the West meant that they learned little about world civilization and spent relatively little time on foreign languages. As a consequence, their education contained a disproportionate amount of material on Russia and especially the great Russian realistic literature of the nineteenth century. Years later many still can recite long passages from memory. The crucial fact for the future was that this Russian literature, and especially the more "progressive" part of it to which the students were exposed, incorporated the values of the Westernized elite of the nineteenth century.

For these reasons it is perhaps not surprising that the denunciation of Western culture in Stalin's last years seemed only to make it attractive as it became available. From the period of their first contact with Westerners after Stalin's death, young Russians sought out Western gum and lapel pins. The older youth also wanted the pins, but they were more attracted to Western music, clothes, and films. A world youth festival was held in Moscow in 1957, and it created a sensation—a feeling of the diversity of the

world and Russia as part of it.[17] Many of the college students
flocked to mass meetings where poets such as Evtushenko read
daring poems that skirted the border of the censorship. Young
intellectuals of the Gorbachev generation led the battle to reintegrate world intellectual currents back into their respective fields.

Gorbachev must have been representative of his generation in a
number of ways to have been promoted so rapidly, but perhaps
the best indirect evidence of his attitudes is the woman he married. Raisa Titarenko came out of a Volga town, reportedly the
daughter of a party official. She was enthusiastic about literature,
and became a college professor of philosophy. She did a sociology
dissertation when that was quite daring. When she traveled
abroad—and she traveled everywhere with her husband—she
dressed fashionably and went to the Yves Saint Laurent show-
rooms. Not only must she have had an impact on Gorbachev, but
his selection of her said something about his original values.

In one respect, however, Gorbachev was a very atypical party
official. Most future officials went to engineering or agricultural
college, but Gorbachev went to Moscow University and took a
social sciences degree in the law faculty. No other high party
official of his generation had such an education, and his choice of
law school was a strange one that is still unexplained. He himself
described it as almost a chance event: "I entered the law faculty,
but at first I preferred the physics. I loved mathematics very
much but also history and literature."[18]

Whatever Gorbachev's reason for going there, Moscow University must have been a revelation for him. Moscow itself was as
different from a Stavropol village of the 1940s as can be imagined
—indeed, more different than any American can imagine. Village
roads were never paved, and villages had few of the city amenities
such as running water or indoor plumbing, and often not even
electricity. Moscow University had provided contact with students of a totally different background and level of intelligence
and sophistication.

Indeed, one of Gorbachev's friends in law school, Zdenek
Mlynar, a Czechoslovakian, was later to become Central Committee secretary in the Dubchek regime in 1968. Mlynar was later to
report, "Gorbachev was completely open to me. It made no dif-

ference to him that I was a foreigner. And that was unusual at the
time because many Soviet students were afraid of us. They didn't
know who we were or what we were doing there."[19] Even the
courses at Moscow University provided more intellectual stimulation than one would have supposed. In an interview, Ivan Frolov
warned against a misinterpretation of the university in those
years. The xenophobia meant that philosophy students like himself were not exposed to post-Marx Western philosophy, but they
did study earlier philosophers, including their actual works.
Moreover, students took seminars every year beginning as fresh-
men, and Frolov insists that students were free to criticize their
instructors on questions of philosophical interpretation.

Gorbachev was in the law faculty and took different courses,
but a German biographer correctly writes, "Even if the interpretations were predictable, Gorbachev and his fellow-students at
least heard and read things that would never reach the ears and
eyes of other students: general constitutional law from Hammu-
rabi to the present day, the history of political ideas, Machiavelli
and Hobbes, Hegel and Rousseau."[20] In a course on international
relations, a professor had discussed Lord Palmerston's view of
foreign policy: "England does not have eternal friends or eternal
enemies, but eternal interests." It was scarcely the simplistic
Marxist view of economic determinism, but it was an idea that
stuck. Gorbachev cited the quotation both on his trip to England
in 1984 and in his press conference after the summit the following
year. And, while it may not have been reflected in class lectures,
the law faculty of Moscow University was one of the centers of
agitation for greater observance of legal norms after 1953, and this
must have informally percolated to the students.

In 1959, Edward Crankshaw, whose extremely critical views of
the Brezhnev generation have already been quoted, had a drastically different view of the Gorbachev generation:

> The Soviet Union's great hope lies in the young—those under
> thirty-five [i.e., born after 1924]... In a dozen professions in which
> Party control is particularly rigid—in the Foreign Service, in the
> Law, in journalism, in economics, in the higher civil service with
> its many branches, in the armed forces, in the university faculties,

you will meet well-turned-out young men in their thirties, usually Party members, relaxed and easy in manner, often with a pleasantly ironical approach to life, and very much in touch with realities of every kind... I have been talking of the cream of the younger men beginning to rise in what are called the liberal professions and the State and Party service. Until the last decade young men of comparable ability would not have dreamt of this sort of career.[21]

But to the extent that this picture was accurate in the late 1950s, how much of it is relevant now? The thirty-year-old of 1957 is in his sixties today, and the twenty-year-old of 1966 is in his forties. Have they rejected the "foolishness" of their youth, or throughout the stodgy Brezhnev period did they increasingly look upon the excitement of their youth with fond nostalgia?

In the one element of the elite with whom we have contact— the policy intellectuals—we can, in fact, observe real generational differences between those who are now in their seventies and eighties and those who are now in their fifties. Even the "liberals" of the older generation tend to think in basic Marxist categories and usually have been quite moderate reformers by Western standards. The intellectuals who are now in their fifties have usually broken in many fundamental although unspoken ways from Marxist categories as they were understood in the Stalin period. Ivan Frolov, for example, has been the leader in treating morality as a more universal humanistic value than simply the defense of class interest.

Unfortunately, we cannot be certain about the attitudes of the middle-level and upper-level officials in the governmental and party apparatus, but the anti-Stalin poet of the 1950s and 1960s, Evgenii Evtushenko, has met many of them, and he has a quite favorable impression. In January 1986 he gave an interview to Rodolfo Brancoli, correspondent of the Italian newspaper *La Repubblica*, in which he recounted his shock at meeting the officials of the Gorbachev generation. "I am used to talking with men in official posts who are all older than me," he said, "and I always see in their eyes that they regard me as a disturber of the peace." Evtushenko had, however, recently met the Georgian party first secretary who had replaced Eduard Shevardnadze.

The first thing he told me was that when he was a student he managed to smuggle his way into the great hall of Tbilisi University to listen to a poetry recital of mine... Do you know what he said to me: "We grew up in the spirit of your poetry." Then in the Urals I met the manager of a large metalworks, so different from the people I was used to meeting that I could not help saying to him: "Pardon me, but you are not in the least like a manager and do not have the slightest appearance of a bureaucrat." Do you know what his answer was? "When I was at high school I won a prize by reciting one of your poems against bureaucrats."[22]

This is, of course, not conclusive evidence, for the younger officials hostile to Evtushenko may well be too polite to speak frankly to him. But there is other evidence. Demitri B. Shimkin, a professor at the University of Illinois, spent four months in 1985 in the remote coal center of Kemerovo, a city normally closed to Westerners. The big event of his stay, he says, was the showing of the American film *Tootsie*. The audiences were standing room only—strikingly different from the audience for a foreign film in an American provincial city, let alone a Soviet film. When the coal miners in this area struck in 1989, they demanded foreign currency to buy foreign goods. Other Soviet fifty-year-olds we meet tend to have a similar attraction to Western culture. They no longer want jeans and rock and roll, but they do want a VCR and the films for it; they want to travel abroad; their wives want clothes like Raisa Gorbachev's.

Gorbachev's Rise

Gorbachev was an excellent student and graduated from Moscow University with honors. He was also politically active. He joined the Communist party at an unusually early age, twenty-one, and he became the Komsomol (Young Communist) leader of his class. Then after graduation, he returned to Stavropol where he entered full-time Komsomol work. Within three years he was selected secretary of the provincial Komsomol committee and then he became first secretary.

In 1962 Gorbachev moved into party work in Stavropol territory. He served briefly as the top party official in a rural county and then was appointed head of the party organs (personnel) department of the provincial party committee that supervised the rural areas in those years. The first secretary of that party committee was Fedor Kulakov, the man whom Brezhnev was to name Central Committee secretary for agriculture in 1965 and the overseer of his pet irrigation and reclamation program.

The rise of Gorbachev's generation was facilitated by a major "generation gap" among those slightly older. Those born from approximately 1919 to 1926 received a high-quality secondary education in the 1930s, but they spent their late teens and early twenties in the World War II period and bore the bulk of the fighting. Large numbers of them were killed,[23] but the impact of the war on their college education had a more important long-term political significance. Veterans had no great trouble getting into college, but a young man who went from high school into the army gradually forgot his mathematics. He found it hard to compete in the rigorous academic atmosphere of the time with those who had spent the war in high school. The biographies of officials of this age group show that a high percentage went to colleges that did not require a strong knowledge of science and mathematics: pedagogical institutes, party schools, in some cases universities or diplomatic schools.[24]

In the United States, the veterans who took advantage of the GI Bill of Rights also had forgotten much of their mathematics during the war, but this had little political significance. In the United States, law has been the route into governmental work. In the Soviet Union, however, Stalin had demanded engineering or agronomy education for the important posts in the administrative and party apparatus, and this practice was continued in the post-Stalin years. Those who did go to engineering school often did so at night.

In a large sample of Soviet officials, only 47 percent born between 1921 and 1925 turned out to have completed college full-time, compared with 65 percent of those born between 1913 and 1916 and 72 percent of the 1926–29 group.[25]

As a consequence, the generational pattern of promotions became quite skewed. A study of regional officials of the Russian

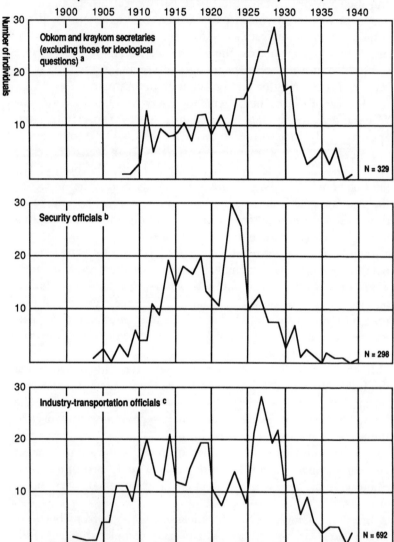

Graph 1. Years of Birth of RSFSR Oblast and Kray Officials, 1965–77

a Including the first secretary, the agricultural secretary, and the two secretaries who divide responsibility for industry, construction, and urban affairs. In earlier years, one of the last two concentrated on organizational matters, but that situation has now changed in almost all oblasts and krays.

b Including the head of the administration of the Committee for State Security (KGB), the head of the internal affairs administration, and the procurator.

c Including directors of important plants, heads of the railroads and their divisions (*otdeleniya,* which tend to correspond to oblasts and krays), heads of ocean and river steamship lines, and (in 1965 alone) chairmen and deputy chairmen of regional economic councils.

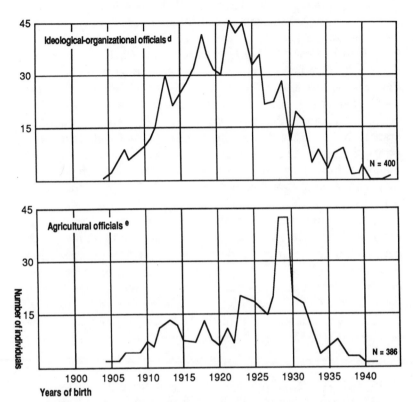

d Including the *obkom* or *kraykom* secretary for ideological questions, the head of the department of organizational and party work of the *obkom* or *kraykom*, the deputy chairman for education and culture and the heads of the departments of culture and of education of the *oblispolkom* or *krayispolkom*, the chairman of the oblast or kray trade union council, the oblast or kray newspaper editor, and the chairman of the oblast or kray people's control committee.

e Including the *obkom* or *kraykom* secretary for agriculture, the deputy chairman for agriculture and the head of the agriculture administration of the *oblispolkom* or *krayispolkom*, and the chairman of the agricultural supply agency *(Sel'khoztekhnika)*.

SOURCE AND METHODOLOGY: The individuals included in this sample were identified, and their ages determined, from lists of deputies to the oblast and kray soviets in 1965, 1967, 1969, 1971, 1973, 1975, and 1977, as drawn from the provincial press. While this methodology does not provide complete coverage of the occupants of the enumerated posts, it does account for an estimated 90 percent of them. Any official who held one of the listed posts at any time during the 1965–77 period and was elected to the oblast or kray soviet in one of the biennial elections is included, but if an official held two posts during the period—e.g., moved from head of the agriculture administration to deputy chairman of the *oblispolkom*, or transferred from one oblast or kray to another (applicable only in the cases of KGB and procuracy officials), he is counted only once.

Soviet Federated Socialist Republic (RSFSR) from 1965 to 1977 showed a normal, bell-shaped distribution of ages of the ideological, organizational, and security officials, with the largest number (as was to be expected) being born in the first half of the 1920s. Technical education was not required for these posts, and the war did not have a distorting effect on promotions. In economic management and in the sections of the party apparatus supervising the economy, however, the situation was very different. A real "generation trough" appeared on the graphs. As those who had been born prior to 1919 retired, they were disproportionately replaced not by persons born from 1919 to 1925, but by much younger men whose education had not been seriously disrupted by the war. (See graph 1.)

As table 3 indicates, the same pattern was repeated among the regional first secretaries of the 1970s, for most of these men must have technical education in the Soviet Union. It was repeated at the end of the Brezhnev era among the industrial ministers. Seventy men served as industrial ministers for some time between 1976 and the end of 1985. Two were born prior to 1906, twenty-one between 1906 and 1912, fifteen between 1913 and 1919, nine between 1920 and 1926, twenty between 1927 and 1933, and three after 1933.

TABLE 3   YEARS OF BIRTH OF NEW RSFSR REGIONAL FIRST
SECRETARIES AND U.S. STATE GOVERNORS, AND OF THEIR
IMMEDIATE PREDECESSORS, 1969–79

Year of Birth	RSFSR Regional First Secretaries	Governors of U.S. States
1901–8	0	1
1909–16	27	18
1917–24	14	35
1925–32	27	28
1933–40	0	15
1941–48	0	1

SOURCE: See Jerry F. Hough, "The Generation Gap and the Brezhnev Succession," *Problems of Communism* 28, no.4 (July–August 1979), 5.

In 1966 Gorbachev became the first secretary of the Stavropol city party committee and in 1968 the second secretary of the Stavropol provincial party committee. In 1970 he was named first secretary of the provincial committee. This post warranted his election as one of the 241 voting members of the Central Committee at the Twenty-fourth Party Congress in 1971. Gorbachev worked as Stavropol first secretary for eight years, and when Kulakov died in 1978, Gorbachev was brought to Moscow as Central Committee secretary for agriculture to replace him.

For many Western observers, Gorbachev's career makes him the absolutely typical party apparatchik—the man who had risen step by step through the party bureaucracy, never having worked for a single day in the governmental or economic administration. Therefore, many thought that Gorbachev was likely to be particularly hidebound when he assumed office.[26]

In fact, Gorbachev's career was one of the most atypical among the party officials of the 1970s. In 1971 he had been the youngest party or governmental official elected a full member of the Central Committee,[27] and only 5 percent of such officials on the Central Committee were within five years of him in age. At the time of the Supreme Soviet elections in 1974, there were seventy-six provincial party first secretaries in the Russian Republic.[28] Their average age was fifty-four, while Gorbachev was forty-three. (Only one of the secretaries was younger.) The typical regional first secretary had joined the Communist party at the average age of twenty-five, while Gorbachev had joined at twenty-one. Only one, besides Gorbachev, had graduated from a university instead of an engineering, pedagogical, or party institute, and only Gorbachev had graduated from the elite Moscow University. (While a party official, Gorbachev had also received a correspondence college degree in agronomy from the Stavropol Agricultural Institute.)

In the Soviet system the main job of the regional party secretaries has been to ensure the fulfillment of the economic plan, and the party leadership has generally selected men with managerial experience in industry, construction, or agriculture, especially in the more important provinces. Gorbachev was only one of nine first secretaries in the Russian Republic in 1974 who had been a provincial Komsomol first secretary before being transferred to party work (another nine had held less important Komsomol posts). In the twenty-five most populous provinces, the first secretaries in 1974 averaged eight years work in industrial or agricultural management and five years work as chairman of a local government.

Thus, the typical party apparatchik in the 1970s and 1980s was not Gorbachev, but his chief rival, Grigorii Romanov. Romanov had worked for eleven years in a shipbuilding design bureau in Leningrad before becoming a borough party secretary at the age of thirty-four. The new first secretary of Moscow in 1985, Boris N. Yeltsin had worked for thirteen years in construction administration before entering party work at thirty-seven and his successor, Lev Zaikov, had been a factory manager until the age of forty-four. The new Central Committee secretary for agriculture, Viktor P. Nikonov, had been the director of a machine-tractor station in agriculture before being moved into party work at the age of twenty-nine.

Many have had a tendency to look upon party officials with a technical background as innovative technocrats and those who rose exclusively in the political sphere as party hacks. In reality, an engineer who has worked for years in industrial production may find it difficult to accept the necessity for a consumer-oriented economy and the chaos of the market. A man with a different education and a political background may be far less hidebound. One of the striking phenomena of the 1970s was a decline in the prestige of engineering education among the brightest teenagers and the rise in the prestige of liberal arts education. It is not surprising that a political elite deeply worried about the future and looking for the man with the best education to lead them in a period of change would now look to an honors graduate of the law faculty of Moscow University with the kind of respect reserved for technocrats in the past.

In other ways, too, Gorbachev must have been special. He has shown a natural political touch in every setting in which he has been seen by foreigners, and he surely had this touch at home as well. He had personal ties to an extraordinary number of Politburo members, and he must have been courting them assiduously. Brezhnev's army had fought in the Caucasus in World War II, and the ideological secretary, Mikhail Suslov, had been first secretary in Stavropol and then head of the partisans there. Television reports of Suslov's funeral showed Gorbachev behaving with special warmth to the dead man's family. Gorbachev's mentor, Fedor Kulakov, had worked closely with Brezhnev's assistant, Konstantin Chernenko, in the early postwar years, and Chernenko must have had a role in Kulakov's promotion under Brezhnev. The chairman of the KGB, Yurii Andropov, was born in Stavropol province and vacationed there and Gorbachev surely even tried to remind Moscow first secretary, Viktor V. Grishin, of his old school ties in his battle with the Leningrader, Romanov.

In recent years, the Moscow rumor network has emphasized Gorbachev's connections with Andropov. It is said that the two had had long conversations while Andropov was on vacation in the 1970s and that Gorbachev had impressed the older man greatly. These rumors are probably accurate, but mythmaking is a part of all political systems. It would be a mistake to forget Gorbachev's other connections with leaders whom he would now like people to forget. Gorbachev was not merely an amiable protégé of Andropov, thrust to power as an accident of history.

Least of all should we forget that Brezhnev was the dictator and Gorbachev's most powerful patron. As shall be discussed in chapter 6, Brezhnev's two closest lieutenants were Andrei Kirilenko and Konstantin Chernenko, the former from his days in Dnepropetrovsk and the latter from his days in Moldavia. Kirilenko had been the more powerful during Brezhnev's first decade in office, but he opposed Brezhnev's decision in the mid-1970s to sacrifice industrial investment to maintain consumption in the face of a decline in economic growth. As Kirilenko's position weakened, Brezhnev gave Chernenko the key responsibility for personnel selection and made him the number two man in the system.

Brezhnev's ability to impose Chernenko on the party and to face down the Kirilenko faction in the Central Committee showed enormous political strength, all the more so since the United States was accelerating its defense expenditures during these years. His ability to have another inappropriate crony, Nikolai A.

Tikhonov, appointed chairman of the Council of Ministers was also extremely impressive.

Nevertheless, Brezhnev had major political problems. The Central Committee, elected in 1976, was composed of officials who had been selected while Kirilenko was the second secretary and who have to have worried about the future if the decline continued. In the late 1970s a knowledgeable Soviet source reported privately that Yurii Andropov had moved into the inner core of the leadership. Andropov had been educated in the same city as Kirilenko in Yaroslavl Province in the 1930s, and, in practice, he took over leadership of the large number of officials who had been beholden to Kirilenko. If Chernenko supported the Brezhnev decision to give "social justice" priority over "growth," then Andropov supported the policy of growth.

Brezhnev's physical strength and mental vigor were declining seriously, and at times foreigners found that his mind hardly functioned. As the rate of economic growth declined along with Brezhnev's health, both the elite and the population developed a real sense of unease. Indeed, Brezhnev himself openly acknowledged the problems in the Soviet economy at the November 1978 plenary session of the Central Committee:

> [There are] shortages of metal and fuel . . . a certain lag of machinery from the needs of the economy . . . the failure of the construction plan to be completed [and] intolerable losses of grain, fruit, and vegetables. . . . A complex situation has developed in transportation. . . .
>
> The chief reason is that the central economic organs, the ministries, and the departments have been slow in achieving a transition to intensive development. They have not been able to achieve the necessary improvement of qualitative indicators or the speeding-up of scientific-technical progress. . . . [There must be] an improvement in the plans, accompanied by measures for perfecting the whole economic mechanism.[29]

The belief that Brezhnev would not live for long reduced the elite's alarm at this situation, but the promotion of old men who opposed an emphasis on growth was deeply frightening to many. (It was precisely at this November 1978 plenum that Chernenko became a full member of the Politburo and de facto the second secretary.) If the elite became convinced that such men would dominate in the future and continue the stagnation, people might decide that Brezhnev himself had to go as the only solution.

Mikhail Gorbachev was, however, also elected a Central Committee secretary at the November 1978 plenum. He was an excellent answer to Brezhnev's problem. Gorbachev had a broad acceptability to a range of people within the leadership, and with a first-class mind and education and a "star" political quality he had all the look of an eventual reforming successor, probably after a transition. This was reassuring to the elite, but at forty-seven in 1978 Gorbachev was far too young and inexperienced to become general secretary "prematurely," as Brezhnev himself had in 1964. The elite could afford to let Brezhnev die in peace while Gorbachev gained experience and was tested for the future.

Just before Gorbachev was selected Central Committee secretary for agriculture in 1978, he met with Brezhnev, Chernenko, and Andropov as they traveled through Stavropol in September on a trip to the Transcaucasus. Other regional secretaries also met Brezhnev on this trip, but only in Stavropol was Andropov announced as being present as well.[30] It was an extraordinary meeting, with four Soviet general secretaries present at the same time. In retrospect, the Soviet leader and the leaders of the two great political machines of the country were looking over a man they saw as a potential long-term successor.

From this perspective, Gorbachev was not the accidental creature of Andropov in 1982, but a kingmaker in that year as much as a protégé. The younger officials on the Central Committee did not constitute a majority, but they were an important bloc within it. Gorbachev was supervising them as the secretary for agriculture, and most of them must have seen him as their champion on a Politburo dominated by the Brezhnev generation.[31] Moreover, to the extent that they saw Gorbachev as being groomed as a long-term heir apparent after a transitional period, they had every interest in jumping on his bandwagon, and the more who did so, the more speed the bandwagon picked up.

Andropov as the new leader of the Kirilenko faction essentially seems to have nailed down his victory by allying himself with

Gorbachev and by promising the younger man the position of personnel secretary that would give him a crucial advantage in the next succession. This deal was temporarily thwarted when Andropov died more quickly than anticipated, and Chernenko was able to win the support of the party leadership as Andropov's successor.

Nevertheless, in long-term perspective, Chernenko's election merely marked one more stage in Gorbachev's rise to power. In the wake of Chernenko's election, Gorbachev was given an extraordinary range of responsibilities—actually all or most of those of four Politburo members in 1980: his own old responsibilities for agriculture and the food industry, Suslov's for ideology (information policy, culture, education, and science, and relations with foreign Communists), Kirilenko's for planning and light industry (but not for heavy industry), and Chernenko's for personnel (but not for the security organs).

The pattern of decisions at the time of Andropov's death strongly suggested that an agreement had been reached on a two-stage succession, with Gorbachev being given control of so many levers of power that he would be virtually unchallengeable after Chernenko's death or retirement. In fact, no change was made in the Politburo membership during Chernenko's year in office that would have weakened Gorbachev's position, and the range of responsibilities of his main rival, Romanov, was not expanded beyond the narrow sphere of defense and the machinery industry. It was Gorbachev who was given the trip to Great Britain and the unprecedented television coverage that built him up as a successor.

Even if the Central Committee had been inclined to reverse the judgment of 1984 when the actual decision to name a successor to Chernenko was made in March 1985, the failure to build up an alternative to Gorbachev left them with few reasonable choices. It was one thing—and dubious enough—to elect Andropov and Chernenko when they were ailing, but after a decade of weak leadership it was something else to pick an unsuitable leader who was healthy enough to live for some time. Andrei Gromyko was seventy-five and had no domestic experience, Viktor Grishin (the Moscow party leader) was seventy-one, had no experience outside of Moscow, and was of mediocre quality at best. Romanov was only sixty-two, but he was poorly educated and very narrow in his experience and outlook.

Gorbachev, by contrast, was intelligent and well-educated. He had been tested in a variety of responsibilities in recent years, and he was of the right age to provide leadership. The younger members of the Central Committee, worried about the future of the system in the face of economic stagnation and the Reagan foreign policy challenge (and many of them hopeful for promotion), had real reasons to select him over his rivals. Gorbachev need not have treated Chernenko's memory with such disrespect in placing his obituary on page 2 of Soviet newspapers, but he, no doubt, wanted to dramatize just how powerful his political position was. In this respect, the gesture was not misleading. It was also not misleading in suggesting that Gorbachev intended to move with great strides over the political landscape.

2

Toward
an Iron Curtain

U NDERSTANDING Gorbachev and his generation requires an understanding of the politics of not just the Soviet period, but of the Russian past as well. If Gorbachev is, indeed, going to lead a major opening to the West, he will not be reversing Russian history, but reversing a limited period in Russian history. He will be representing forces that have been fighting for decades for such a reversal, already with some success.

For many Westerners, Russia was always separate from and alien to the West, at least after the Mongol conquest in the thirteenth century. From this perspective, anti-Western groups such as the Slavophils represented the essence of Russian thought and political culture, and Lenin's Bolsheviks were a natural expression of this tradition. The implication is that Russia's relationship to the West is immutable, not subject to political conflicts or political process.

But this view is highly misleading. The Slavophils were not the spokesmen of either the tsar's court or the bureaucracy, but a conservative protest against them. After the end of Mongol rule in 1492, Russia had increasingly become a part of the West. Even the establishment of an autocratic state in Russia really followed the normal Western line of development at the time. Hans Rogger of UCLA reminds us that the growth of national consciousness in the seventeenth century was itself "one of the elements and one of the signs of Russia's westernization." Russia, Rogger writes, "was singularly receptive to every current of ideas which emanated from Western Europe."[1]

The great Russian leader of the eighteenth century, Catherine the Great, had actually been born in Germany and continued to speak Russian with a heavy German accent. During her reign, French became the normal language of discourse among the aristocracy, and, in the words of Suzanne Massie, "Many ordinary Russians spoke several European languages as a normal part of their lives; merchants and shopkeepers found it essential, and even coachmen tried their luck in broken Italian and German."[2]

The repeated efforts of Catherine the Great and her successors to initiate modernization and Westernization policies in order to strengthen national defense and Russian power never, of course, went unchallenged.[3] During the reign of Peter the Great, the conservative protest was violent, and he dealt with it violently. As Rogger points out, many Russians in the interior, especially in the old capital of Moscow, continued to see Peter's new capital as an evil, Westernizing force (a German state, Alexander Herzen called it in the mid-nineteenth century):

> St. Petersburg early became a symbol of all that was resisted and feared as strange, novel, and threatening to established interests and ways of life. The new capital of Peter became for many the "foreign" city, the home of an essentially non-Russian court, populated by ministers and courtiers whose interests were thought to be only rarely those of Russia. From it, there spread all over the country not only the "French kaftan," and the "German frack," the powdered wig, the mincing walk, the clean-shaven face, and the Prussian uniform, but also deceit, waste, and corruption. However naive and crudely expressed this feeling may have been, it was to have a lasting effect.[4]

The debates heated up in the second half of the nineteenth century. The "West" had never been a uniform entity. Spain was very different from England, and France had been continually racked by controversy over the type of political institutions to adopt. Hence the question of Westernization in Russia always involved asking—which West? The elite often had been divided on whether to follow the French example or the Prussian, and the increasing emphasis on universal suffrage in nineteenth-century Western Europe intensified these disagreements.

After Russia's defeat in the Crimean War in 1855, Tsar Alexander II began introducing serious reforms. Political reform soon waned, but the last two tsars, who were otherwise very reactionary, presided over the most "radical" industrial policies. Alexander III began large-scale railroad construction, which his successor, Nicholas II, accelerated. For the first time Russia began to assume a large foreign debt to finance this and other projects. Foreign investment was encouraged, and Russia began to be dotted with foreign-owned factories. This was the program that led B. H. Sumner to write about the profound change in the economic structure of Russian life that "westernized it to a far greater extent than previously."

Lenin and the West

The suggestion that the Bolshevik and Khomeini revolutions were analogous reactions against the process of Westernization will jar most readers, for one of the revolutions is seen as "left-wing" and "radical" and the other as "right-wing" and "reactionary." Moreover, it is not usual to emphasize the anti-Western character of the support for Lenin's Bolshevism. We basically have accepted the Marxists' definition of themselves and of socialism as the culmination of Western economic and political development after capitalism, rather than a substitute for it.

Yet, the old totalitarian model always emphasized the similarities between left-wing and right-wing extremism. Communist revolutions have never occurred in advanced capitalist societies, but only in countries at relatively early stages of industrialization.

In the Third World, the radical revolutionaries have been explicitly anti-Western. Just because Russian Communists did not speak in these terms at the beginning of this century does not mean that the Bolshevik Revolution was different.

Marx can have many different meanings in an underdeveloped country. In Western Europe, Marxism had been both a serious attempt to understand historical development and a deeply moralistic critique of capitalist society. In an underdeveloped country, these two aspects of Marxism do not fit comfortably together. If history moves inexorably by stages, a revolutionary in a "feudal" country is fighting to establish a capitalism he considers morally repulsive. Moreover, if the revolutionary accepts the inevitability of stages, this, in practice, means that the country will follow the Western line of development, accepting its "superstructure" as well as its "bases"; if the revolutionary goes directly to socialism, the economic forms and social relations of the West are being rejected.

Those who actually introduced Marx into Russia did, in fact, explicitly reject the European path of industrialization, or, in milder versions, insisted that peasants be treated more gently and that industrialization progress more slowly. Such intellectuals—Lenin labeled them "the Populists"—used Marx's works to document the horrors of capitalism that they thought Russia should avoid. They demanded that Russia adopt different—and more communal—institutions and follow its own path of historical development.

Then in the 1890s a large number of Russian intellectuals began looking to Marxism for its historical analysis. These people—who came to be called "legal Marxists"—spoke about an ultimate socialist society, but their immediate political goal was to push Russia along the West European line of development. Since Russia was at the feudal stage, they saw Marxism as an effective doctrine that said Russia must and should become capitalist.

Although Lenin strongly criticized the Populists, he essentially found Marxism appealing for the same reason that they did: Marxism's condemnation of capitalism and its "superstructure" in Western Europe. Lenin continually expressed contempt for the cultured, Westernized men of his society—the liberals, the professors, the businessmen, and the bureaucrats. The hallmark of his political career was a consistent refusal to cooperate with those who wanted to move Russia along a Western European path. When he came to power, he adopted a policy of industrializing Russia with different institutions and social relationships than in Western Europe, thereby proving that the Populists were right in saying it could be done.

The social base of the Bolshevik Revolution, as of the Khomeini revolution in Iran, was provided by former peasants streaming into the city. As in the developing societies of the twentieth century, the peasants in nineteenth-century Russia had little contact with the major urban centers and life within them. This changed with the industrialization and modernization during the second half of the nineteenth century. An improvement in medical care led to a decrease in the mortality rate and a rapid increase in population. The resulting pressure on the land produced real rural hardship—including a famine in 1891—and migration into the city. Industrialization furthered this process by creating job opportunities that served as a magnet as well.

In Russia many peasants who did not emigrate to the city worked part-time in it. The non-black-earth lands in the center of the country had poor soil, and a family could hardly support itself from agriculture alone as the population increased. So the men often worked for months in the city, often hundreds of miles from their native village. Many traveled with their horses all the way to the Donbass coal fields in the Ukraine to work in the mines.

The peasants of central Russia had been serfs less than a half century earlier. Even after the abolition of serfdom they had continued to be members of a village commune that both limited their freedom and provided them security and stability. Sudden exposure to the city, to factory life, to strange secular values, and to the insecurity of market forces came as a real shock to many. Like the new urban population in Iran in the 1970s, they associated these alien values with the West and the Westernized elite in control of the country. It was a particularly easy association in Russia because of the wave of foreign investment and importation of foreign managers that had occurred in the decades before the revolution.

Leonid Brezhnev was a typical product of this period. His father came directly from the village to the largest steel plant in the Ukraine in 1900, and Leonid was born in 1906. Seventy-five years later he still had vivid, bitter memories of his youth:

> Our family lived in the workers' settlement called "The Lower Colony"... To the southwest of the village, in "The Upper Colony" was a totally different world... The factory administration consisted of Frenchmen, Belgians, and Poles... Entry by the workers to the "Upper Colony" was forbidden. Cabs on pneumatic tires would roll up and important ladies and gentlemen get out of them. It was as if they were a different breed of people—well-fed, well-groomed, and arrogant. An engineer dressed in a formal peak cap and coat with a velvet collar would never shake hands with a worker, and the worker approaching an engineer or foreman was obliged to take off his hat. We workers' children could only look at "the clean public" strolling to the sounds of a string orchestra from behind the railings of the town park.[5]

It was the fathers and older brothers of the Brezhnev generation who gave Lenin his victory. The Bolshevik Revolution was no sudden coup d'état by a tiny conspiracy. By 1907, the revolutionary Marxists and Lenin's group within them were receiving the support of large numbers of Russian workers in the elections to the consultative assembly, the Duma, formed after the Revolution of 1905. In the next years just prior to World War I, Lenin's Bolsheviks had increasingly taken over the trade unions, again through elections. And after the Bolshevik Revolution, in the relatively free election to the Constitutional Assembly in December 1917, Lenin's party received nearly 30 percent of the vote. Although this was far from a majority, the Communists had a majority of the Russian workers and a majority or near majority of the peasants in the center and the west of the country, where migrant work was so prevalent. Lenin lost among white-collar employees and among peasants who still had little contact with the cities.[6]

There were many reasons for the support that Lenin's extremism received. Serfdom left a real sense of class polarization among the peasants, and the Bolsheviks' theme of class exploitation struck a responsive chord among workers with the attitudes Brezhnev expressed. Lenin's program—and even more the form of Communism that developed under Stalin—provided a simple answer and sense of certainty that insecure people were craving, and in a direction that corresponded to the communal values they had known in the collective village mir.

A key reason for Lenin's support, however, was the anti-Western implications of his program. Lenin damned the Populists as he fought with them, but he was as determined as they were that Russian industrialization would take place under institutions very different from those in Western Europe. To a Russian audience, Leninism represented a repudiation of the institutions and values of Western Europe—and, of course, of the Westernized elite that was ruling Russia.

Many suggest that if professional revolutionaries and workers inside Russia were perceiving an anti-Western element in the analysis and appeals that Lenin was issuing from exile in Western Europe, then Lenin himself was unaware of what was happening. The son of a high provincial educational official, Lenin viciously denounced the Asiatic side of Russia and certainly was eager to transform rural Russia with industrialization based on large factories. After the revolution, he named an education minister (Anatolii Lunacharsky) who had joined the Bolsheviks only in 1917 and who was quite Western-oriented. Lenin sometimes spoke admiringly of America in comparison with the Western Europe he knew.

Unquestionably Lenin was a complex man, and it is impossible to believe that he would have carried Russian xenophobia to the heights that Stalin did. Nevertheless, we should be careful about glorifying Lenin. The French historian, Alain Besançon, may have painted an extreme picture of Lenin's attitude to the West, but, if so, only in its shadings:

> Lenin's tastes were ... those of the generation of the sixties ... Of modern art he knew nothing and wished to know nothing. A contemporary of Max Weber, of Freud, of English logic and of German critical philosophy, he knew nothing of any of them. He was wary of the Russian literary *avant-garde*, even when it claimed to be

revolutionary . . . Valentinov, who knew him well in Geneva . . . asked him whether he had read Shakespeare, Byron, Molière, or Schiller. He had not. Of Goethe, he had read *Faust*, and that was all. Amongst the Russian classics, he had read Pushkin, Turgenev, Tolstoy, and Goncharov, but only in the manner in which the critics of the intelligentsia, Bielinski and Dobriolubov, understood them. . . . He happily ignored Dostoevsky. "I haven't got time for this rubbish!" he declared . . . The vicissitudes of exile led him to visit all the brilliant centres of European civilization at its zenith. He disregarded them. In London he disdained "*their* famous Westminster," the Westminster of the class enemies . . . He hated Paris.[7]

Everybody in Russia in 1917 understood that Lenin was the great extremist on the political scene, and there were few illusions about the thrust of his policy. Although many Westerners treat the gutting of democratic institutions after 1917 as a betrayal of the revolution, Lenin had never promised Western democracy. He always treated members of the Westernized elite—even members of other socialist parties—as implacable class enemies, and he was determined to have a political system in which they would play no role.

The surprise of the 1917 Revolution was Lenin's ability to survive in power. People looked to the French Revolution for their analogies, and Lenin was seen as a Robespierre who would be overthrown and eventually replaced by a military officer like Napoleon. But World War I had fatally weakened the other Russian institutions, especially the army, and the anti-Westernism in Lenin's program had a far stronger appeal to the generations of Brezhnev and his father than the Westernized elite (including the other socialists) ever suspected.

After the revolution Lenin continued to show his basic attitude about Russia's relationship to the West in a number of ways. One was symbolic. Almost immediately he moved the capital from Petrograd (as St. Petersburg was then called) to the anti-Western Moscow, and returned to the site of the Bolshevik Revolution only once during the rest of his life—for the funeral of his brother-in-law.[8] Then when Lenin established the Communist International, or Comintern, to direct foreign Communists, he named the party leader of Petrograd as its chairman. Peter's city was still the window between Russia and the West, but now it was to be a window through which Russia brought Europe to a higher level of civilization rather than the other way around.

The crucial test came in foreign economic policy in the early 1920s. After the end of the Civil War, Lenin decided to follow a New Economic Policy (NEP) to try to restore the economy. Private agriculture was legitimated, and compulsory delivery of agricultural products by the peasants was abolished; some small factories were denationalized; free artisans and some private trade were permitted.

A large number of high officials pushed for an extension of NEP into the realms of foreign trade and investment. The industrial and financial authorities wanted to limit the Commissariat of Foreign Trade's monopoly of foreign trade and to control trade with tariffs and customs instead of administrative measures. While Lenin was ill in 1922, virtually the entire Politburo supported a partial change in policy. In addition, the Commissariat of Finance, whose counterpart under Count Witte had pushed industrialization in the 1890s on the basis of foreign credits, retained an interest in a similar policy in the Soviet period.

It was precisely the debts from the tsarist period that raised the key question. These debts were huge, and in the heady days after the revolution, the Communist party had repudiated them and had nationalized foreign property without compensation. As the Civil War ended and Russia began reestablishing diplomatic and trade relations, Westerners demanded that the Bolsheviks reverse these policies. The United States even made this a condition for establishing diplomatic relations.

Even aside from ideological considerations, the Soviet Union faced an awesome dilemma. On the one hand, as two highly respected Western economists were to write in 1924, the repudiation of the debts and the nationalization without compensation "uprooted so far as Russia was concerned the whole economic system based on private contract and by rejecting the very foundations upon which international credit and commercial intercourse among civilized nations are built, isolated Russia from the rest of the world." On the other hand, the annual payments on the debt would have been so high that "a thriving agricultural, commercial, and industrial Russia would be quite out of the question."[9]

Since the industrial countries—and David Lloyd George of Great Britain in particular—wanted Russia to recover so that it could serve as a market, the obvious solution was for Russia to recognize the legality of the debts and the principle of compensation, but for the West to accept that the payments would not be made in full. At the Genoa Conference in 1922, Lloyd George suggested such an arrangement and the Soviet foreign trade minister and the top two officials of the foreign ministry—all on the delegation in Genoa—strongly and repeatedly recommended to Moscow that it be accepted. Lenin's answer could not have been more negative and emotional. His notes to his delegates at the Genoa Conference were almost hysterical, filled with underlinings and exclamation points to emphasize his distress. He was able to brush aside his subordinates' pleas.[10]

Foreign debt and the foreign trade monopoly were logically separable issues, but at their heart they were the same—the relationship to the European economy. Lenin's position on the monopoly of foreign trade was the same as on the debt. His personal secretary has described the extremely "intensive" attention he gave this question, despite rapidly deteriorating health. He "was convinced that a rejection of the monopoly of foreign trade... would mean going on a fatal path for Soviet power."[11] In response to a defense of a compromise Politburo decision by *Pravda* editor, Nikolai I, Bukharin, Lenin presented an impassioned plea for autarchy:

> Our border is maintained not so much by customs or border guards as by the monopoly of foreign trade. This Bukharin does not see— and this is his most striking mistake... that no customs policy can be effective in the epoch of imperialism and of the monstrous difference between poor countries and improbably wealthy ones. Bukharin refers several times to customs protection, not seeing that any of the rich industrial countries can completely break this protection. It is enough for it to introduce an export subsidy for the importation into Russia of those goods that are covered by our

customs protection. Any industrial country has more than enough
money for this, and, as a result, any industrial country will surely
break our indigenous industry . . . Russia can be made an industrial
power not by any customs policy, but exclusively by a monopoly of
foreign trade. Any other protectionism is in contemporary conditions completely fictitious—a paper protectionism . . . We should
struggle against this with all our might.[12]

Even in precarious health, Lenin was able to get the Central
Committee (and the majority of Politburo members who stood
behind it) to reverse their policy. The monopoly of foreign trade
stayed in place and, indeed, was strengthened.

A number of American historians have argued that at the end
of his life Lenin had come to accept NEP as a permanent gradual
path to socialism rather than a temporary retreat,[13] but Lenin's
position on foreign economic questions calls this view into real
doubt. The emotional character of his argument betrays an extraordinarily negative attitude toward the market and private
property, and it is difficult to see how this was compatible with a
long-term continuation of NEP. Moreover, Lenin's refusal to cooperate on the foreign debt left him few options in financing the
rapid industrialization he was demanding. The domestic sacrifices
required could only be justified by continuing hostility toward
the West and its institutions.

Finally, while Lenin had insisted that relations with foreign
nations were necessary, he always justified them in purely tactical
terms. In March 1919 he told a party congress: "We are living not
merely in a state but in *a system of states*. It is inconceivable that
the Soviet Republic should continue to exist for a long time side
by side with imperialist states. Ultimately one or the other must
conquer. Until this end occurs, a number of terrible clashes between the Soviet Republic and bourgeois states is inevitable."[14]
He argued that the inner nature of their capitalist economy would
drive the Western governments to war with one another, and it
was only these "contradictions" that gave the Soviet Union some
maneuvering room. But nothing in the analysis suggested that
diplomacy would provide more than a temporary respite.

Stalin and the West

Western scholars presented with the analogy between the Bolshevik Revolution and the Khomeini Revolution have reacted with varying degrees of enthusiasm and skepticism. A common response, however, has been that the Khomeini of Russian history was not Lenin, but Stalin.

There is much to be said for this argument. Stalin was the man Lenin chose to be his closest political assistant, and this choice was no bizarre aberration. Nevertheless, Stalin's personality and background were different from Lenin's. Lenin had lived for seventeen years in Western Europe, but Stalin remained inside Russia except for several very brief visits abroad for party congresses. He was one of the *komitetchiki* (committeemen), who, as professional revolutionaries, had organized the workers at home for the leadership in exile. In 1911 Stalin reported to an associate that "the workers are beginning to look upon the emigration [and their tempests in teacups] with disdain: 'Let them crawl on the wall to their hearts' content; but as we see it, let anyone who values the interests of the movement work, the rest will take care of itself.' "[15] In the 1920s, he contemptuously described the party leaders who had been in exile abroad as "literati."

Moreover, Lenin was an ethnic Great Russian, while Stalin was a Georgian who spoke Russian with an accent until the end of his life. Stalin associated himself strongly with Russian nationalism, however, and showed real xenophobic strains. Robert Tucker, the American political scientist, believes that his identification with Russia was deep, but some Georgians think that he adopted this stance to protect himself from the suspicion of favoring the non-Russians. Yet no one doubts the depths of his anti-Western feelings.

Stalin spoke as a Russian nationalist from the early days. In 1907 he called the Bolsheviks the "true Russian faction" and the Mensheviks "the Jewish faction." Instead of seeing the Russian Revolution as part of the world revolution, Stalin publicly declared in August 1917, "The possibility is not excluded that Russia will be the country that blazes the trail to socialism. It is necessary to give up the outworn idea that Europe alone can show us the way." In the mid-1920s he referred to Leninism as the highest achievement of "Russian culture," not of the European philosophical tradition, and he enunciated the doctrine of "socialism in one country," emphasizing Russia's ability to do the job without the help of the world revolution.[16]

When Stalin explained to a party congress in 1923 why foreign policy could not be discussed in public, he presented a chilling picture: "We are encircled by enemies. That is clear to all. The wolves of imperialism who encircle us are not dozing. There is not a moment when our enemies do not try to seize hold of every little crack in order to slip through and harm us... In such a situation, is it possible to bring all questions of war and peace out onto the street?" The image of wolves stayed with Stalin. At least twice in important meetings with Westerners during World War II he was seen drawing wolves. The same thing happened in his last meeting with a foreigner (the Indian ambassador) several weeks before his death.[17]

When Stalin gained control of foreign relations in the late 1920s, he demanded that the Comintern refuse cooperation with non-Communists abroad. Moderate socialists were said to be "social fascists"—even worse than the avowed fascists because they only pretended to represent the workers.

The test came in Germany. Hitler had glorified war and had even written of the need for more *Lebensraum* (living space) for Germany, with the Soviet Ukraine being Germany's natural breadbasket. The German Communist Party was large, but Stalin refused to change Comintern policy. So the German Communists still voted in the parliament against measures that would ameliorate the Depression—and often were on the same side as the Nazis. The only possible explanation for Stalin's policy is that he really did believe that Western governments were completely the tool of Big Business, so it didn't matter whether a "moderate" or a Hitler was the political leader. Perhaps an open fascist would be easier to overthrow in a revolution than a "social fascist" who could fool the workers.

When no revolution occurred and Hitler gave indications that his foreign policy might be as dangerous as his words suggested, Stalin did permit his foreign minister to pursue a vigorous collective security policy against Germany. In 1935 the Soviet Union actually signed a military alliance with France against Hitler. The Comintern in 1935 also approved a "Popular Front" policy that encouraged the Communists to cooperate not only with the social democrats, but with anyone to the right of them who opposed Hitler.

From the perspective of American conservatives in the McCarthy period of the early 1950s, all of this anti-Hitler "front" activity looked like liberals and moderates being tricked by Communists. Men dedicated to a Communist revolution, however, could see it as Communists being trapped into cooperation with moderate forces for short-term foreign policy goals and being distracted from their revolutionary goals at a time of great depression.

As a result, many people contended that a fundamental change had occurred in the relationship between the Soviet Union and the capitalist West. Leon Trotsky wrote of the "revolution betrayed." The Soviet Union, he asserted, was eager "to seem a moderate, respectable, authentic bulwark of order [and] in order to seem something successfully and for a long time, you have to be it."

> The bureaucracy has arrived at the idea of insuring the inviolability of the Soviet Union by including it in the system European-Asiatic *status quo* . . . The Communist International systematically paints up the episodical allies of Moscow as "friends of peace," deceives the workers with slogans like "collective security" and "disarmament," and thus becomes in reality a political agent of the imperialists among the working classes.[18]

Nicholas Timasheff of Fordham University, scarcely a Trotskyist, treated these developments as a "great retreat" and contended that "in the course of The Great Retreat, the Russian nation has broken the backbone of the Communist monster."[19]

In reality, neither the hopes of Timasheff nor the fears of Trotsky were to be realized. The Soviet Union was still not part of the West. The foreign minister, Maxim M. Litvinov, might talk and even think in Western terms, but the language of the country's two top leaders, Stalin and Viacheslav M. Molotov, remained quite ideological. Even during the Popular Front period, the Communists did not abandon their revolutionary goals. Many wondered, for example, if the victory of the Republican government in Spain over Franco would not simply result in a Communist Spain. And, of course, the Great Purge of 1937–38 created an enormous sense that some deeply alien and awful force was controlling Russian policy. The American diplomat, George F. Kennan, expressed the feeling vividly a quarter of a century later:

> Russia was never really available, in the sense that Western liberals thought she was, as a possible partner of the West in the combatting of Nazism... Russia herself was, throughout these years, the scene of the most nightmarish, Orwellian orgies of modern totalitarianism... Her purposes were not the purposes of Western democracy. Her possibilities were not the possibilities open to democratic states. The damage that had been done with the triumph of Bolshevism in Russia went deeper than people in the West supposed.[20]

A number of Westerners have argued that the Great Purge, which wiped out virtually the entire administrative elite, was motivated by Stalin's desire to kill potential opponents in a pact with Hitler that he already had in mind (and that he actually signed in August 1939). It is far more likely that Stalin feared that a prolonged Popular Front with foreign moderates would legitimate liberalism at home unless he destroyed all opposition.

In any case Stalin's attitude toward contact with Western ideas was made abundantly clear in his recruitment policy after the purge. When he removed domestic policy officials, Stalin normally tried to replace them with men in their thirties with worker and peasant backgrounds and the appropriate specialized education and experience for the job, even if the experience was extremely short. He followed an identical policy in the military, except that the new commanders were in their forties. (In practice, most of the World War II generals had been at the corporal or sergeant level during World War I.)[21]

The men Stalin selected for the diplomatic corps, however,

were very different. They were, to be sure, in their mid-thirties on the whole,[22] but they almost never had experience dealing with foreigners. Charles E. Bohlen described meeting Gromyko, for example:

> He came to lunch at Spaso House [the American embassy], and I think it was the first time he had ever had a meal with foreigners. It was quite apparent that Gromyko, a professor of economics, had virtually no knowledge of foreign affairs. He was ill at ease and obviously fearful of making some social blunder during the luncheon.[23]

Rather than insisting that diplomats have the kind of expertise that he demanded of governmental and economic administrators as well as military officers, Stalin clearly felt that the contact with the West necessary for such expertise was deeply corrupting. The diplomats of the Gromyko generation were, of course, allowed to go abroad, but their contact with Westerners was carefully controlled. Stalin continued to see the world as an alien place.

The Debate on the Cold War

The Nazi invasion of the Soviet Union on June 22, 1941, brought Stalin back into the arms of the Western democracies. The war was no longer described as an imperialist one, driven by the capitalist competition for colonies, but one between the imperialist powers and the peace-loving countries, prominently including the United States and Great Britain.

The Grand Alliance of World War II inevitably left many crucial decisions to be made when the war ended. Each of these policy decisions was marked by a major debate that emerged from behind closed doors to appear in the censored press in muted form.[24] Publicly Stalin was pledging a continuation of the wartime alliance in the postwar period. Therefore, whatever he was actually thinking, many people in the Soviet establishment could argue for a postwar world that embraced the West. Substantial parts of the educated elite—even among "ideological specialists" within the party apparatus, who are thought to be the most reactionary men in the Soviet system—remained attracted to a relaxed posture toward the West.

Many pushed such a policy in a number of different ways permitted by the censorship. For example, the philosophers, under the leadership of Georgii Aleksandrov, the head of the Propaganda Administration of the Central Committee, respectfully emphasized the Western philosophical roots of Marxism-Leninism.[25] Many historians wrote in a similar vein about nonradical figures from the past.

Others tried to create the impression of a less threatening outside world by treating Western governments as partly responsive to moderate forces. Even in late 1946, when relations with the United States had already become very bad, Eugen Varga, the director of the Institute of the World Economy and World Politics, wrote that "the democratic forces in all countries" had such a strong political impact on governmental policy that "the relationship of the capitalist countries to the Soviet Union will not be the same as it was in the prewar period." In 1947 he expressed scorn at the idea that "the working class and the Labour Party have no influence on the policy of England, that the financial oligarchy makes all the policy."[26]

One of the most important of the ideologists, Petr Fedoseev, who was appointed chief editor of the Central Committee journal, *Bolshevik*, in the late summer of 1945, implicitly attacked the Leninist idea that the drive for colonies inevitably led to war. He said that World War II was very different from World War I, for the issue of colonies was not involved. Germany was simply seeking world domination. He insisted that "Leninism does not consider war inevitable, even in present conditions. War can be averted if the peace-loving nations act in concord." Fedoseev's contention that "the goals pursued in the war determine the policy of these states after the war" seemed reassuring about American aims.[27]

The most comprehensive and authoritative published statement of the moderate position appeared in a two-part article by Andrei Vyshinsky in *Pravda* on April 21 and 22, 1945. Vyshinsky had been the prosecutor in the show trial of the 1930s and had been chosen to install a Communist regime in Romania in February

1945, but in these articles he suggested that the Soviet state had strong support and could adopt a more moderate policy at home, especially with regard to the peasants.

Vyshinsky said little directly about foreign policy, but one sentence in Vyshinsky's discussion of the formation of the Soviet federation seemed to summarize his position on relations with the West at the present: "Comrade Stalin warned against the danger of an attack on us from the outside, against the danger of economic isolation for our federation, and also against the danger of an organized diplomatic boycott." In the context of the rest of his program, Vyshinsky certainly appeared to be saying that a moderate policy, including in Eastern Europe, was necessary to avoid isolation in the postwar period.

All of these views, to repeat, came from very high officials, and they did pass the censorship, but they never went unchallenged. The conservatives damned men like Varga for revisionism and said that Western governments were "completely subordinated" to the monopolies and, therefore, driven to war to acquire colonies. The conservatives described the British Labour party as being as bad as or worse than the Conservatives, for it tried to fool the workers. They said that to treat the Western philosophical tradition with respect was to forget that these pre-Marxist philosophers were agents of their respective ruling classes. For most of the conservatives the roots of Lenin were not to be found in Western Europe, but in radical Russian philosophers such as Nikolai Chernyshevsky.

The most comprehensive early statement of the hard-line position came in a two-part article that began in the same April 22 issue that contained the second part of Vyshinsky's article. If Vyshinsky wrote about the state, then Pospelov wrote about the Communist party. It was a "heroic party"—one with "its ideological implacability, its organized nature, and its iron discipline." The party won its authority by its mobilizing character, by its struggle against "foreign invaders" and "the bourgeois-landlord counterrevolution." Pospelov said little about foreign policy directly, but again and again he attacked "social-democratic parties of the West" that had "sunk into the bog of opportunism" and represented "Marxism in words" alone, and this implied no possibility of a moderation in Eastern Europe. Pospelov's sharp criticism of the social democratic parties seemed a way of implying that there were no moderate forces in the West who might reduce governmental hostility to the Soviet Union, even if the latter wanted détente. "Millions," Pospelov asserted, had been inspired by "Stalin's theory of the possibility of the victory of socialism in one country," and this conveyed precisely the opposite message from Vyshinsky's warning about economic isolation or diplomatic boycott.

For the historian, the really fascinating question is the significance of these debates, and especially their continuation well into the period when the Cold War was heating up. They add fuel to the debate about whether there was a real chance of avoiding the Cold War. My own sense, however, is that it would be a mistake to believe that a good relationship between the United States and the Soviet Union was realistically possible at this time.

In talking with the Western leaders and to his own public, Stalin seemed committed to continuing the wartime alliance in the postwar period, but there is reason to doubt that Stalin really had strong hopes of maintaining it. From 1943, the former foreign minister, Maxim Litvinov, was pessimistically warning American acquaintances about the depth of the Soviet leader's suspicions.[28] When President Roosevelt acquiesced in the removal of Henry Wallace as vice-presidential candidate in the election of 1944 and his replacement by Harry Truman, these suspicions can only have become darker. In June 1941, when Germany had invaded the Soviet Union, Truman had told *The New York Times* that "if we see that Germany is winning, we ought to help Russia, and if Russia is winning we ought to help Germany and that way let them kill as many as possible."[29] Truman had probably forgotten this flip remark, but it surely did not disappear from Soviet files and affected judgments about Roosevelt's intentions. Stalin himself was telling the Yugoslavian Communists: "This war is not as in the past; whoever occupies a territory also imposes on it his own social system. Everyone imposes his own system as far as his army can reach. It cannot be otherwise."[30]

Stalin conceivably might have accepted the status quo and a

reasonably correct détente between the two blocs if the West had calmly accepted the Communization of Eastern Europe.[31] Conceivably his appeals for a maintenance of the Grand Alliance were a sincere expression of a desire for a stable division of Europe. Yet, if he had such thoughts, he was being totally naive. A West that had gone to war in September 1939 when Germany invaded Poland would never calmly accept an outcome of that war that left Poland Communized and a Soviet satellite.

The official signs of a return to orthodoxy and an ensuing xenophobia began with a 1944 Central Committee decision that condemned a favorable treatment of Hegel. Marx had come out of Hegelism, and this decision began the denial of the European roots of the Bolshevik Revolution. Then in May 1945 the top scholars of the Academy of Sciences were given medals on its anniversary. The directors of the institutes and the academicians were given the highest medals, but Eugen Varga, although he was both, ranked so low that he did not make the list published on the first day in *Pravda*. As a guarantee that the insult would not be missed, the published list was broken precisely at the point where his name appeared in alphabetical order so that his was the first name to be seen on the second day and was very visible. Medals are a serious business in the Soviet Union, and such a decision had to be taken at the top. Varga could still publish his views, but in May 1945 they were not really respectable.

Gradually, and seemingly inexorably, events moved toward the awful xenophobia of the last years of Stalin's life. In 1946 Stalin personally described the origins of World War II in traditional Marxist terms. He criticized Aleksandrov's history of philosophy, and a conference was called to condemn it. When the criticism was not strong enough, scholars were brought in from the provinces who felt no constraints. In 1947, the big conference dealt with Varga's book, and when he persisted in expressing his views, his entire institute was closed.

In the last years of Stalin's life, the two great sins became "cosmopolitanism" and "bending low to the Western ideas and practices," different ways of saying the same thing, although most "cosmopolitans" turned out to be Jews. The guilty person was soft on Western ideas, on capitalism, on the United States. He was not sufficiently patriotic and socialist. He was calling into question Russia's ability to go it alone and lead the world.

In countless ways, Western influences were denied or memories of them were erased. In Leningrad, the restaurant Nord (French for "North") was renamed Sever (Russian for "North"). The bread called Frantsusky (French) became Gorodskoi (Russian for "city"). Scholars no longer studied Marx, but focused on Lenin and on his Russian predecessors. The vast majority of modern inventions and achievements (even the game of baseball) were said to have originated in Russia. Except in the defense industry, real limits were even put on the ability of Soviet engineers to read Western technical publications. Cybernetics, the basis of the new computer industry, was said to be anti-Marxist.

The xenophobic campaign reached the point where the students at Moscow University told a joke about it. A contest was held, they said, to find the best book on the elephant. The Frenchman submitted one on the love life of the elephant, the Englishman one on "The Elephant and the Empire," and the German a seven-volume treatise on the metaphysics of the elephant. The Russian's entry was "Russia: The Homeland of the Elephant." To the professors, it was no laughing matter.

The last four months of Stalin's life featured a growing campaign of "vigilance." It began with the uncovering of a plot by doctors (mostly with Jewish names) to kill Soviet leaders, but it was extended in an ominous way to a wide range of dangerous ideas and activities done at the behest of the West. In his last work, *Economic Problems of Communism*, Stalin categorically rejected all continuing pressure for change. Wars between capitalist states were inevitable, he asserted. The Western state was completely subordinated to the monopolies, the Third World bourgeoisie had sold out completely to the West, and the objective laws of socialism (the code phrase for an insistence on the status quo in the Soviet Union and its rigid application to Eastern Europe) were all-powerful. A number of policy-oriented intellectuals who had been suggesting otherwise had to recant. The most prominent was Petr Fedoseev, who in 1945 had tried to suggest a continuation of the Grand Alliance was possible. Now he had erred by questioning the binding character of the laws of social-ism.

Nicholas Timasheff may have unwittingly put his finger on the major reason for this pathological trend. In predicting a moderate development in 1946, he noted that "for the past 150 years every major war, whether successful or unsuccessful, has pushed Russia further towards the liberalization of her institutions."[32] Stalin too read Russian history, and he may not have liked the pattern. That men like Vyshinsky were pushing both for an easier foreign pol-icy and a moderation of governmental repression at home may not have reassured him. Americans as different in their approaches as George Kennan and Adam Ulam, the Harvard political scientist, have emphasized the importance of this factor. They have ex-plained the origins of the Cold War in substantial part by Stalin's need for an outside menace because of (in Kennan's words) "the necessity of explaining away the maintenance of dictatorial au-thority at home."[33]

For us in the 1980s, however, the really crucial thing is not the explanation for the Cold War and the deepening xenophobia. It is that the drive to reintegrate Russia back into the West was actu-ally quite strong in the 1940s. Even in the heart of the Stalin era, less than ten years after Stalin had liquidated virtually the entire elite in the Great Purge, some very substantial people were insist-ing that Russia was part of the West and should not cut its ties. They were daring to fight the growing tendency toward xeno-phobia. They were trying in one way or another to combat the old ideological division of the world into separate black-and-white parts.

Think about the people we have been discussing. A very sub-stantial part of the Communist party members of the Moscow intellectual community, let alone the non-Communists, were for liberalization. However, the men who have been quoted were at the center of the repressive and propaganda apparatus: Vyshinsky was the prosecutor at the show trials, Aleksandrov was number two in the Central Committee apparatus in the realm of idea con-trol, Fedoseev was one of Aleksandrov's chief assistants, and Varga was a thoroughly political scholar.

Indeed, even within the Politburo, there is a real paradox about the Russian xenophobia at the end of the Stalin period. Stalin was not a Russian, but a Georgian. The same was true of his secret police chief, Lavrentii Beriia. In the last three years of his life, Stalin had an inner core of four top lieutenants: Beriia and three ethnic Great Russians—Georgii M. Malenkov, Nikita Khrushchev, and Nikolai A. Bulganin. These Russians were opposing the worst aspects of Stalin's policy of xenophobia and began reversing it within six weeks of his death.

3

The Costs
of the Stalin System

AT the time of Stalin's death, most Western observers predicted that the totalitarian system would remain unchanged or become even more totalitarian. Yet the new Soviet leaders were determined from the very beginning to change course. They signaled their intentions in the lead article in the obituary issue of the leading Central Committee magazine, *Kommunist*, which was "signed to press" (passed the censor and sent to the printer) only four days after Stalin's death. The article, written by a Malenkov assistant, Eduard Burdzhalov, praised Stalin, but its purpose was to bury him ideologically as well as physically. As the article progressed, it increasingly mentioned Lenin and Leninism more than Stalin:

The tactics of Leninism do not exclude reform, compromises, and agreements. Under certain conditions they are necessary. V. I. Lenin indicated that, in leading a long and complicated struggle against the bourgeoisie, it is unreasonable to refuse to maneuver, to

> take advantage of differences between enemies, or to make compro-
> mises with allies, even if they are temporary, unreliable, wavering,
> and conditional... This is like climbing an uninvestigated and un-
> climbed mountain and refusing beforehand to make zigzags some-
> times, to turn back sometimes, to change direction... The tactics
> of Leninism have a flexible, maneuvering character.[1]

Six weeks later, the first authoritative attack on Russian chau-
vinism appeared in *Kommunist*. It was certain to attract attention
because its author was the same Fedoseev who had written in
favor of détente in 1945 but had been denounced in *Pravda* at the
end of 1952. His message was also attention-getting. Praising
Russian achievements, he said, "does not mean that the Soviet
people shut themselves off from the culture of foreign countries."
He pointedly criticized "the monopolists of the USA [who] want
to isolate the toilers of the USA completely from the outside
world," and indicated that this was inexcusable.[2] At the same
time the harsh propaganda line toward the Western power in the
Soviet press was also moderated.

These verbal changes were reinforced in July by an actual end
to the Korean War and the arrest of the hated secret police chief,
Lavrentii Beriia, who seems to have been the major adviser to
Stalin pushing a xenophobic policy. So the wild xenophobia of
the previous six years was going to be curbed, although it was
still not known (and still had not been decided) how much. To
some extent Russia was going to turn once more toward the West,
and since this posture was closely associated with tolerance of
Western ideas at home, Russia was going to move away from the
harsh repression of the Stalin years.

But why was this happening? Why had Western predictions
been so wrong? Western scholars had been seeing "totalitarianism" or "the Soviet system" as having a life of its own. They had
forgotten that the Soviet leaders were real men with personal interests and values, and that the system Stalin had created had
enormous costs for these leaders. Some of these costs were purely
political or ideological, but a new generation of leaders also had
reason to fear the repression of the Stalin period for personal reasons.

In addition, the Stalin system suffered a fatal economic contradiction. Stalin had promised that autarchy and repression would allow the Soviet Union to catch up with the West rapidly. In reality, the autarchy that protected an insecure Russian people from market forces and strange Western ideas also protected Soviet industrialists from foreign competition. Consequently the Soviet economy failed to match that of its rivals in vigor and innovativeness. The Soviet system helped the Soviet Union to win World War II, but it was the losers of that war—Japan and Germany—that surged forward economically out of the destruction of the war, not the Soviet Union.

Political Costs

The first reason that the new Soviet leaders were moved to change Stalin's system was simply because they were afraid for their lives. During collectivization or the incorporation of new territories, Stalin had killed or imprisoned many ordinary people, but in more normal periods, the Soviet dictatorship was most repressive toward the educated elite and the top political officials. The most powerful 50,000 to 100,000 officials in 1937 were decimated in the Great Purge, and the top officials in 1953 were the ones who most feared a new purge.

The Politburo members, above all, had to deal with Stalin and his whims on a daily basis. Stalin was a truly awful man who seemed to delight in teasing or laying a trap for an unsuspecting subordinate. For example, he recommended to Gromyko that he improve his English by going to church while ambassador to the United States. Nikolai Bulganin, whom Stalin trusted to supervise the military and the defense industry, once remarked to his friend, Nikita Khrushchev, "You come to Stalin's table as a friend but you never know if you'll go home by yourself or if you'll be given a ride to prison." Khrushchev noted that "Bulganin was fairly drunk at the time, but what he said accurately depicted how precarious our position was from one day to the next."[3]

Whatever the Politburo and the Central Committee members might think about repressing the average citizen, if they permitted one of their own number to gain absolute power over the population, how could they prevent that power from being turned against themselves? So they eliminated Beriia and began restricting police and other controls in order to increase their own personal security. They also worried about the safety of their families. The children of the elite tended to go into intellectual or professional jobs and to be attracted to Western culture. Severe repression could catch them up in it—and with it their fathers.

Second, we should not discount the possibility that new leaders simply had different values from those of their predecessors. A lust for total power and a willingness to kill millions of people are not normal, and a stable society does not permit those with such values to rise to the top. Men who are willing to endure the hardship of exile or prison for their ideology can be fanatical and ruthless, but the second and especially the third generation of leaders in radical countries are almost always more moderate.

Instead of rebelling against the established order into which they have been born, postrevolutionary generations have been driven to succeed within it, and they have been conventional enough to do so. They have worked for years within a bureaucratic hierarchy. They have learned to play committee politics, to accommodate the various interests of their subordinates and their bosses. If they had been too single-minded, they would have offended someone at some time in their careers and would have been shunted aside. Hard-driving, even ruthless people obviously can do well in a bureaucracy, but their personality differs from that of men who go underground and captivate people by their oratory and charisma.

Many of Stalin's Politburo lieutenants, not to mention lesser officials, must have found some of Stalin's policies repulsive. Marxist-Leninist ideology had treated socialism as a more just and freer society than capitalism. Party doctrine had enshrined a "democratic centralism" that called for free discussion of alternatives before a decision was made. The Politburo members were scarcely tempted to renounce one-party rule and call free elections, but we should not assume that the dreams of Marxism-Leninism had no meaning for them.

Nikita Khrushchev, for one, seemed to have a strong personal commitment to improving the lot of the peasant, and he appeared to be deeply offended by Stalin's attack on the Communist party. Khrushchev was willing to loosen censorship to a considerable degree. Moreover, he had a powerful faith in the superiority of socialism over capitalism. He really thought that the Soviet Union could easily surpass the United States and begin making the transition to the less repressive and higher stage of Communism. Georgii Malenkov, Khrushchev's chief rival in 1953, seemed to be more of a representative of the educated middle class—"a man with a more Western-oriented mind than other Soviet leaders," the American ambassador, Charles Bohlen, reported.[4]

A third political reason for the new leaders to change Stalin's system of rule was, paradoxically, that it undercut the real control of the top leaders as much as it strengthened their position. When Westerners talk about control by the party in the Soviet Union, or by the dictator, or by Moscow, they often use words whose implications they have not fully considered. For a dictator— whether an individual or a collective Politburo—the strengthening of control over society as a whole can give excessive power to the instruments of control and administration rather than to the dictator. The danger is particularly great in a thoroughly socialistic country in which each branch of the economy is under the control of a single ministry.

One problem is the scale of the leaders' responsibilities. Although the leaders have the power to issue any decree to the ministries and to remove any official, they don't have the time to exercise consistent detailed control over them and prevent them from following their own self-interest. In June 1985, Gorbachev was very blunt on this point when he complained that "the ministries in their present form . . . have no interest in the economic experiment. . . . They have vast experience and ability in swaddling up everybody and interpreting the decisions of the Central Committee and the government in such a way that after their application . . . nothing is left of them." His audience applauded, and Gorbachev retorted sarcastically, "If the ministers are applauding too, the ice has begun to shift."[5] This produced both laughter and applause.

Another problem is just as serious. A new revolutionary leader may be convinced that he knows what to do and how to do it. Later, less fanatic leaders are far less self-confident. In 1957, Khrushchev asserted that "it is laughable to seek in Marx or Engels instructions on, for example, how to proceed with requisitions of agricultural products from the private plots of collective farmers."[6] Andropov openly admitted that we "still have not uncovered the laws that are inherent to [socialist society], especially economic ones."[7] Gorbachev in July 1986 made the point even more strongly: "No one, not only in Khabarovsk, but also in Moscow, in the ministries, in Gosplan, in the government and in the Politburo, has ready recipes that can guarantee acceleration for us."[8]

Stalin had a number of ways to obtain information and advice. In 1923 he spoke about creating a system of "barometers" instead of a "simplified apparatus." The Central Committee apparatus, the trade unions, the Ministry of State Control, the scholarly community, and, of course, the secret police—all of these overlapped the ministries in a way that was supposed to reduce Stalin's dependence on the latter in the policy process.

To some extent, Stalin's system served its intended purposes. Nevertheless, if the party apparatus is to be effective in controlling specialized ministries, it must also be staffed with specialists who will have the same professional biases as the ministries. It hardly matters whether military officers are in the Ministry of Defense, the Central Committee apparatus, or the staff of the Defense Council; they are going to believe that a serious defense threat exists and that military expenditures need to be increased. Doctors in the institutions overseeing the Ministry of Health are not likely to call for a fundamental change in the health system, while agricultural administrators, wherever they work in the system, will not usually favor a decollectivization that leaves agricultural administrators unemployed.

Thus freer discussion in the press is necessary for leaders who want to receive information and advice. Fundamental criticism of the health system or the military is far more likely to come from nonprofessionals, or from iconoclasts within a profession, than from established institutions. Such people need the media to get their views to the leadership. An isolated letter to the Central Committee or even an isolated critique in a professional journal will not do the job. But through the press, the leadership can be convinced that the criticisms are responsible enough to represent a respectable consensus.

When the leadership is conducting a xenophobic campaign against foreign ideas, the problem of adequate information becomes especially great. Important new ideas always come from a variety of countries, and cross-fertilization is especially vital for a developing country, as the Soviet Union was in the 1950s. One advantage a backward country has is using foreign experience cheaply rather than having to invent everything from scratch.

But a developing country that refuses to borrow in the name of patriotism is dooming itself to a backward position. By 1953, for example, the Soviet Union was not making the transition from steam locomotives to diesels because of the notion, prevalent in the 1930s, that petroleum would soon be exhausted. The discovery of petroleum in the Middle East changed this consensus abroad, but the new ideas never percolated into the Soviet Union. In agriculture, the growing importance of soybeans was not recognized. In defense, the military was not being exposed to Western thinking on the implications of nuclear weapons.

Finally, the controls on the flow of information and ideas from the West interfered with the building of popular support for the leadership. An American study of emigrants who left the Soviet Union during World War II found that the police were the major source of dissatisfaction and suggested that the reduction of terror would benefit the system.[9] And so it proved to be. The liberalization after 1953 only increased public satisfaction at little political cost.

For all these diverse reasons, the Politburo members of 1953— or at least the sophisticated ones who comprised a majority— sensed that loosening censorship and restrictions on Western ideas would increase their power by allowing them to take advantage of Western technology. It would increase their support among the population, and increase their control over the ministries and over any future general secretary with dangerous ideas about a purge.

The trick, of course, was to loosen up without letting the situation get out of control. In his memoirs, Khrushchev said, "We in the leadership were consciously in favor of the [cultural] thaw, myself included, but... we were scared—really scared. We were afraid the thaw might unleash a flood, which we wouldn't be able to control and which would drown us."[10] Nevertheless, the dangers of action were not as great as those of total inaction. The Politburo had ample levers to permit gradual movement and to reverse the flow of events to a limited extent, if necessary.

The Defects of the Economic System

Stalin's obsession with investment in heavy industry meant extremely low living standards, even eight years after the end of World War II. This policy not only betrayed all the promises of abundance contained in Communist ideology, but was increasingly counterproductive for growth as well. So little was being paid to the peasants and so little investment was being made in agriculture that low agricultural productivity was beginning to threaten industrial growth.

A change in investment patterns was not inherently difficult. Soviet standards of living could be improved without drastically changing the system. As we shall see in the next chapter, the improvement over the next three decades was, in fact, substantial. Food consumption and housing conditions rose significantly under Khrushchev, and this trend continued in the Brezhnev years, when the Soviet Union became an appliance society and took the first steps toward becoming an automobile society.

But other economic costs of Stalin's policies were imbedded in the system itself. Nationalization under Stalin had gone to extraordinary lengths after 1929. Peasants were permitted to have private plots (really gardens around their cottages) and to sell the produce on the free market. Old private homes were permitted, until they were razed for high-rise construction. But that was about all. It was not legal to establish a private restaurant, a private kiosk on the street, or a one-man private repair service. The owner of a private car could not legally use it as a taxi. And a person with an idea to produce a Hula-Hoop, a personal computer, or any other product could not create a private business.

It is not just that industry was nationalized. A government might own the factories but control them as loosely as U.S. stockholders control, say, IBM. Or government financial institutions might make capital grants to entrepreneurs with new ideas and the state might share the profits with the manager-entrepreneur, as occurs with many absentee owners in the West. Or nationalized trade organs could grant franchises to independent managers, as Exxon or McDonald's.

The Soviet economy does not, however, function in this way. State ownership has meant control over the various branches of the economy through a series of ministries that occupy a monopoly position in their respective branches. Any new product must be provided by a state enterprise under one of these ministries. Any new store or restaurant must be built for and operated by the Ministry of Trade (except for company cafeterias or commissaries operated by other ministries). Any new hybrid plant must be developed by a state institute or experimental farm, and it is introduced into the state farms or collective farms only with the approval of the appropriate administrative agencies.

As a result, many spontaneous developments that we take for granted in the United States become very difficult in the Soviet Union. If Vietnamese immigrants move into an American city, Vietnamese restaurants and stores spring up. If IBM does not develop a personal computer or Eastman Kodak an instant camera, an Apple Computer or Polaroid Corporation can be created. Acreage devoted to soybeans or a new breed of corn can soar if the products seem profitable. If someone in the United States thinks that a pet rock might sell, he does not have to go through a corporate board.

In the Soviet Union, all such decisions on investment in new products, new factories, and new restaurants must go through a monopolistic ministry and even (if the sums are large) through the State Planning Committee (Gosplan). Consequently, the innovator faces far greater problems than the natural inertia found in any large bureaucracy such as IBM. The sheer volume of decisions to be made and the cumbersomeness of the planning process severely restricted any hope of flexibility in the Soviet Union. In the electronic age, this is extremely costly, for products may become obsolete within a year or two, or even months.

Not only was new investment funneled through noncompeting ministries, but the planning system severely limited the flexibility of existing firms and the competition among them. The managers worked under very detailed plans that included not only gross sales targets, but also the numbers of different items to produce. The plans also included the amount of supplies that would be received (so much steel, so much petroleum, such and such machinery, etc.). The actual customers (plants or wholesalers) that were to receive the output in each quarter were specified, as were the actual suppliers of raw materials and parts.

Once the managers were given a fixed plan, they were awarded a bonus for overfulfillment of the plan and were punished for underfulfillment. As a consequence, they had an incentive to work well, as judged by a large number of indicators (although the gross sales target was most important). However, they really could not overfulfill the plan by much, because they couldn't find the extra supplies, and they had little incentive or possibility of shifting production from an item that was unpopular to one more popular. A publishing house, for example, had a plan including titles and their press run, and it could not obtain the paper even if it could sell much more of a given title. Hence, a best-seller became defined as one that disappeared from the shelves in a few days.

To be sure, there was some flexibility and wheeling and dealing in Soviet management. The ministries could change orders in their plants when new priorities arose (e.g., when the government decided to increase investment in the petroleum industry in the late 1970s), or when other plants failed to fulfill their plans. Suppliers and their customers could make a few informal deals. For example, if a garment factory agreed to take cloth of a slightly different type or lower quality than specified in the plan, the textile plant might give it quicker delivery. Nevertheless, the flexibility did not extend to the ability to change suppliers if the original one produced low-quality materials, and the flexibility usually involved cutting corners or lowering standards.

Indeed, the one major form of flexibility built into the economic system produced the greatest problem of all. Since the State Planning Committee could not know all the details of the work of all the plants in the Soviet Union, it had to bring the managers into the planning process, by giving them some general guidelines at the beginning of the planning year and then having them submit draft plans for the coming year. How much did they propose to produce, how much of various supplies did they need, how many workers, and so forth? The job of higher officials was to balance the many proposals into an integrated plan.

In the Soviet press of the 1930s, the 1950s, or the 1980s, one continually finds almost identical stories about the consequences of this planning system. Fulfilling a fixed plan did not result only from good work. The simpler way was to start with an easy plan. Indeed, if the original plan wasn't reasonable, even the best manager would never be able to fulfill it.

The managers were not fools, so when they submitted their draft plans, they proposed as low an output plan as they conceivably could get away with. The managers also demanded as many supplies and as large a work force as possible. They could not keep the difference between the amount they earned on sales and the amount they paid in costs, nor were they judged by such a ratio. Once supplies or workers were officially included in the plan, they were "free" to managers who were judged by their ability to meet their output plan within the limits imposed.

In this situation, the job of Gosplan, like that of the budget office in a university or other bureaucratic institution, was to bring the inflated requests into line with resources. Since the resources were the proposed output plans of the different plants, Gosplan also applied pressure for an increase in output. Therefore, the planners took last year's figures and called for a more or less arbitrary increase, following what the American economist Joseph Berliner, on the basis of interviews with managers of the 1930s, called the ratchet principle.[11]

This system had a number of unfortunate outcomes. First, while a manager might dream of a big bonus for a major overfulfillment of the plan (if he could only find the supplies), he knew that this higher level of production would only become the base for next year's ratcheting. If he was producing for the consumer market and was tempted to take advantage of a fad like Hula-Hoops or Hush Puppy shoes, he knew that the demand would soon drop. Since he was working for a bonus rather than for profit, he could not even make a real killing, and he would be in deep trouble the next year when demand dropped. He had an interest in overfulfilling the plan by 1 or 2 percent, but not by much more.

Second, if the manager economized on supplies and labor, these new low figures would also be the basis for next year's plan. He had an incentive to utilize all of the supplies he was allocated in a given year, so that his plan would not be cut in the future. His incentive was particularly strong to retain as many workers as he could. Bonuses were awarded on a monthly basis, and irregularities in the supply system could lead to pressure to produce at top speed—"to storm"—at the end of each month to meet the plan, and this required extra workers. So long as they were part of the base plan, they were no cost to the manager.

In the past, an incentive system that encouraged managers to hoard workers was one of the great strengths of the Soviet system. Developing countries usually have had a major unemployment problem (and Russia did in the 1920s), and the Soviet incentive system solved this difficulty and ensured that everybody could find work. There was even a labor shortage. It was not a problem to waste labor when it was unskilled and would have been underutilized in any case. But it was something else to waste labor that was becoming more and more skilled and educated. And, when the supply of new entrants into the labor force slowed to a crawl in the 1980s, the incentive system became disastrous.

Third, the planning system created extremely low incentives for innovation. A new product or technological process will inevitably have bugs in it, and it will complicate the fulfillment of that year's plan. Since the new product or reduced level of costs would simply be included in next year's plan as the target to meet, there was no advantage to the plant over a plan in which the preinnovation situation is the target.

This problem was particularly great in the capital goods area.

Consumers' demand for particular items is finite. There are only so many watches or television sets that the population wants. If one factory produced especially low-quality or undesirable goods, customers would buy the products of a competitor, and the Ministry of Trade would put on real pressure. When manufacturers produced for other factories, however, they found that the demand was virtually infinite. The requests to Gosplan for supplies were always greater than the available production, and allocations included in the plan were "free" to the manager. It usually was better for a manager to accept a relatively low-quality or inefficient machine instead of nothing. Hence there was a continual sellers' market in which manufacturers had little direct incentive to improve their product.

To be sure, these defects of the Soviet incentive and planning system were no secret to top Soviet planning officials. We get our information from the same Soviet press that they read (and write in). The planners naturally tried to counteract the tendencies of the incentive system. Besides applying the "ratchet" to managerial requests, they could order a manager to introduce this or that product, this or that new machine. They tried to introduce an indicator for innovation. However, pressure met constant and pervasive foot-dragging—a problem that was intensified by the fact that the ministries had virtually the same interests as their plants and were also resisting pressure.

Indeed, sometimes both the producers and their customers were dragging their feet simultaneously. The Soviet response to the energy crisis of the 1970s is a perfect example. In the capitalist world, the drive to economize on fuel quickly led to the development and purchase of energy-efficient machinery. In the Soviet Union, by contrast, the machinery plants had a captive market for their existing machinery and had no incentive to go through the hassle of producing a new energy-efficient machine. The customers of the machinery manufacturers received their petroleum by chit, and its price was fundamentally irrelevant to them. Hence they had nothing to gain from installing a new machine and working the bugs out of it. They would simply be allocated the lesser amount of petroleum that it required. And, in fact, in a decade in which every wasted barrel of petroleum was a loss of much valuable foreign currency, the Soviet Union was the only major country that made almost no progress in lowering demand for energy.[12]

One should not, of course, exaggerate. Machinery that broke immediately and produced nothing was a minus, and if the quality of materials was too low, the customer-managers would complain and get action. The pressure from higher authorities for improved innovation did have some impact. Indeed, the quality of Soviet production has been improving over the years, and sometimes fairly substantially. The problem is that other countries have been improving far more rapidly.

The Problem of Protectionism

The United States has a number of inefficiencies and distortions built into its economic system, but in comparison with other economies, it still provides a relatively free and competitive environment for its manufacturers. Moreover, while the United States lacks certain raw materials and needs to import certain tropical agricultural products, it has such a large domestic market that it is not driven to trade simply to create large, efficient factories with enough customers for their goods. Nevertheless, when American industries are protected from foreign competition, they often become sluggish and inefficient. The automobile industry is the example that is familiar to everyone, but there are many others.

An enormous amount has been written about the relationship of the Soviet Union to Western technology, but most of it has missed the point. The Soviet Union is criticized for relying on foreign technology through copying, buying, or stealing, as if this demonstrated a fundamental flaw in the system. Actually the Soviet Union has been a developing country, and all developing nations (and all developed ones to a large extent) use foreign technology in one way or the other. It would be foolish for an India or a Mexico to spend money to reinvent the tractor or even to develop a new oil drill or computer, and they seldom do.

The problem is not that the Soviet Union has utilized foreign technology, but that it has done so in a very truncated and flawed manner. Most developing countries do not just copy or buy old technology, but try to use direct foreign investment, joint companies, joint production, licenses, or the like. But the Soviet leaders did not want to permit foreigners to share in or obtain profits inside the Soviet Union. During the exaggerated xenophobia of the last years of Stalin's life, Soviet scientists and engineers even found it difficult to read Western technical literature and to steal or copy Western ideas.

When Brezhnev opened the Soviet economy more to the West, severe limits remained. For a long time, a deputy minister of foreign trade complained in 1984, the prevailing view in the Soviet Union had been that "the importation of licenses shows the technological backwardness of the purchasing countries and lowers its prestige." He asserted that Japan pays 3.1 times more for licenses than it receives and West Germany twice as much, and noted that "the psychological barrier of underestimating the significance of licenses is still not overcome everywhere."[13] Moreover, machinery would not be imported if comparable machinery were produced inside the Soviet Union.

When Americans think of protectionism, we apply the word to practices—tariffs and quotas, for example—that governments undertake to thwart the natural working of an existing market. Lenin, as we have noted, insisted that this was not enough. Instead, the Soviet Union established a monopoly in which foreign trade had to be conducted directly through the Ministry of Foreign Trade. Because the Soviet Union has not followed traditional protectionist practices, we do not see it as protectionist, but Lenin was right when he told Bukharin that the Soviet system provides a stricter protectionism than provided by tariffs. The Soviet Union makes Japan look like an open society.

Even if the monopoly of foreign trade were abolished, the basic planning and incentive system protects Soviet manufacturers from foreign competition, especially in the capital goods industries. Since managers request as much machinery as possible in the planning process, the requests for machinery and other supplies always exceed the amount available. Even when Brezhnev began importing manufactured goods and whole factories, no domestic manufacturer had to lose any business. Even inferior goods still found a customer, and no manufacturer had to raise quality to compete with foreign goods.

Finally, the Soviet Union had forgone the advantages of a vigorous export strategy. The most rapidly developing countries in recent decades—notably in East Asia—have attacked protectionism indirectly through such a strategy. Toyota did not have to compete with General Motors in Tokyo; it competed in California, with the same effect. Countries such as Japan, Korea, and Taiwan began exporting not when they had reached the most advanced technological level, but when they were relatively backward. It was by selling products in the world market at cheap prices that they broke into these markets and, thereby, forced their manufacturers to raise the quality of their goods to world levels and to innovate to meet changing demand.

The Soviet incentive system, however, gave the managers little reason to produce for the export market, unless forced by Gosplan. Since the manufacturers of equipment and raw materials had a virtually unlimited domestic demand, they were not forced to go abroad to find markets. Instead, any intelligent manager avoided the export market at all costs, especially the non-Communist export market. The higher quality and technological level required for the foreign market would make gross production plans harder to fulfill. Variations in foreign demand, unless completely absorbed by the Ministry of Foreign Trade, would introduce variability into the plan or into plan fulfillment, if foreign sales were to become a key indicator.

Thus, the Soviet Union had to take a series of steps if it wanted to overcome the impact of autarchy on Soviet economic performance. First, in the mid-1950s, it had to relax the restrictions on the reading of foreign technical journals and end the campaign against "bowing low to the West" in the technical sphere. Then the Soviet leaders had to overcome their resistance to foreign trade. They had to permit ever more trade representatives and economic administrators to travel abroad to sell and buy things. This began in the Khrushchev period, and Brezhnev added political concessions (notably to the West Germans) to increase the flow of technology from Western Europe.

Nevertheless, Brezhnev's policy of importing foreign technology was basically a failure. Some Western economists guess that it improved the annual rate of Soviet economic growth by 0.5 percent, but even this is not certain. The annual rate of economic growth was 5.0 percent in the late 1960s before the import policy was instituted, but fell to 3.0 percent in the first half of the 1970s and to 2.3 percent after 1976. The basic problem was that the industrialists still enjoyed almost total protection from foreign competition and that the major benefit in the trade of manufactured goods was sacrificed.

Consequently, if Gorbachev is serious about raising Soviet technology to world levels, he must not only conduct domestic reform, but also attack the protectionism enjoyed by Soviet manufacturers. He must break away from autarchy in a way that has barely been attempted, and the Russian economy must be at least partially exposed to the rigor of the business cycle. Russians must be exposed much more fully to Western ideas and must be freer to travel to the West so that they can develop a feel for Western markets. Soviet citizens of Moslem background must develop a similar feel for the Middle East if they are to be used to penetrate that market.

In short, the close relationship between the Soviet Union's economic ills and protectionism means that serious economic reform must involve a real break with the intellectual and cultural isolation associated with the Russian form of Khomeinism. Such reform depended on a totally new relationship between Eastern Europe and Western Europe and so aroused fears among the conservatives that went well beyond economics.

To subject the managers to foreign competition also means to subject the workers to harsher discipline—to force them to work more productively than the foreign workers whom they have been told are exploited under capitalism. Economic reform may also expose the workers to unemployment if the Soviet integration into the Western business cycle becomes fairly complete. And economic reform will have these consequences at the same time that it requires an attack on subsidized prices and acceptance of greater inegalitarianism in income distribution.

It is small wonder that Brezhnev, especially in his declining years, was unwilling to undertake radical economic reform. Gorbachev would surely like to avoid it too. Nevertheless, the costs of the present system are extremely high. They threaten the Soviet Union's military position, they undercut the effectiveness of its foreign policy, and they utterly destroy the legitimacy of an ideology that claims socialism is advanced and capitalism is backward. A Gorbachev who hoped to rule in the year 2000 could not let things drag on.

4

The Politics of Reform: Group and Institutional Interests

WITHOUT question, political and ideological obstacles to reform *do* exist in the Soviet Union. Officials never like reorganizations and workers do not like the fear of unemployment. Communist ideology has emphasized egalitarianism and freedom from unemployment as the supreme human rights, and radical reform would threaten both. Hence it raises doubts not only among the workers, but also among those who take the ideology seriously.

Moreover, the Soviet Union is a multinational society with some twenty ethnic groups that have their own native language and are large enough and live in a compact enough area to think of national independence. Estonia, Latvia, and Lithuania actually were independent states between the wars. Russians who have been accustomed to thinking in Marxist terms must wonder whether a decentralization of economic power will lead to a decentralization of political power as well.

Many Westerners look at these economic, political, and ideological obstacles and assume that reform is impossible. Yet, Gorbachev has most emphatically pledged himself to radical reform. He has not simply talked about improving consumer services (the easiest part of reform), but about bringing Soviet technology to world levels (the hardest part). Since he hopes to rule until the end of the century, he must be serious, or else his promises will lead to public disillusionment long before then. If we are to understand Gorbachev's options and strategy, we should be asking ourselves why he thinks he can succeed and how he intends to do so.

Gorbachev's task is to build a shifting series of coalitions as he moves from one stage of reform to another. It is true that the vast majority of Soviet citizens have some reason to fear radical economic reform, but it is also true that the vast majority also have some reason to favor it. Since everyone will have something to gain and something to lose, Gorbachev must keep the attention of the majority at any one time on the positives rather than the negatives. He must take care not to arouse all the opposition at once, and he must use old language to make new steps seem less threatening. And as he warned us in his interview with the editors of *Time* magazine he must manipulate his foreign policy so that it contributes to the realization of his "grandiose" domestic program.

Institutional Interests

The institutional interest has long had the greatest legitimacy in the Soviet Union. As we have seen in chapter 3, the budgetary process has required each institution to press its demands for more funds and supplies, and top Soviet leaders have generally held that administrators should believe in their programs and fight for them. Stalin criticized an aircraft designer who conceded that another design bureau's airplane was better than his. "A designer should love his own plane,"[1] Stalin said. Similarly, Khrushchev in his memoirs explicitly refused to criticize the military for pushing for new weapons and the funds to build them. "That's their job," he wrote.

Indeed, the decision-making process is based on the assumption that institutions have interests that must be taken into account. The head of the staff of the Council of Ministers has been frank in acknowledging that "the representatives of the interested ministries and departments" are named to the interagency committees that draft legislation.[2] In 1986 the government even named the institutions that were to participate in a series of laws to be enacted in the coming years. A law that expanded the rights of people to engage in individual labor was drafted by a committee with representatives from the various legal organs, the trade unions, the Ministry of Trade, the Co-ops, the State Planning Committee, the Ministry of Finance, the State Committee for Labor and Social Problems, and the Academy of Sciences.[3]

In addition, when one institution leads the drafting of a more specific law or decree, it "must be cleared beforehand with the interested (*zainteresovannye*) ministries, state committees, and departments."[4] Frequently the interagency committees may not meet formally, but the practice of requiring "a second signature" or "third signature" from other interested organizations is fairly common. For example, no changes can be made in wage scales without the signature of the relevant trade union as well as the economic administrative agency involved.

To a very large extent the institutional interests in the Soviet Union are perfectly recognizable to anyone familiar with Western bureaucracy. For example, Americans who participated in Law-of-the-Sea negotiations found the representatives of the Soviet Ministries of Geology, Fisheries, Merchant Marine, and so forth taking quite predictable positions. The participants in Soviet environmental politics act in expected ways.[5]

Even when Soviet institutions behave in different ways from their American counterparts, the incentive system usually explains why. Thus, the Ministry of Health runs the hospitals, which are funded on the basis of the number of beds and doctors. Even though the Soviet Union has far more hospital beds per capita than the United States (which itself has too many), the number in the Soviet Union keeps rising because of the budgeting formulas. In order to justify these increases, the ministry keeps patients in the hospital an inordinately long time—for example, two weeks for a normal delivery of a normal baby—despite the fact that this is totally uneconomic and drastically increases the danger of infection. Medicines and equipment produced by another ministry are neglected. Indeed, this bureaucratic self-interest—and the ability of the ministry to enforce its interests—is surely the major cause of high Soviet mortality rates.

A similar difference in behavior is found in the defense industry. The American defense industry is very susceptible to the military's desire for expensive, high-technology weapons and to constant changes in plans and design, for manufacturers are paid through cost-plus contracts. The higher the costs, the larger the profits. The Soviet defense industry administrators, by contrast, are judged primarily by their ability to meet a fixed plan, and they have an interest in as easy a plan as possible—and in weapons that are uncomplicated and do not change frequently.[6] Yet, as in the case of the Ministry of Health, the difference in behavior from the American counterpart's simply proves that Soviet bureaucrats defend institutional interests in the basic way that we would expect once we understand the incentives under which they work.

Institutional interests in the Soviet Union can also affect attitudes toward the West. It will come as no surprise that the newspaper of the Ministry of Defense takes a very hard-line view of the Western "threat," while the Ministry of Foreign Affairs likes negotiations and the Ministry of Foreign Trade likes foreign trade. Scholars in the Institute of the U.S.A. and Canada tend to favor a bipolar Soviet policy that concentrates on relations with the United States, while the Institute of World Economics and International Relations (which has a large concentration of scholars working on Western Europe) tends to favor a multipolar policy that concentrates on Europe and Japan.

Domestic institutions can also have interests in the posture that the Soviet Union takes toward the West, but these can be complex. Obviously the defense industry has an interest in a foreign threat that is not shared by the oil industry, which wants freer importation of advanced drilling equipment. Even in the defense industry, the producers of high-technology items have more ambivalent interests than the tank manufacturers, for détente may lead to defense funds being shifted from tanks to research and development. The Ministry of Culture generally has an interest in ideological control, which justifies its continued administration of cultural institutions, but the ministry's theater administrators profit from the importation of foreign films that increase the size of their audience, even (or especially) if such films are ideologically suspect.[7]

Soviet institutional interests with respect to economic reform are also complex. In general, of course, few institutions in any country really like any reorganization, for their officials have become accustomed to functioning within a system that they know. Nevertheless, some have more to lose than others, while still others may actually hope to benefit once the dust has settled.

Certainly everyone agrees that the institutions with the most to lose from reform are the economic ministries in Moscow. They have a comfortable monopoly position within their respective branches of the economy and protection from foreign competition, and reform challenges both.

Tatiana Zaslavskaia, a sociologist in favor of reform, agreed with Gorbachev's assertion that "the ministries, in their present form... have no interest in the economic experiment." She distinguished among three levels of officials: (1) those at the highest level, (2) "the employees of the branch ministries and departments and their territorial administrations," and (3) "the employees of the enterprises." In her view, economic reform "raises the prestige and influence of the first and third level, and lowers that of the second." By implication, she warned that the ministerial officials would have to be attacked. "Self-interest always lies at the base of behavior, whether it is conscious or unconscious. But it determines the main actions."[8]

Gorbachev had emphasized the ministers, but Zaslavskaia was right in talking about a wide range of officials within the ministries. The middle-level officials of the ministries have as much to lose as the higher ones. They are essentially production-oriented engineers rather than specialists in sales and marketing, and they issue vast numbers of directives relating to production and supply. A sales-oriented, consumer-oriented society would be a shock for them. The agricultural officials have more to lose than the industrial ones. Even capitalist industry has many bureaucratic jobs in the headquarters of giant corporations, but decentralization of farming decisions to the family level would leave many agricultural officials with no comparable administrative jobs to assume.

The military has reason to be ambivalent about reform. It tends to be basically conservative, and the ideology in which it indoctrinates its officers and troops is old-fashioned. It knows that it has been given top priority in a centrally directed system, and it fears that a system giving more power to the consumer would reduce its primacy. And, of course, if reform requires an opening to the West, the military would not like either the lessened sense of threat or a reduction in military spending.

Yet, in an era in which weapons take years or even decades to develop, the military has the responsibility of assessing threats in the fairly distant future, and it is trained to take a worst-case perspective. Increasingly in recent years, it has had a reason to worry that the computerization of Western conventional armies and the Strategic Defense Initiative might be at least partially effective. It must fear that at some point Chinese modernization will have a major impact on Chinese military capabilities, and that a Japanese GNP that is now moving ahead of the Soviet GNP might be translated into military strength if Japanese politics change.

The Soviet military knows that the technology of its weapons has often lagged behind the American. The Soviet defense industry took twenty years longer to produce an effective solid-fuel intercontinental ballistic missile, a high-orbit satellite system, and the capacity to catch film ejected from space. Nuclear submarines have been too noisy, and cruise missiles are still primitive. Even if the defense industry produces computerized weapons, the military must wonder how an army composed increasingly of Central Asians can cope within them unless Central Asia is computerized too. If the military—or a substantial part of it—became convinced that only economic reform would bring Soviet technology to world levels and create a population that could use it, it might conclude that economic reform, whatever its drawbacks, is indispensable.

In a system without competitive elections and with strong civilian control over the military, the Communist party is the only institution with the power to challenge the ministries. In much of the Western literature, this fact has been taken to mean that reform is impossible. Party officials are often described as an especially conservative and ideological group who are counterposed to a more reform-minded, pragmatic group in the governmental machinery.

In reality, the traditional Western interpretation should be reversed. The Central Committee apparatus, headed by the Central Committee secretaries, has some fifteen hundred officials, who are directly supervised by the general secretary and have a special relationship to him. Moreover, many of these officials do not have a power comparable to that of the ministries and develop a resentment toward them. The largest number of party officials work in the provincial party committees at different territorial levels. As we shall see in chapter 7, the regional party secretaries tend to be an integral part of the general secretary's political machine, and thus are naturally inclined toward him for political reasons. And their institutional interests strongly support any measure that decentralizes power from the ministries into the provinces.

The provincial party secretaries are much stronger in local matters where they sometimes have direct control, but they can only make appeals to the ministries in Moscow as supplicants. A decentralization that left more decisions to the marketplace would reduce the functions of many minor party officials. But the republican and regional first secretaries are the closest Soviet equivalent to American state governors, although with more power. If economic reform freed them from minor details (e.g., detailed involvement in procurement of supplies) and gave them more power to influence the course of development in their province, they would be enthusiastic.

The regional first secretaries also have the prime responsibility for political stability in their respective regions, and nothing would lead to their removal faster than a major riot. Hence their central concern about economic reform would be the same as the general secretary's: how to bring it about without undermining political stability. But they are also acutely aware that an absence of economic reform might also undermine stability. The man who raised this danger most insistently at the Twenty-seventh Party Congress was Boris Yeltsin—first secretary of Sverdlovsk Province in the Urals for over eight years and then first secretary of Moscow.

In addition to self-interest, the provincial party officials also have an emotional stake in the issue. The provinces really detest the ministries. Imagine the attitude of the Western American states to "Washington" or the Western Canadian provinces to "Ottawa." Imagine that, moreover, all the stores, theaters, factories, and farms were run from Washington through highly restrictive directives emanating from a highly centralized apparatus. Imagine that in 82 of 166 "states" the majority of the inhabitants had a native language other than English.[9] In this situation it would be easy to see outright dominance, not just overcentralization. So the ministries become the scapegoats for all local defects. Not surprisingly, almost every article published by the provincial party secretaries for thirty years has contained complaints about the ministries and the State Planning Committee. If "their" general secretary calls for the support of the provincial first secretaries in an attack on the ministries, their sheer pleasure will overshadow any lingering doubt about their own self-interest.

Income and Occupational Interests

A second major cleavage in Soviet society is produced by differences in occupation and "class." Well before Karl Marx, political philosophers from Aristotle to James Madison pointed to conflicts between the rich and the poor as the major source of political conflict in society. In the Soviet Union, too, some people have more income, status, and privilege than others and this affects their policy preferences. Yet the general American understanding of this aspect of Soviet life and policy could not be more fundamentally wrong. We speak incessantly about elite privilege, but the basic problem in the Soviet Union is not too much elite privilege, but too much egalitarianism.

Living standards under Stalin were extraordinarily low, but his successors began improving them for several reasons: a fear of unrest, a sense that the Soviet model would not be attractive unless life improved, a belief that better incentives were necessary to maintain growth, and, in many cases, a personal distaste for the level of poverty that existed. They began a war on poverty that involved shifting resources from investment to consumption. (This was one reason that economic growth slowed.)

As table 4 indicates, the new Soviet policy raised Soviet living standards steadily and markedly. The Brezhnev era in particular was the one in which the Soviet Union became an appliance society, in which people moved from a one-room apartment to a one-bedroom apartment, and in which meat consumption (despite a temporary plateau in the late 1970s) moved toward British levels. In addition, Khrushchev and Brezhnev followed a persistent policy of promoting social egalitarianism, at least with respect to workers and peasants. (They were much more insensitive to the

TABLE 4 SOVIET LIVING STANDARDS, 1960–1985

End of Year	Kilograms of Meat Consumed Per Capita	Square Meters of Urban Living Space Per Capita	Percentage of Families with			
			Refrigerators	Washing Machines	TV Sets	Cars
1960	39.5	8.9	4	4	8	—
1965	41	10.0	11	21	24	—
1970	47.5	11.0	32	52	51	2
1975	56.7	12.0	61	65	74	5
1980	57.6	13.0	86	70	85	10
1986	62.4	14.3	92	70	99	16

SOURCES: *Narodnoe khoziaistvo SSSR v 1964 g.*, *Statisticheskii ezhegodnik* (Moscow: Statistika, 1965), 610; *Narodnoe khoziaistvo SSSR, 1922–1972 gg.*, *Iubileinyi statisticheskii ezhegodnik* (Moscow: Statistika, 1972), 367 and 373; *Narodnoe khoziaistvo SSSR v 1975 g.*, *Statisticheskii ezhegodnik* (Moscow: Statistika, 1976), 576, 594, 595; *Narodnoe khoziaistvo SSSR za 70 let*, *Yubileinyi statisticheskii ezhegodnik* (Moscow: Finansy i statistika, 1987), 471, 472, 517.

problems of lower white-collar and service personnel, who are overwhelmingly women.) To a very large extent, they presided over a relative leveling in income distribution that is quite unappreciated in the West.

Obviously some Soviet citizens today live much better than others. The manager of a major Soviet plant receives 500 rubles a month, plus bonuses and privileges such as a chauffeured car. The person working at the minimum wage receives 80 rubles and has no bonuses and privileges. The difference between life in a big city and a small town or village goes far beyond money. It is simply unimaginable to the American who takes paved streets and shopping malls for granted even in a small town.

Moreover, higher bureaucrats have one kind of privilege that has relatively few counterparts in the West—access to special stores with goods that are not available in the regular stores and are sometimes sold at reduced prices. Except in military commissaries and exclusive clubs and executive dining rooms, every dollar in America tends to be equal to every other dollar. In practice, most Americans can't afford to shop at Tiffany's, but if they have the money to spend and want to spend it, the doors are open. In the Soviet Union, intellectuals and lower officials often have the money to buy goods, but don't have the access to the stores where they are available.

Soviet privilege must, however, be kept in perspective. There are differences in income and privilege in all societies; the crucial question is the size of the gap. The difference between the well-to-do and the poor in the Soviet Union is, in fact, considerably less than in the United States. As Konstantin Simis, the author of the highly critical *USSR: The Secrets of a Corrupt Society*, acknowledges, Soviet officials receive such low salaries that they cannot begin to live on a reasonable level without special stores or outright corruption.[10]

Consider one of the most famous stories of Soviet privilege—that chronicled by Vladimir Voinovich in *The Ivankiad*. Voinovich lived in a cooperative house—already a sign of privilege—but he had the only one-room apartment (one room, not one bedroom) in the building. He was at the top of the list to receive a two-room apartment, and one opened up when a family emigrated to Israel. However, the man supervising the publication of belles lettres throughout the Soviet Union—one of the top fifteen men in publishing in the Soviet Union—had a three-room (that is, two-bedroom) apartment adjoining the vacant one and wanted an extra room. There seemed to be a solution. A woman with a two-room apartment in the cooperative lived with her grown son who wanted to live alone, and she was willing to trade her apartment for two single rooms. If the wall between the vacant two-room apartment and the publisher's apartment were knocked down, one of the empty rooms could be attached to his, and the other could be turned into a one-room apartment. The woman would get the latter and Voinovich's old room, and Voinovich would get her two-room apartment. Except for the fact that the latter was not as spacious as the vacant two-room apartment, everyone should have been happy.

But Voinovich, in fact, was not happy with this arrangement. He wanted the better apartment, and he resented the privileged position of the publisher. (As a man with a wife and child, the publisher was entitled by law to 47 square meters, or approximately 425 square feet, of living space. He already had 50.5 square meters in his three-room apartment, and the addition would raise him to 68.) *The Ivankiad* describes the ensuing struggle in detail, including the various strings the publisher pulled (even the intervention of the mayor of Moscow and another Central Committee member), to get the cooperative to give him more than the law permitted.

No doubt, the struggle of the publisher violated the norms of Soviet society. No doubt, he should not have tried to pull strings, and his friends should not have intervened. Yet if one steps back and looks at the incident from afar, it is mind-boggling. Here is one of the top publishers in the country—perhaps on the level of the publisher of Simon and Schuster. In what other society would a man at that level be forced to live in a three-room apartment (each averaging about 12 by 12 feet) and have to fight with all kinds of semilegal means to obtain a fourth room—that is, a three-bedroom instead of a two-bedroom apartment, so that he

could have a study? And he lost! The cooperative eventually supported Voinovich, and the publisher was left with his two-bedroom apartment.

The relative egalitarianism of Soviet society is achieved in a
number of ways. First, in a thoroughly socialist society, the regime can forbid people from setting up businesses that would
make them wealthy. The state owns most housing, and it can
allocate rooms as it wants. Second, the state pays wages, and it
has followed a very egalitarian wage policy. Workers in industry,
construction, and transportation—and especially male workers—
do very well in comparison with managerial and technical personnel, and the gap narrowed in the Brezhnev period. In agriculture,
prices paid to farmers vary by region in order to compensate for
different growing conditions (see table 5).

TABLE 5 MONTHLY WAGES WORKERS AND MANAGERIAL–
TECHNICAL PERSONNEL, 1965 AND 1982 (IN RUBLES)

Industry	1965	1982
Workers	101.7	196.1
Eng.-Tech. Pers.	148.4	220.2
Ratio	1 to 1.46	1 to 1.12
Construction	1965	1982
Workers	108.4	224.3
Eng.-Tech. Pers.	160.7	221.0
Ratio	1 to 1.44	1 to .98
Agriculture	1965	1982
Workers (Peasants)	72.4	158.3
Agron.-Tech. Pers.	138.4	193.1
Ratio	1 to 1.91	1 to 1.22

SOURCE: *Narodnoe khoziaistvo SSSR v 1982 g.*, *Statisticheskii ezhegodnik* (Moscow:
Finansy i statistika, 1983), 370–71.

Pressure to permit more private enterprise in agriculture, trade, and the services has been resisted in substantial part because the leaders know that some people would become quite rich as a result, and they have a real distaste for "speculators." They realize that in China some artisans and peasants have earned a great deal of money since the reform. And in Hungary, the granting of royalties to inventors has led the inventor of Rubik's Cube (Mr. Rubik) to have a million dollars in hard currency in foreign banks.

A third instrument of egalitarianism in the Soviet Union is pricing policy. Americans take for granted that prices reflect the forces of supply and demand, except for indirect effects of governmental subsidies and protectionism. Scarce supplies are rationed by ability and willingness to pay. In a thoroughly socialist country, the state also sets prices, and it can try to ensure a more egalitarian distribution of goods by setting prices so that anyone can afford them.

In fact, the Soviet Union has followed its own version of "to each according to his needs" by heavily subsidizing the prices of necessities. Rent is fifteen dollars a month, meat and bread are sold well below cost, mass transportation is a nickel, medical care and college education are free, and cultural items are heavily subsidized (movies are under a dollar, books a dollar or two, and plays several dollars). Items that are considered luxuries (including cars) are sold at very high prices.

A fourth instrument of egalitarianism—or at least subsidy of the worker—is the use of the factory as a provider of services. Much of the country's housing, day-care centers, school equipment, and even stores are financed through the industrial ministries. They then are able to provide these services to their employees—workers as well as administrators—who, as a consequence, do far better than those in other sectors.

Work-centered services have been particularly important in food distribution. Unlike other industrial countries, the Soviet Union retains the noon meal as the big one of the day, and makes a real effort to ensure that meat (or, occasionally, fish) is always served in the cafeterias at work, even when it is not sold in the stores. This has been a way of making meat available to everyone, for cafeteria prices are low. Meat to take home has also often been sold at work—and rationed at four pounds per worker per week.

Finally, in talking about the position of workers, we cannot forget "managerial prerogatives." The Soviet leaders have been eager to avoid the slightest unemployment, even to the point of encouraging hoarding labor. There are fairly strict trade-union and legal safeguards against unwarranted firing. Managers surely hate this policy, as an infringement on their authority. All of the talk about "discipline" and "expansion of enterprise rights" in the Soviet Union is mostly about what has been called "managerial prerogatives" in the West—the power relationship between managers and workers.

Thus, in the urban areas, the Soviet Union has realized far more of its socialist goals than Americans have recognized. In agriculture, the situation is more complex. The average collective farm has 480 persons working on it, ranging from managerial and skilled farm-machinery drivers, whose earnings are comparable to those of urban workers, to unskilled field workers, who are the bottom of the whole country's status system. Except among the old, however, the number of unskilled farmers is declining, and as table 5 showed, there was also a leveling of wages between the peasants and the technical-managerial personnel in agriculture.

Yet, while peasants as a whole are still poorer than industrial workers in the Soviet Union, the situation looks rather different in worldwide perspective. Free market agriculture tends to drive the incompetent from the farm into unskilled city jobs, while it can reward the successful farmer quite well. If the Soviet Union moved fairly drastically toward market pricing and greater family independence on the collective farms, the skilled on the farms would do far better than they do now. They certainly have in China. Moreover, they would have the satisfaction of far greater independence. The incompetent or untrained, who are really being subsidized now, would have a tough time, and this "subsidy" is an important, if implicit, part of social policy.

If we fail to understand all these positive social characteristics of the Soviet economic system, we will never understand why it has been quite stable.

Unfortunately for the Soviet leaders, social policy as it developed under Khrushchev and especially Brezhnev had a series of negative consequences as well. First, by pricing many desirable items so low, the Soviet leaders have created a bigger demand than can be filled. The result is shortages and lines. If the United States priced steak at one-third cost, we too would have trouble keeping it in the stores. Instead of rationing by price, the Soviet system often rations scarce items by willingness to stand in line. The result is an enormous waste of time.

This is unacceptable to the well-to-do and even to the state, but the informal "solutions," such as the special stores, have seriously undercut the moral legitimacy of the system. At a writers' congress, the poet, Evgenii Evtushenko, bluntly expressed a widespread feeling: "Any sort of closed distribution of foods and goods is morally impermissible, including the special coupons for souvenir kiosks that lie in the pocket of every delegate to this congress, myself included."[11]

In addition, just as there is corruption in the United States (scalping) when a ticket to the Super Bowl or a rock concert is priced below the supply-and-demand equilibrium point, so the subsidized Soviet prices encourage black marketeers to obtain goods illegally or semilegally and to sell them at higher prices. This "second economy" increased substantially in size in the Brezhnev period. The Central Statistical Administration estimated that it provided 1.5 billion rubles of services—3½ percent of the country's total.[12]

In short, even more so than in the United States and Great Britain in the 1960s and the 1970s, economic growth in the Soviet Union was sacrificed to social welfare. We spoke of excessive exploitation of the workers under socialism, but by the end of the Brezhnev period, the problem had become excessive coddling of workers. Thus, to a very substantial degree, economic reform in the Soviet Union must embody large elements of Reaganism and Thatcherism—more benefits to the well-to-do, an attack on trade-union and worker privilege, less welfare and more investment, and, of course, a greater role for market mechanisms.

These various aspects of social policy are absolutely crucial to keep in mind if we are to understand group attitudes toward reform.

Intellectuals are generally enthusiastic about economic re-form. They would benefit from the liberalization associated with computerization and greater access to Western markets. A movement toward market mechanisms would end the hated special stores. A reduction in worker privilege would also be pleasing. (It really rankles young Moscow scholars with Ph.D.s to see the many advertisements for bus drivers offering 100 rubles a month more than they themselves earn.) But those who work in the state sector are on fixed salaries, and they fear inflation enormously.

The bureaucrats are very ambivalent. On the one hand, they will have to make the greatest adjustment in their work life. Some who functioned quite effectively in the old economic system will not be able to adjust to the new conditions. At a minimum, many will have to change jobs. When five agricultural ministries were merged into one in late 1985, some three thousand employees lost their jobs. They were paid a three-month severance pay, but the experience cannot have been any fun. In late 1987 it was asserted that 60,000 officials in the central ministries would lose their jobs in the coming reductions. In 1986 a top Soviet economist estimated that the plans for increase in labor production implied that thirteen to nineteen million fewer persons would be employed in material production by the year 2000, and he raised this estimate to twenty million a year later.[13]

Though Zaslavskaia suggested that factory managers would benefit from reform, they too would be very ambivalent. The enterprise directors are production engineers, and they are not used to a sales-oriented, consumer-oriented economy. They also would not enjoy foreign competition any more than the ministries. Hence their increased power and freedom would come at a very heavy price.

Yet managerial personnel at all levels will be as enthusiastic about the changes in social policy as American businessmen are about Reaganism. They resent the narrow gap between their wages and those of the workers. They are angry at the lack of worker discipline and at their inability to do anything about it. And though everyone likes subsidized prices, higher-income peo-

ple benefit less from them than lower-income. They would benefit more from a reform that puts a large variety of high-quality
consumer goods in the stores. Moreover as Wolfgang Leonhard
points out, bureaucratic privilege is never secure but depends on
grace from above. Only ownership of property, which cooperatives would provide, gives real security.[14] Finally, administrators
are college-educated men and women. Like bureaucrats everywhere, they would like to read newspapers with political gossip,
and they would like the freedom to travel. We should not forget
that the individual bureaucrat feels the sting of the dictatorship as
much as—or more than—the average citizen.

The group that has the most to lose from reform is the
workers, for they had benefitted the most from the Brezhnev "social contract."

No one likes the threat of unemployment. The workers' enthusiasm for tougher discipline would be limited, and they will think
that foreign competition is outrageously unfair. Similarly, Soviet
workers never will believe that meat prices need to be doubled or
tripled, especially if their wages are rising more slowly than those
of managers. The workers will exaggerate what is going on, and
they will resent the peasants, artisans, and traders who suddenly
become well-to-do, accusing them of exploiting the workers, as
they have been told for decades that this is what free enterprise is
all about. (This is already happening in China.)

Yet, we must not exaggerate. The workers are consumers, and
they would appreciate more goods in the stores. They would applaud the abolition of special stores. But most important the
workers of the 1980s are not the workers of the 1930s, let alone of
1917. In 1939, only 7 percent of workers had as much as an incomplete high school education. In 1970, by contrast, 20 percent
had a high school diploma, and this figure soared to 42 percent a
mere nine years later.[15] As a result, worker attitudes are becoming
more middle-class, and many would welcome the chance to enter
the middle class more "officially" by setting up their own shops,
repair services, contracting firms, and the like.

In my judgment, the prevailing Western analysis of the Soviet
social forces of the 1980s has been extremely flawed. In empha-

sizing the conservative nature of "bureaucrats" and workers, Westerners write as if Russians today are the same people they were decades ago. We know that industrialization has been extremely corrosive of dictatorship when countries reach the level of economic development of Argentina, Brazil, Greece, South Korea, and Spain, but we assume that Russians are totally different. There is no reason, other than the persistence of old stereotypes, to make this assumption. In a democratic system, older people have the vote to exercise their influence, but in a dictatorship, the people in their teens, twenties, and thirties who have the energy to demonstrate and even riot are the ones with potential power, and they are the people with the most education, with the most "modern" attitudes in the 1980s and 1990s.

The prevailing Western image has been of a Gorbachev who is on a hill, trying to push the huge boulder of Russian society up toward reform with only a few intellectuals helping him. My image is that Gorbachev is, indeed, on a hill and dealing with a huge boulder of social forces. But he is on the down slope of the hill trying to bring the boulder down gradually to reform without letting it roll over him. The intellectuals are his biggest opposition, for they are pushing on the other side of the boulder.

Ethnic Interests

Ethnic differences are important in every country, but in the Soviet Union they are crucial. In the United States, different ethnic groups come to the country knowing that their children or grandchildren will assimilate into the predominantly English-language culture. In the Soviet Union, by contrast, the twenty some largest ethnic groups have lived in separate areas as long as the Russians have in Russia. Like the French in Quebec, they cling fiercely to their identity. In fact, the Soviet Union has established "republics" for these nationalities, with the constitutional right to have their native language as an official language, to promote their native culture, and even to secede from the USSR. The latter "right" has no meaning, but the others do. The ethnic identification is further intensified by the fact that domestic passports, which every citizen must carry, list nationality. The non-Russians are officially identified on their passports as Estonians, Ukrainians, Georgians, Uzbeks, Jews, and the like.

The multinational character of the Soviet Union and the requirements of maintaining stability are always on the minds of the Soviet leaders, and of all Soviet citizens who think about political issues. Non-Russians have a strong tendency to want more autonomy from Moscow, and some would like to leave the federation, even if it were democratic. The non-Russians are sensitive about the question of Russification and about the implications of any policy for it. For example, many Central Asian economists have not wanted large heavy-industry investment in their republics for fear that only Russian workers would have the necessary skills and would have to be imported.[16] In Kazakhstan, students rioted in 1986 when a Russian was appointed first secretary of the republic.

Russians for their part tend to be as dedicated to "the preservation of the Union" as the American North was in the 1850s and 1860s. Some want very tough control over the non-Russians, others favor a looser federation, but almost none wants the breakup of the Soviet Union. Even Russian liberals who would like Western democracy for themselves usually are very uneasy about its suitability for the Soviet Union, for they fear that it would mean separatist parties and movements in twenty different republics. On balance, the 1986 Kazakh riots were a favorable development for Gorbachev, for they dramatically reminded the Russians of the consequence of pushing for more liberalism than Gorbachev wants.

Many Americans, especially in the last two administrations, have looked at the multinational character of the Soviet Union, have seen the ferocity of ethnic conflict around the world, and have concluded that ethnic conflict in the Soviet Union will soon be the source of major instability. Special attention has been paid Soviet citizens of Moslem background, many of them located in Central Asia, who have been thought to be especially susceptible to the Islamic fundamentalism that has been so popular on the

Soviet Union's southern border. Some Americans have had the
secret hope that American pressure might crack the Soviet
Union.

It would be a mistake, however, to exaggerate the potential for
ethnic instability in the Soviet Union in the near term. Ethnic
and religious conflicts that become explosive—the French in
Quebec, the Catholics in Northern Ireland, the Shiites in Lebanon, the blacks in America in the 1950s and 1960s, the mestizos
in Central America in the 1970s—occur when a group with a
rising education level finds its mobility into better jobs blocked
by another group.

The Soviet leadership has long exercised great skill in avoiding
this problem.[17] Recognition of the local language (along with Russian) as an official language of instruction and work in each republic defuses the most explosive issue. (When French was
installed as the primary language in Quebec, separatism lost
much of its force.) Moreover, the Soviet Union has long followed
a vigorous affirmative action policy of promoting local persons
into top political and administrative jobs within each republic.
Some key posts—often the party second secretary—are restricted to Russians to ensure control, but the number of such
slots is not large enough to take many jobs away from local persons.

The Soviet leaders have taken several additional steps to
strengthen political stability among the non-Russians. First, they
have required party membership for those who want to advance.
Such membership is easy to obtain for hardworking persons who
do not go to church or become politically dissident, and it has
become very widespread. (Fifty percent of all men with college
education are party members.) And once the educated Moslem
population has been admitted to the Communist party, it has to
fear Islamic fundamentalism, even if it is attracted to it. If a Khomeini won, he might not distinguish between "good" and "bad"
Communists.

Second, the Soviet leaders have coupled these powerful incentives to avoid dissidence with severe penalties for those who
don't. Frequently Moscow dissidents are handled a bit gingerly,
with warnings first and arrest only if dissent continues. But in the

non-Russian republics, organized nationalist dissidence can be dealt with very harshly. Two of the activists in the Kazakh riots were convicted within six weeks.

Though the Soviet leadership has been successful in keeping the non-Russians under control, it still worries about the impact of economic reform on nationality relations. From the earliest days of the century, a strong centralized party and then a strong centralized state were associated with stable control over the non-Russian borderlands—and were justified in those terms. In fact, control over the borderlands has been stable, and many Russians with the image of seething borderlands may think that this stability results from the centralized state rather than the controlled social mobility emphasized here.

And, of course, integration into the world economy means more than exposure to the West. A Soviet export capability and strategy should give the country real access to Middle East markets. The number of people with Moslem backgrounds who speak the languages of the Middle East will give Soviet sales personnel a real advantage in dealing with Middle East customers—while causing many Russians to be nervous.

Obviously the various nationalities contain the full range of social strata and institutions, and, hence, each has a full spectrum of views that are represented. Ultimately, however, the republics are far from Moscow, and they have the same institutional interests as other regions in a decentralization of power from Moscow. In addition, there is also an emotional element. Especially to the extent that Marxists think that political power reflects economic power, it is hard for non-Russians not to feel that economic reform is better for their own autonomy and dignity.

The Inadequacy of Interest Analysis

All these social cleavages provide the environment in which a leader must function. Various Western specialists on the Soviet Union may argue with this or that assessment of the attitude of different groups toward economic reform. Other specialists would like to know—as would I—how the different interests interact. Does the support of managers for a change in social policy outweigh their concern about their ability to function in a new environment? Does national feeling outweigh the concerns of the Uzbek and Ukrainian worker about reform, or is the "class" worry more important?

But the real problem with interest analysis is that it can lead to the belief that the status quo is immutable. Group interests tend to remain the same over time, and if policy is the product of group pressures, then the configuration of forces that produced current policy will likely produce a similar policy in the future.

Yet, policy changes. Sometimes the change can be explained by simple group analysis. Perhaps a new class has arisen during industrialization, perhaps a new ethnic group has immigrated to a country, perhaps a formerly subservient ethnic group has acquired education. The early stage of industrialization, for example, always features a rapid expansion in the number of workers and in the priority given to industrial values. The more advanced stages of industrialization feature a decline in the proportion of workers in comparison with professional, managerial, and service personnel. Preferential treatment for workers becomes more difficult to defend, and as other classes grow in size, they present their own demands. This factor is important in explaining Western politics in the 1980s, and may be important in explaining Soviet politics as well.

Nevertheless, such "objective" changes explain only a proportion of change. We know full well that in the West nationalism or religious fervor or national pessimism can affect a broad range of social groups simultaneously. We know that there are times of intense political activism in the United States and of deep political apathy or at least quiescence. We know that some upper-stratum American conservatives see their interests promoted by economic growth, which expands their wealth, while others see their interests promoted by environmentalism, which sacrifices growth to preserve the status quo.

The same is true in the Soviet Union. The balance of institutional and group forces, conventionally defined, do not explain why a Gorbachev was selected general secretary over a Grishin or a Romanov, who would have been more comfortable to the institutions and classes that have dominated Soviet politics for the last forty years. They do not explain why Gorbachev talked with such urgency about reform, when he could have guaranteed himself a quiet five to ten years in office at a minimum by taking a slow and gradual approach. To understand the broader politics of reform in the Soviet Union—and especially its implications for the West—we must go beyond the analysis of group and institutional interests.

5

The Politics of Reform: Intellectual Currents

SUCH a fundamental and far-reaching question as Russia's relationship to the West cuts across the normal institutional and group lines in Soviet society, and it touches the most basic of values. The "politics" that concerns these values is the politics of broad intellectual currents. It takes place in a great variety of settings—in novels and literary journals, in newspaper columns, in scholarly articles and books, in films and film reviews, in conversations in college dorms and at parties, in efforts to form groups to preserve historical monuments or the environment.

It is an extremely subtle politics, but in the long run enormously important. The decline in the rate of Soviet economic growth over the last quarter of a century is not simply the result of problems in the economic system. It also reflects a shifting of resources from investment to consumption, as well as increasing attention to environmental concerns. When the Soviet leaders picked three new leaders after Brezhnev's death, not one of them was an engineer, and this was not a chance occurrence. The political elites are part of society and are influenced by its values in some respect. They also must take societal values into account as they try to maintain support for the regime and its policies. We too must be acutely aware of the shifts that take place in the broader intellectual currents of society.

Marxist-Leninist Ideology

When Americans think of broader ideas in the Soviet Union that transcend institutional and group interests, they generally focus on Marxist-Leninist ideology and its ability to overcome the pragmatic forces that favor reform and liberalization. Almost no one gives any thought, however, to what Marxist-Leninist ideology actually is. It is seen as synonymous with "dogma," and as supporting all aspects of the status quo—except, perhaps, policies with a liberal or semiliberal character.

Without any question, there are dogmatic ideas in the Soviet Union and powerful persons who support them. Nevertheless, Marxism-Leninism is actually a powerful force both for the preservation of the status quo and for drastic change. Many persons whom we would call ideologists or dogmatists have often been quite uneasy about Marx. He was not only a Westerner, but a German Jew, the worst of all foreigners to a Russian xenophobe. He became a virtual nonperson during the late Stalin period when Lenin and his Russian precursors such as Chernyshevsky were emphasized.

Even today "ideologues" still tend to emphasize Lenin, while great attention to Marx usually implies a Western orientation. Brezhnev did not quote Marx once in his four reports to the party congresses during his reign, but Andropov wrote (or at least signed) a long article on Marx on the occasion of the ninetieth anniversary of his death.[1] Gorbachev's report to the Twenty-seventh Party Congress began with a survey of the world that quoted Marx (or referred to Marxism) five times. He quoted Lenin in this section only when he was referring to Marx. All of these decisions by the different general secretaries were meant to be powerful symbols.

Although each Soviet leader has tried to say that his interpretation of Marxism-Leninism is "the" ideology, Marxism-Leninism is actually quite ambiguous. For example, it has two major and contradictory views of historical development. Marx did a great deal of scholarly research to demonstrate that the "laws" of feudalism inexorably lead to the rise of capitalism. At Marx's funeral, his colleague, Friedrich Engels, compared him to Darwin: "Just as Darwin discovered the law of development of organic nature, so Marx discovered the law of development of human history."[2] The classics contain some virtually absolute statements about economic determinism and about the role of classes in shaping decisions. These statements could be and were cited when a leader like Stalin wanted to say that American foreign policy was inexorably driven to war or that East European countries must follow the Soviet path precisely.

Yet, Marx's detailed journalistic and historical work showed a keen awareness of the importance of political factors and, at times, their independence from direct economic influences. For several decades he toyed with the notion of an "Asiatic mode of production," which clearly implied that the same laws of development did not function in Asia as in Europe. He wrote letters to Russian revolutionaries around 1880 in which he agreed that Russia might have a socialist revolution before the establishment of full capitalism.[3] Moreover, Lenin believed that an underdeveloped country such as Russia could go directly to socialism, and he acted in 1917 on the basis of this belief.

What, then, are the implications for the Third World today? Are the forces that permitted Russia to jump the capitalist stage dominant in all newly industrializing nations in the twentieth century? If so, the Soviet Union is wise to support revolutionary forces. Or was Marx's argument about historical development right, except perhaps for a few exceptions produced by the destruction of war, and does feudalism naturally give rise to capitalism in the Third World? If so, the Third World countries are generally on a West European path, and a Soviet policy of promoting revolution is foolish—"defeatist" as Gorbachev said in 1987. In fact, Marxism-Leninism leads to both interpretations.

Even on the question of the market, Marxism-Leninism does not imply a single direction in the 1980s, though the market has always been regarded with great suspicion. Profit as a legitimate reward for enterprise was basically a very foreign idea, and very easy to equate with price-gouging, speculation, and exploitation of the customer. Marxism-Leninism contains no faith in the "hidden" hand of the market. It glorifies planning. And, of course, the conception that unemployment might be necessary or even desirable is totally alien.

Nevertheless, Marx was writing in the mid-nineteenth century, and his vision of the future had little in common with the Soviet system of the last half-century. He spoke of the withering away of the state, not the creation of state monopolistic ministries. Indeed, the combination of planning, public ownership of factories, and withering away of the state he foresaw seems less like the Soviet Union of the 1980s than the United States with its Federal Reserve Board and regulatory agencies controlling publicly owned cooperatives such as IBM and General Motors.

In addition, Lenin at the end of his life was moving Russia away from the total nationalization of the Civil War period. No one will ever know what form of socialism Lenin would eventually have introduced, for he probably did not know himself how he would react to the impending problems and crises of the late 1920s. It is, however, easy to interpret his statements of the early 1920s as evidence that he was proposing a long-term "cooperative socialism" (in Gorbachev's words) rather than the system Stalin established.[4]

For these reasons, Marxism-Leninism can provide the basis for a radical economic reform—a reform that even could result in a system that the Soviet Union would call socialist but that would have many similarities with the system that we call capitalism (though capitalists of 1850 would not have called it that). In fact, even some of the moral outrage that Marx and Lenin felt about capitalists can be turned against the contemporary socialist ministries. It is natural for a Soviet Marxist to think that the managers of the means of production in the Soviet Union are no better than the owners—really the managers—of the means of production in an IBM (this is the main reason that the sense of a privileged bureaucracy in the Soviet Union is stronger than it should be in worldwide comparison) and to call for a virtual "Marxist" revolution against them.

The greatest ambiguities in Marxism-Leninism regard repression and freedom. The emphasis on rigid scientific laws can breed intolerance, for a person who feels certain about "laws" naturally feels that it is foolish to defer to the uneducated. Moreover, Marxism-Leninism treated the early stage of industrialization as "a primitive stage of accumulation" which was inherently exploitative and painful, and this created the sense that a painful policy by the Communist party, while regrettable, might be unavoidable.

One can go further. Marx treated culture, religion, philosophy, political institutions, and the like as the "superstructure" of the economic base—as reflections of the interests of succeeding exploiting classes. If this is taken to its extreme, then Greek and Roman civilizations are the superstructure of a slave-owning class, the culture of the Middle Ages (or of China and India) the superstructure of a landlord class, and modern philosophy and culture that of the bourgeoisie. By implication, what we call Western civilization has little value, and there is little reason not to suppress that which is not useful to the new proletarian ruling class.

As has already been argued, it is precisely the rejection of the Western superstructure that may account for the popularity of extremist forms of Marxism in Third World countries, including Russia. Lenin, we have seen, was rejecting West European economic and political institutions and especially the Westernized elite that was ruling Russia. The xenophobes of the postwar period were extremely explicit in denouncing pre-Marxist philosophers as evil because they reflected the values of the ruling class of their time.

Nevertheless, Marxism-Leninism still remains on its face one of the most utopian, liberal doctrines ever developed. It promised the withering away of the state and of all oppression. Socialism would end restraints on individual freedom imposed by powerful classes as well as by the government. Only socialism would allow the full development of the personality, and eliminate poverty, for each would receive according to his needs. However much we may dismiss these aspects of Marxism-Leninism, they are explicit in the ideology, while repression is only implied. The Soviet press emphasizes these liberal aspects in response to Western criticisms, and students must be especially struck by Marx's and Lenin's statements about freedom and the development of the personality under socialism when they read them in school. Many who came of age in the Khrushchev era have seen these promises as ideals to be attained. For the young, the original utopianism of Marx and Lenin continues to live, even if—or perhaps especially if—it is not reflected in reality.

All of these ambiguities in Marx and Lenin have led to a vast Western literature on what Marx and Lenin *really* meant. Those who have wanted to discredit these men have traced all the most repressive aspects of Soviet society to their doctrines. Those who have liked the Marxist ideals and criticism of capitalism have argued that the Soviet Union is simply a perversion of Marxism-Leninism (or Marxism alone) produced by power-hungry men in a backward Asiatic country.

Even inside the Soviet Union itself, by the late 1970s major scholars could freely publish very different interpretations of Marxism-Leninism. Instead of seeing history as moving inexorably from the tribal to the slaveholding to the feudal to the capitalist stage, many scholars described a single stage between tribal society and capitalism, frequently defining it in quite nontraditional terms. Instead of seeing capitalist economies in the Third World as leading to deformed and dependent economic growth, most economists openly indicated that such economies grew more rapidly than those in countries of a "socialist orientation." A number began to describe international relations as being based not on implacable conflict between classes (and, therefore, between socialism and capitalism), but on cooperation between nations. All of these commentators found appropriate quotations from Marx and Lenin, as did their opponents.[5]

Nationalism and Patriotism

Americans often ask whether ideology is giving way—or has given way—to nationalism as the major force in Soviet society, but the question is based on a misunderstanding. The antagonism between ideology and nationalism is obvious in a country like Poland, where Communism was imposed from the outside and meant the loss of national identity. It is obvious in the American Communist party, which has totally supported Soviet rather than American foreign policy. However, in Russia as well as Albania, China, Cuba, Vietnam, and Yugoslavia, where Communists came to power essentially by their own efforts, their leaders have allied themselves closely with nationalism and patriotism. Indeed, their victory depended on that alliance.

Certainly Soviet leaders have closely associated themselves with Russian patriotism. The defeat of Russia in the Crimean and Russo-Japanese wars and its dismal performance in World War I were crucial in the collapse of the tsarist regime. During the Civil War, Lenin went out of his way to depict the Bolsheviks as championing Russia against foreign intervention. In the 1920s and 1930s the Bolshevik commitment to industrialization and Stalin's espousal of "socialism in one country" were efforts to identify the party and its leaders with nationalism. The victory in World War II clearly has been used to strengthen this tie in the postwar years. And, as we have seen, conventional wisdom holds that the centralizing character of the Bolshevik party has meant tight Russian control over the non-Russian borderlands, which has pleased Russian nationalists.

Yet Russian nationalism or patriotism, like ideology, is ambiguous. One stream has focused on the Russian past and glorified the peasant, the Russian soul, the communal tradition. It protests the inundation of old Russian villages and churches by lakes produced by hydroelectric dams as well as the destruction of old buildings to make way for the construction of skyscrapers. This stream of nationalism is the heir to the Slavophil or at least Populist criticism of the state. In men such as the writer Aleksandr Solzhenitsyn, it can lead to anti-Communism less because of Soviet repression than because of Soviet pell-mell industrialization.

In its extreme forms, this history-oriented stream of nationalism can be virulently anti-Western and xenophobic because the West is the source of the "modern" ideas (including industrialization) that destroy the old Russia.

Many Westerners became very alarmed when a number of highly anti-Western nationalists appeared in print in the late 1960s, many in the journal *Molodaia gvardiia*. Some observers thought that they were associated with several Politburo members, and that their virulent nationalism was the hidden agenda of the general conservatism of the Brezhnev era, perhaps even of the moderate conservatives.[6] The same concern arose in 1987 when an extreme group called *Pamiat* became publicly known.[7]

But this fear has been grossly exaggerated. Dmitrii Poliansky, the Politburo member most often rumored to represent extreme nationalism, was removed from the Politburo to be ambassador to Japan. Aleksandr Shelepin, persistently rumored to be the Stalinist on the Politburo, was in decline throughout the Brezhnev period before being retired in disgrace. And those associated with *Molodaia gvardiia* were removed from their posts, while the nationalists found it extremely difficult, if not impossible, to publish elsewhere. The freedom for Pamiat to speak out—and to be severely criticized—has more to do with the freedom of *glasnost* than with Pamiat's power.

However, this form of patriotism can also take quite benign forms. Dmitrii Likhachev is the leading academician who studies ancient Russia, and he is privately labeled a moderate Slavophil by another scholar. He has asserted that "a distinctive and great culture existed in ancient Russia," and is scornful of the idea that Russian culture was backward and could become even slightly respectable only by "punching through a window to Europe." He damned the "self-denigration" of Russian culture that was fashionable in the nineteenth and early twentieth centuries in Russia. Nevertheless, in a book whose second edition had a printing of fifty thousand copies, Likhachev fervently distinguished between "nationalism based on a hate of other peoples and a patriotism based on love of one's own":

> If you love your own people, your own family, the more you will love other people... Nationalism which fences itself off from other cultures ruins its own culture and dries it up. Culture should be open....
>
> If everything is going well in a family, then other families are pulled into the life of the family. They visit and participate in family holidays. Happy families live in a social, hospitable, and joyous manner. They live together. These are strong families, solid families.
>
> So it is in the life of peoples. Peoples in whom patriotism is not replaced by nationalistic "acquisitiveness," by greed, and by the misanthropy of nationalism, live in friendship and peace with all peoples... Nationalism is the manifestation of the weakness of a nation, not of its strength.

It is no accident that in 1986 Likhachev strongly endorsed a book of poems by Boris Pasternak, including several from his suppressed novel, *Doctor Zhivago*. Openness in culture in a "healthy family" goes beyond receptivity to other cultures.[8]

A second stream of Russian nationalism or patriotism has been concerned with Russian national power. It is less concerned with the defense of preindustrial values than with the defense of the Soviet Union pure and simple. Those who hold this view do not object to industrialization, but favor it because it is necessary for national power. This is the stream of nationalism with which the Communist party has associated itself over the years.

This second stream of nationalism, like the first, has different variants. One emphasizes military power in order to protect Russia from a hostile world or to provide the means for expansionism to achieve some manifest destiny. Another embodies a determination to make Russia equal to or better than other countries not so much in the military realm, as in the economic or cultural one. Patriots of this type may not like it that other countries are not following the Russian lead in contemporary art or music or fashion. They may think that Moscow should be one of the world's great industrial and intellectual centers and that this is not possible unless Moscow opens itself to world intellectual currents.

The three really important developments in nationalist or patriotic feelings during the Brezhnev era were actually far less ominous than many Westerners thought. The first was an enormous emphasis upon the victory in World War II as a legitimization for the Soviet regime. The war had been the great achievement of the Brezhnev generation, which had risen to very high levels just before the war and had led the country to victory. Brezhnev and the heir apparent Andrei Kirilenko had been political officers in the army; Suslov had headed the partisans in Stavropol; Ustinov and Kosygin had been top industrial ministers in Moscow; Gromyko had been ambassador to the United States. Their propaganda effort gave the military great press, but glorifying a defensive struggle long in the past at least did little to legitimate—or suggest—activism in the present.

A second development in the Brezhnev era took place at the citizen level rather than in regime propaganda. This was the beginning of a real search for roots. Bolshevism had rested on nativist resentments of the West, but it had also embodied a populist rejection of the old Russian elite and its institutions. Since the revolution, censorship had played havoc with a detailed exploration and understanding of many aspects of the past, especially the post-1917 past. Paradoxically, a Russian in the post-Stalin period could learn a great deal about the tsarist period through nineteenth-century literature and through Soviet historical works and novels, but even the names of most former Soviet leaders could barely be mentioned. It was even impossible to publish a meaningful anthology of poetry from the Soviet period—poetry that at one time had already passed the censor.

The search for roots really centered on the village. Probably the most vital literature of the Brezhnev period—and some of the most popular—was written by the so-called *derevenchiki*—the village writers, who tended to concentrate on the most backward villages. Russians who were only a generation or two from the village began to have romantic views about it and about farm life. The destruction of the village was increasingly felt as sacrilegious. At the same time, historical novels became even more popular.

The most fashionable painter, Ivan Glazunov, used a style reminiscent of religious icons, and his work could be found in the apartments of Central Committee members.[9] Many people became interested in genealogy, and social studies and the humanities superseded engineering as the prestigious college major. Environmentalism and preservation of historical monuments (including churches) became mass movements.

Although this deep interest in the past can take pathological forms, it has had many liberalizing sides. It has been a protest against a drive for industrial growth and national power at all costs. It has insisted that other values are important and must have a role in policy. Implicitly it has represented a deep protest against the censorship that has prevented honest discussion of Soviet history.

The interest in the past also eroded old ideological dogmas. The "superstructure"—culture, religion, and tradition—had been dismissed as unimportant in favor of class factors, but an emphasis on history reverses this interpretation. And if the superstructure is relatively autonomous, then the values of Western civilization have an autonomy from the interests of the respective ruling classes in Western history. It is but one small step from this point to say that the values of Western civilization are good—a step that all the intellectuals were taking in one way or another.

Thus, a summary volume published in 1983 on the Third World, coedited by the top official on Third World studies at the top Soviet institute (IMEMO), focused on "the spiritual-cultural peculiarity" of different societies rather than the dominant class in power. "Taken together, these enumerated elements of the individuality of the analyzed sociohistorical type of society were deposited in a specific *social-genetic 'code'* of their development. It is as if this 'code' absorbed in itself the stable instruments of heredity of each stage of history of the given societies, passed through each change in their evolution, and influenced the whole course of social development."[10] Such language is a long, long way from an analysis that says stages of history, based on different owning classes, are qualitatively different from each other.

The third important development in the Brezhnev era was the growing sense that the old economic system interfered with the achievement of national goals. In the past, the economic system, despite all its flaws, still contributed to rapid growth in heavy industry and defense. But as the world has evolved toward the "third industrial revolution" based on computers and electronics, the old system has not adapted well. Japan and Russia began industrialization at the same time. Now, Japan, with half the Soviet population, has equaled Soviet GNP. It can export high-technology products while the Soviet Union cannot, and hence the Japanese model is more attractive in the Third World (and even the United States). In 1986–87, South Korea began challenging Japan with its goods in the American market. It is a real affront to national honor that Russia has not only remained inferior to Western countries, but is falling behind Asian ones.

But more than pride is involved. National defense can also be affected by technological backwardness, as Marshal Nikolai Ogarkov, then chief of the Soviet general staff, pointed out in an interview in *Red Star* in May 1984. Ogarkov began by stating that nuclear weapons are essentially unusable. No first strike can be so successful that it prevents massive retaliation, he said. Only a person who is "incompetent from a military point of view" can believe that an opponent's command-and-control system could be knocked out and retaliation thwarted. Moreover, Ogarkov asserted, limited use of nuclear weapons was impossible because escalation almost inevitably would ensue. Ogarkov explicitly drew the obvious conclusion—that conventional weapons and what he called weapons based on new physical principles would be decisive in any new war. He warned that NATO was modernizing its conventional weapons to such an extent that they were becoming as powerful as nuclear ones, and that SDI-related research might produce a real breakthrough. And although Ogarkov didn't mention it, Chinese modernization over a period of decades might give military technology of high quality to over a billion hostile people on the Soviet border.

Ogarkov quoted a statement by Engels that nothing depends on the economy more than the military. He clearly implied the need for a major improvement in economic performance. Clearly he was calling for a change in social policy and investment—and perhaps even for economic reform. Chernenko did not approve of either those ideas or a top general who was so urgent in his commitment to them, so Ogarkov was demoted from the General Staff to be commander of the European theater of operations. But he was allowed to repeat his statements about nuclear weapons (but not about conventional weapons and the economy) in an article with broad circulation.[11]

Even if the dangers of a militarily disastrous technological breakthrough were discounted, the foreign policy consequences of Soviet technological backwardness are already clear. Stalin and Khrushchev expected Third World countries to follow the Soviet path—and Soviet foreign policy leadership—because sustained balanced growth in the Third World countries with capitalist systems would be impossible. They thought that the nationalistic drive for true independence would push Third World elites toward socialism, but the opposite occurred. Autarchy and the Soviet model in the Third World did not produce as good economic results as Third World economies that retained a private sector and that exposed themselves to the world market. And if the Soviet Union had been able to export Japanese-quality goods, it would be dominating the Middle East borders as much as, or more than, the United States dominates Latin American markets, with political lines of influence tending to follow economic ones.

Several times during 1985 Mikhail Gorbachev referred to this aspect of foreign policy. In October 1987 he dramatized the point by referring to testimony before the U.S. Congress on why "Gorbachev's reforms" were bad:

If the Soviet Union achieves the goals set by the 27th Party Congress, this will strengthen its prestige on the international arena, raise the authority of the Communist Party inside the country and abroad and . . . thus increase the threat to the national security of the USA. . . . The success of the restructuring can weaken the political and economic unity of Western Europe since the USSR will enter its markets. The political influence of the USSR in the developing country will widen, since it can increase its military and other aid to them and since some of them will want to adopt the model of the Soviet economy if it becomes competitive with the economy of the USA. . . . The restructuring is dangerous because it will strengthen the position of the USSR in international financial and economic organizations. . . . Listen to the conclusion they draw: the failure of the social-economic policy conducted by the USSR under the leadership of the CPSU and the Soviet government would answer the national interests of the USA.[12]

The implications for the Soviet Union were certainly clear enough.

The Relation to the West

Lenin and Stalin, like the tsars, were for industrialization. As we have seen, Stalin and his successors transformed Russia from a country of peasant villages into a country of cities. They took a society in which 44 percent of the population was literate in 1920 and turned it into one in which in 1987, 71 percent of the population ten years of age and older had at least seven years schooling and 51 percent had a high-school degree or better. They took a traditional society in which life was usually very confined geographically and turned it into one in which almost every family had television.[13]

So despite all the differences between capitalism and socialism, despite all the censorship and the restrictions on travel, the average urban Russian has a life that is closer to that of the average American today than to that of his grandfather in a preindustrial village at the turn of the century. Our first impression of Moscow is its differences from New York and London, but Gorbachev's grandfather would notice the similarities in the buildings, in the nine-to-five schedule in the factory or office, in the electric lights and gas stoves, in the presence of television and movies, in the people traveling by mechanized means rather than by horse. A Brezhnev who began his life envying the strange Westernized life of the elite in Upper Colony could end it with a sense of satisfaction that the average urban Russian of 1982 had a more "modern" and "Western" life than the elite in Upper Colony in 1915. And a Solzhenitsyn who shared Lenin's rejection of the modern West could feel that the Soviet leader had been instrumental in ruining old Russia.

But just as the increasingly Westernized part of the population in tsarist Russia and the shah's Iran pushed for even further Westernization, so have many in the new Soviet Union wanted to go further in adopting Western ways. To some extent they have done this simply by wearing Western forms of dress, (symbolized by blue jeans), by seeking out Western culture. In the early 1980s, S. Frederick Starr concluded a superb history of jazz and rock and roll in the Soviet Union and young people's reception of it in the following manner:

> The Soviet Union...has maintained uniform policies, to be sure, even totalitarian ones, but in the field of popular culture it has proven absolutely impossible to implement those policies effectively. Far from being docile and malleable, Soviet jazz fans have shown themselves to be independent and resourceful. Those who like jazz find ways of playing or hearing it, whatever policy may be. Nor are members of the Party and government immune to public tastes... It is no wonder that, in the long run, the government had to make its peace with jazz...
>
> Cultural phenomena from abroad are no longer immediately pigeonholed by political or class origin... The exercise would be pointless today: few people care if a new form of jazz or popular music is labeled bourgeois, and there is no way of keeping jazz out of the USSR anyway, for modern communications have rendered popular culture completely transnational.
>
> The present young adult generation is the first in Soviet history to share fully in European and American popular culture. When, in the future, members of this generation gather together to reminisce about their youth, they will dredge up many of the same "golden oldies" that would come to mind at a similar session in Hamburg, Lyons, Birmingham, or Milwaukee. Many of the old stars whose names they will recall will be foreigners: Duke Ellington, the Beatles, Michel Legrand, the Nitty Gritty Dirt Band, and others... The young people will feel at home in conversations about music with contemporaries from any other industrial society.[14]

Many of the Soviet intellectuals, of course, have continued to argue for even freer contact with the West and for greater assimilation of Western practices. Brezhnev adopted the discussion of

the "scientific-technical revolution" as a watchword for his regime. The phrase implied, first of all, a more "scientific" and
orderly approach to policy and decision making than had existed
under Khrushchev. It meant a reduction in his emphasis on
worker and peasant participation and greater reliance on the advice of the "specialists." Since the "specialists" were really the
specialized ministries, reliance on their advice tended to imply a
policy that would not challenge the status quo. For the military
(and, indeed, for many of the ministries), the "scientific-technical
revolution" meant improving the technological sophistication of
its supplies—and, therefore, an increase in their budget to purchase them.

Yet, the Westernizers were able to use this framework to advocate the adoption of Western ways. Emphasizing science and
technological progress hinted at an attack on traditional ideology,
since science was not part of the means of production, and scientists were not the proletariat, except by the most tortured definition. Liberals tried to make the point, as clearly as they dared,
that emphasizing the scientific-technical revolution as a driving
force in history meant turning away from the owners of the
means of production and from the proletariat.

This position also legitimated the adoption in the Soviet Union
of features of Western life that had once been regarded as the
counterrevolutionary result of capitalist development. If they
were instead the product of the scientific-technical revolution,
then the Soviet Union inevitably must adopt them, for it too is
subject to the laws of that revolution. The late Nikolai Inozemtsev, the director of IMEMO, expressed the point very clearly in a
prizewinning textbook on the capitalist world that he coedited:

Marxist investigators naturally ask themselves the question: What
has produced these changes [in capitalism] and what do they reflect—the objective needs of the development of productive forces,
or the nature of imperialism and the features that are inherent in it?
We, of course, have a fundamentally different attitude to these two
groups of factors. The socialist states cannot ignore the objective
laws of the development of productive forces.[15]

Some of the consequences of the scientific-technical revolution —or industrialization, as we would phrase it—are obvious: urbanization, lower birthrates, a highly educated population, higher priority to scientific research, and so forth. But anything at all in the West could be attributed to "the objective laws of the development of productive forces"—greater investment in the housing sector, a large increase in services and service personnel, greater citizen participation, or whatever. Those in the Soviet Union who favored a more open relationship to the West could contend that scientific-technical progress required a freer exchange of information, an international specialization of labor, and an integration of the world economy.

Naturally there have been other ways to debate the relationship of Russia and the West in the Soviet Union. Traditionally, discussion of the past and of the Western tradition have been favorite methods. It continues today. After the election of Gorbachev as general secretary, for example, the major Soviet journal on world history carried a long discussion on the transition from feudalism to capitalism in Europe. The question seemed arcane, but it really concerned whether Russia and Eastern Europe were part of the West.

Similarly, if Western states are described as nothing but instruments of class domination, then long-term cooperation between Soviet and Western governments seems impossible. Peaceful coexistence and détente can be no more than temporary expedients. In the words of a conservative theorist, "ideological struggle is not a military battle. Nevertheless, it is just as tense, and it demands a maximum mobilization of forces and resources."[16]

However, if the state arose not because of class domination but because of society's need to have certain vital functions fulfilled, if the "superstructure" of culture or tradition or politics is more powerful than economic forces, or if (as Georgii Arbatov, the future director of the Institute of the U.S.A. and Canada said in 1955), "the masses in our day display a vital interest in foreign policy" and "the imperialist governments cannot fail to take their opinion into account to this or that extent,"[17] then normal dealings and even cooperation with the West are possible. The driving force of international relations can be seen as national interest.

For most people in the Soviet Union, the issue of the relationship to the West is a fairly simple one. Should the Soviet Union adopt Western ideas and institutions (notably at the present-time market mechanisms)? Should it be open to Western cultural influences? For most people, the answer to this question has correlated fairly closely with their basic foreign policy posture. The more a person has been willing to accept Western influences, the more he has been inclined to favor good relations with the Western governments, most prominently the United States, and a reduction in military spending.

Within the top political and intellectual establishment, however, important variations are possible. The conservatives, for example, can be essentially isolationist or, by contrast, messianic in spreading world revolution. More interesting from our point of view are the variations among those who want a more open relationship to the West. In the nineteenth century, as we saw, the Russian elite argued about which Europe to emulate—Prussia or France? Today this debate seems to have died almost completely, but it has been replaced by an analogous one about which West —the United States or Western Europe?

A man of Andrei Gromyko's age remembered both World War I and World War II. His father's generation fought in the Russo-Japanese War, and he himself remembered the full-scale clashes on the Soviet-Chinese border in the 1930s and the fear that Japan would move toward Siberia rather than Southeast Asia. The notion that the Soviet Union should risk concessions to Germany and Japan in order to conduct an effective multipolar policy was a frightening one. It made more sense to deal with the United States, and let it control Germany and Japan and keep them from acquiring nuclear weapons.

There were a number of ways to defend this policy in public.[18] The most direct was to write repeatedly about German "revanchism" and Japanese "militarism," for if these were the main dangers, then Gromyko's foreign policy was the only intelligent one. The more indirect way was to emphasize the unity of the Western alliance and the dependence of the Allies upon the United States. If this were true, then a policy of playing to Europe and Japan is a hopeless one.

Events of the 1970s, however, raised serious questions about the old assumptions of a link between good relations with the United States and liberalization. Brezhnev coupled détente with the United States with a conservative domestic policy, and even this détente proved extremely difficult to maintain. The Europeans turned out to be much more forthcoming. Hence those in the Soviet Union who wanted to justify relaxed tension at home by relaxing tension abroad had an increasing incentive to deal with Europe rather than America.

The emphasis on Europe also had tactical advantages for a liberal. It permitted the wrapping of reform in the cause of national defense by insisting on the need for the information revolution and an opening to the world economy in order to bring technology to world levels. It permitted a strong America-bashing that furnished a defense against the charge that the liberals who promoted Westernization were soft on capitalism. It allowed "bad" Western values to be attributed to the United States, while an opening to Europe would only bring in the "good" Western values—as if Paris did not have Pigalle and "Dallas" were not a top-rated show in Great Britain.

Those who began to push this policy used two lines of argument. One was essentially a foreign policy one. Instead of emphasizing ally dependence on the United States, the proponents of a Europe-centered and Japan-centered policy talked about "contradictions" within the capitalist world. Instead of emphasizing German revanchism and Japanese militarism, they focused their attention on "American fascism." Many began to use contemporary international relations language, speaking of "triangles," "quadrangles," "multipolarity," and the like. They talked of national interests, and Gorbachev himself quoted Lord Palmerston, "England does not have eternal friends or eternal enemies, but eternal interests."

The second line of argument focused on Europe as a positive entity. In traditional ideology, Eastern Europe was "good" socialism, and Western Europe was "bad" capitalism. Now even Central Committee officials might speak about "we Europeans" or about a "European civilization that transcends the division be-

tween East Europe and West Europe."[19] Consider the following
words and think about how it differs from a traditional Marxist-
Leninist view:

> Whatever aspect of the development of human civilization we take,
> the contribution made by the Europeans is immense. We live in the
> same house, though some use one entrance and the others another.
> We need to cooperate and develop communication within that
> house.
> The European home is our common home where geography and
> history have intimately linked the destinies of tens of countries and
> peoples. We proceed from the belief that Europe, which has given
> the world so much in the sphere of culture, science, technology,
> and advanced social thought, is also capable of setting an example
> in the solution of the most complex problems of contemporary in-
> ternational life.[20]

With the traditional anti-American arguments of the conservatives being co-opted by some of the strongest reformers, the
center of gravity in the debate about the relationship with the
West changed drastically. With the reformers able to say that the
old economic system was no longer providing the basis for world
leadership, there was little answer to them. The really significant
fact about the long quotation about Europe just cited is that it was
made in 1985 and that it was made by the new general secretary,
Mikhail Gorbachev.

6

Kremlin Politics
Prior to Gorbachev

M ANY in the West assumed that the policies of Brezhnev
and then Chernenko represented the balance of group interests in the bureaucracy and that, consequently, the death of
these two men would change nothing. Originally many saw Gorbachev as a clone of the aging Politburo of the 1970s and, therefore, a cautious, conservative man himself. Or perhaps they saw
him as the accidental protégé of Andropov and hence very weak
as he sought to consolidate power. They saw a united and conservative bureaucracy as having gutted the earlier Kosygin reforms
and being so strong that Gorbachev could not introduce the radical economic reform or major change in foreign policy he seemed
to want.

But to an extent that is not recognized, this is a striking reversal
of our older view of the Soviet leadership. Westerners used to talk
about a totalitarian dictator or perhaps Politburo, totally insulated
from and unresponsive to other forces in society. When the totalitarian model reigned supreme in the 1950s, we did not speak

about an all-powerful bureaucracy, but an all-powerful political leadership that conducted a permanent purge of the bureaucracy. We did not talk about a Soviet political culture that glorified privilege or an easy life, but one that glorified sacrifice in the name of national power. The essence of Leninism, we said, was a denunciation of "trade-union consciousness" (the workers' desire to have a good life today rather than to sacrifice for the revolution) and an insistence on the workers doing what the party leadership considered necessary. We did not speak of a conservative ideology, but one that was dedicated to ruthless transformation. The basic distinction we made between a totalitarian dictatorship and an authoritarian dictatorship was that the former was dedicated to change and the latter to the preservation of the status quo.

This book takes a fairly traditional view of the power of the general secretary. Social forces are important in determining who will be selected general secretary. They influence the course he considers it wise to undertake and the strategy he must adopt to overcome resistance. Nevertheless, the Soviet system has weak institutional restraints on the general secretary. In my view the Kosygin reforms of 1965 failed not because of the power of the bureaucracy, but because they were not the Brezhnev reforms and were opposed by the general secretary. In my view, the stagnation at the end of the Brezhnev period was also the result of his great power and his determination to prevent change. By that time the bureaucracy was not a monolithic conservative body, but embodied a multiplicity of interests. It had become increasingly Westernized and wanted modernity for Russia and more freedom for itself.

Moreover, if, as suggested in chapter 1, however, Brezhnev was quite happy for reasons of his own security to have a young innovator in the Politburo who could be seen as a long-term leader after a transitory one, then the direction of Gorbachev's thinking and his enormous power would not have come as a surprise. Gorbachev's consolidation of power both before and after his election was an absolutely classic one using the old mechanisms of power.

Basically in the 1980s we came to rely too heavily on Moscow rumors, often deliberately leaked to influence Soviet public opin-

ion and even the succession itself.[1] We need to go back to the
esoteric communication of political detail and to an understanding
of the interests of the various contenders. And, most of all, we
need to understand the way in which issues arise in Soviet politics. If we see simple dichotomies between détente and entente or
liberalism and conservatism,[2] if we ignore the issue of social justice versus industrial growth, we will continually make mistakes
when we try to draw conclusions from the limited pieces of information at our disposal and will be confused about Kremlin alignments.

Khrushchev's Policies

During the 1960s a very dramatic image of the politics of the
Khrushchev era became widely accepted in the West. Khrushchev was seen as leading an embattled liberal faction seeking
greater political freedom, a major improvement in the standard of
living, and détente with the United States. They were thought to
be opposed by a conservative group headed by Frol Kozlov (the
heir apparent), Mikhail Suslov (the ideologist), and Marshal Rodion Malinovsky (the defense minister).[3]

Without any question, the policies followed in the Khrushchev
period were very erratic and sometimes inconsistent. Khrushchev
would make promises and then back off from them. Policy initia-
tives were taken and then reversed. All of this was interpreted as
the result of mighty battles within the Politburo. For example, in
1960 Khrushchev flew to Paris for a scheduled summit meeting
with President Dwight Eisenhower, even though an American
spy plane had been shot down over the Soviet Union. Once in
Paris, however, he refused to meet Eisenhower. The American
press spokesman, Charles Bohlen, said that the decision was the
result of pressure from Suslov and Malinovsky.

This image of the politics of the Khrushchev era was much
oversimplified. Khrushchev's two top lieutenants at the end,
Leonid Brezhnev and Aleksei Kosygin, were said to be the core of
Khrushchev's liberal faction. In reality, they led the effort to overthrow him in 1964 and then instituted a more cautious policy.

The first problem was that the conventional analysis of the Khrushchev era never adequately distinguished between conflicts over policy and conflict aimed at a change in leadership, between policy conflicts among persons seeking to influence the leader and policy conflicts between the leader and independent political powers. In the United States in 1984, the Democrats Walter Mondale and Gary Hart had relatively few policy differences, but their conflict was fierce and even became personally bitter. From 1981 to 1984, David Stockman, the director of the Office of Management and Budget, energetically fought the president's policy on the deficit—and, therefore, on defense and taxes—but no one would say that he was trying to overthrow the president, or even that he opposed him in the sense that Mondale did. Such distinctions are vital to keep in mind in any analysis of the Soviet Union.

Most analysts assumed that the Politburo conflict of the Khrushchev era was often of the Reagan-Mondale or Reagan-House Speaker Tip O'Neill type. If a presumed Khrushchev ally or "liberal" was demoted, that was seen as a power loss for Khrushchev. If anyone seemed to be opposing one of Khrushchev's policies, he was then part of the opposition to Khrushchev.

This was a gross misinterpretation. When Mikhail Suslov, the conservative ideologist, was chosen to give the indictment at the time of Khrushchev's removal in 1964, this did not prove that he was a leader of the opposition. Suslov had taught in the Industrial Academy in 1931 when Khrushchev was party secretary there, and almost surely had a long political relationship with him. In the Soviet Union a political ally may be called upon to perform at such a public event as a sign of loyalty to the party. Similarly, Rodion Malinovsky, the minister of defense who was thought to be part of the conservative opposition, had fought alongside Khrushchev at the Battle of Stalingrad, and the two had lived in adjoining tents for a month. Khrushchev surely chose him as defense minister because he considered him a trustworthy friend.[4]

As we saw in chapter 2, in 1945–46 Stalin selected for the top ideological apparatus subordinates who had a range of policy views. At the end of his life, two of Stalin's top three lieutenants —Khrushchev and Malenkov—were far more moderate than the dictator himself, while the third, the secret police chief Lavrentii Beriia, seems to have been very hard-line. This in no way demonstrated that Stalin was the leader of an embattled faction. Rather it showed that he was a dictator who was intelligent enough to want advisers offering different opinions from which he could choose, rather than yes-men around him.

We should not think Khrushchev—or subsequent Soviet leaders—did not also understand the need for diversity among their subordinates. It surely is true that Suslov and Malinovsky argued against some of Khrushchev's policies, and, no doubt, from a conservative perspective. Sometimes they may well have persuaded him, for they were old friends who knew how to appeal to him. But they could no more force Khrushchev to cancel the summit with Eisenhower than could one of Reagan's subordinates defeat him in a test of power.

Another part of the misunderstanding of the leadership conflict in the Khrushchev years resulted from a failure to distinguish style from substance. Various Politburo members disagreed with different parts of Khrushchev's policies, but they all hated his way of operating. Khrushchev was impulsive. He conducted a new reorganization every year. He announced decisions without having the staff investigate and prepare them properly, let alone the Politburo fully discuss them. In short, he was a lousy boss to work for, even if you agreed with many of his policies. A good deal of the so-called conservative opposition to Khrushchev simply wanted a more cautious approach—that is, more consistency, more consultation, less risk-taking. Much of the early analysis of the Brezhnev period labeled it "Khrushchevism without Khrushchev." That generalization had important elements of truth, until Brezhnev's health began deteriorating and policy became frozen.

Most basically, however, the liberal-conservative image of Khrushchev-era politics was misleading because Khrushchev was no simple liberal. His major opponent after Stalin's death, Georgii Malenkov, seemed much more like a real Westernizer. Some of Malenkov's closest assistants (e.g., Georgii Aleksandrov and Eduard Burdzhalov) were quite radical, and the changes that he introduced almost immediately when he served as leader in March 1953 suggest that he would have pushed policy more consistently in a liberal direction if events had worked out differently. As has been noted, Charles Bohlen, the American ambassador to Moscow in the mid-1950s, called Malenkov a "man with a more Western-oriented mind than other Soviet leaders. He at least seemed to perceive our position, and, while he did not agree with it, I felt he understood it." With Khrushchev, by contrast, "there was no meeting point, no common language. Like trains on parallel tracks, we went right by each other."[5] Edward Crankshaw made the point in another way: "Malenkov could read, and did read, Horace and Robert Burns. Khrushchev was in his twenties before he could read or write."[6]

The British ambassador to Moscow, Sir William Hayter, painted a similar picture of the leadership at a meeting with the British Labour party leader Aneurin Bevan in August 1954. "The first impression was alarming...[Khrushchev] seemed impulsive and blundering, and startlingly ignorant of foreign affairs. Bevan tried to put some quite simple United Nations point to him and he totally failed to grasp it, in spite of expert interpreting, until it was explained to him in words of one syllable by Malenkov."[7] At that time Khrushchev had already been leader of the Central Committee Secretariat for seventeen months and was already replacing Malenkov as the leader.

In other contexts too, Khrushchev scarcely came across as a pure liberal, eager to integrate the Soviet Union more into the West. In December 1962 he was taken to an abstract art exhibition, and it clearly offended him. One painting, he said, "looked, if you will excuse me, as though some child had done his business on the canvas when his mother was away and then spread it around with his hands." To the abstract artists as a whole, he declared, "Just give me a list of those of you who want to go abroad, to the so-called 'free world.' We'll give you foreign passports tomorrow, and you can get out. Your prospects here are nil. What is hung here is simply anti-Soviet. It's amoral." Khrushchev's views on other Western cultural trends were no more favorable: "I don't like jazz. When I hear jazz, it's as if I had gas on the stomach... Or take these new dances which are so fashionable now. Some of them are completely improper."[8]

Although Khrushchev's impulsiveness and utopianism certainly make it misleading to call him a moderate, his views appealed to diverse constituencies. At Stalin's death, there clearly were Politburo members—including his former chief lieutenant, Viacheslav Molotov—who wanted to continue most of the old dictator's policies, while Malenkov and others almost surely would have gone further in the direction of Westernization. Khrushchev had elements in his program that appealed both to conservatives and liberals.

Nevertheless, the alignments varied by issue. Molotov and Malenkov had worked very closely with Stalin. Molotov had talked like a really bloody-minded person in the 1920s and the 1930s, while Malenkov had very dirty hands in a 1949 blood purge. In varying degrees they might have liked to see police terror relaxed, but they absolutely did not want the purges discussed. Khrushchev, by contrast, wanted to push this aspect of de-Stalinization vigorously, perhaps out of a desire to discredit both Molotov and Malenkov, perhaps out of a deep revulsion at what had happened, probably out of both impulses.

In social policy, Malenkov identified himself with the better-educated part of the population—the managers and the intellectuals. His economic program centered on consumer goods, from which this group would especially benefit. He never would have talked about art and jazz in Khrushchev's crude terms. Both when he was personnel secretary in the late 1940s and in 1953–54, admission to the Communist party was limited in size and heavily favored those with higher education.

Khrushchev's policy was directed at the values and interests of the workers and peasants. He pushed higher payments to peasants and a more egalitarian wage policy in the cities. He encouraged worker participation against the managers, and he drastically expanded the number of workers and peasants admitted into the Communist party. He conducted a major education reform that gave preference to those with worker and peasant backgrounds and forced all elementary and high-school students to acquire work experience.

Khrushchev's values came out clearly in his advocacy of education reform:

> Young people entering educational institutions quite frequently say that after they have won in the admission competition, the competition among the parents begins, and it is this that often settles the matter. This creates inequality in admission to higher and specialized secondary educational institutions.
>
> If a boy or girl does not study well, the parents and those around the child frighten him by saying . . . he will not be able to get into a higher educational institution and will have to work at a factory as a common laborer. Physical work becomes something with which to scare children . . . Such views are insulting to the working people of a socialist society.[9]

In his social policy, Khrushchev was defending some quite traditional Marxist-Leninist values. His response to the problem of education, for example, was to draw "all students without exception into socially useful work at enterprises, collective farms, etc., after completing the seventh or eighth grades . . . Neither parents' status nor their pleas will exempt anyone from productive labor." On these social issues, Khrushchev apparently was quite close to a man such as the "conservative" ideologist, Suslov, who also took egalitarian values very seriously. The contempt that virtually all educated Russians expressed for Khrushchev was the product not just of his relatively uncultured style, but also of his social policy. (It is amusing to see in the 1980s how this was reversed, and Khrushchev is remembered as a liberal hero.)

Khrushchev was also not a pure liberal in his economic policy. He associated himself with improved food and housing from the beginning, and in the late 1950s and early 1960s he made some quite extreme statements in defense of the consumer and against the "metal-eaters" who simply wanted to expand the steel industry. Yet, when he defeated Malenkov, Khrushchev's closest associate was Nikolai Bulganin, who had been Stalin's top lieutenant for defense, and the issue was Malenkov's support of consumer goods over heavy industry. Khrushchev reduced the size of the armed forces, but he pushed modernization of its equipment and the construction of rockets. His words probably expressed his hopes and attempts to curry popularity while the budgets reflected his priorities.

In questions of economic organization, Khrushchev could be a wild experimenter. At the end of his reign the resulting administrative structure was a bizarre patchwork that embodied his incompatible ideas of the previous decade. In the early 1960s, Khrushchev permitted a fairly vigorous debate on economic reform that would use more market mechanisms. (These were known in the West as the Liberman debates, after the economist, Evsei G. Liberman.)

Conceivably the pressure for a more market-oriented reform, coupled with Khrushchev's inclination to reorganize and take chances, eventually might have led to a major reform. Nevertheless, Khrushchev's own instincts seemed strongly opposed to private property and markets, and to the income differentiation associated with them. In the 1950s he had opposed the creation of family-sized "links" on the farm. While in power, he was limiting the number of privately owned cows and expressing suspicion of the private plot of ground. He even was dubious about collective farms and was pushing for their transformation into state farms because the latter embodied a "higher" form of property.

Khrushchev also had very mixed ideas about the West. He loved to travel abroad and to see new things. A disproportionate amount of space in his memoirs is given to reports of these trips. He was eager to learn from the West on technological and agronomical questions. He seemed genuinely committed to peaceful coexistence, and Charles Bohlen believed that travel changed many of his ideas.

Yet Khrushchev also seemed deeply committed to transforming society in directions that would take it away from the Western model. His brand of utopianism opposed the values of professionalism and expertise, of the market and private ownership, of class differentiation. His famous statement, "We will bury you," never was the threat that many Westerners thought (a better translation would have been "We will be present at your funeral"), but it bespoke his deep conviction that history was on socialism's side— and not some centuries in the future. He took for granted that socialism was a vastly superior system to capitalism and that it soon could surpass it economically, and he was proud to say, "We communists are men of vigorous revolutionary action, we see our task as one of transforming the world and building a communist society."[10]

Khrushchev challenged the West in foreign policy too. He competed vigorously in the Third World with large foreign aid programs to countries such as Egypt and India, and he seemed deeply to believe that the revolutions in China, Vietnam, and Cuba represented the wave of the relatively near future. In Europe, he issued ultimatums over Berlin, and he tried to change the nuclear balance with a dangerous installation of missiles in Cuba.

The Politics of Détente

In his last years, Khrushchev forced through policies that offended almost every major institutional interest in the country, and his social policy was inimical to the interests of the entire administrative-political elite. Khrushchev's ability to enact so many unpopular decisions testified to his enormous strength, but by angering all of the party leaders in so many different ways, he eventually provoked them to unite against him and throw him out of office.

The man selected to replace Khrushchev, Leonid Brezhnev, clearly was more cautious. One former Soviet colonel said contemptuously in private, "He was chosen because he had never made a decision in his life and was incapable of making a decision." As time passed, it became obvious that his top priority was to avoid being overthrown, for he took care not to challenge any of the major power centers of the Soviet system. At least temporarily, the Soviet Union changed under his leadership from a totalitarian or semitotalitarian system based on an ideology of transformation into an authoritarian system dedicated to the preservation of the status quo.

The top priority of the new leadership had to be economic. Khrushchev had launched his major industrial reorganization, including the abolition of the industrial ministries, because everyone recognized that the old economic system had real problems.

The Liberman debates were a signal that the leadership realized that the Khrushchev reforms had not worked. Now the new leadership was essentially reconstituting the old ministerial system. It had to claim that it was doing something to ensure that the old problems—especially the lag of Soviet technology behind the West—would be corrected.

One alternative for the new leadership was a substantial economic reform that would change the incentive system for the managers, introduce some semblance of a private sector in agriculture and the services, and subject the new ministries to foreign competition to offset their reconstituted monopolies in their respective branches. The last of these would have involved a tariff-type mechanism rather than direct control by the Ministry of Foreign Trade to protect local industry, and it would have meant a real opening to the West. This alternative was being explored seriously by Hungarian and Czechoslovakian economists, and it had cautiously expressed support in the Soviet Union as well, even in *Pravda*.[11] The director of a big international relations institute declared privately that the monopoly of foreign trade did not mean the monopoly of the Ministry of Foreign Trade.

It is unclear how much support reform had at the Politburo level. The new chairman of the Council of Ministers, Aleksei Kosygin, had been an industrial administrator in the old system for thirty years, and surely he did not want to dismantle it completely. Nevertheless, he is reported to have approved a plan that would have partially reintroduced NEP in the services. Nikolai V. Podgorny, the third of the inner three in the Politburo in the mid-1960s, was very closely associated with key reformers. A leading sponsor of intellectual liberalization, Aleksei Rumiantsev, had been Podgorny's ideological secretary in Kharkov in the early 1950s, and Liberman was a prominent economist in Kharkov at the time. In 1967 the young Gorbachev apparently saw the balance of forces tilting so strong to reform that Brezhnev would be a brief, transitional figure.[12]

All of the evidence, however, indicates that Brezhnev was always skeptical about fundamental economic reform. The first additions to the Politburo in November 1965—Aleksandr Shelepin and Petr Shelest—were conservatives who could be counted to vote against Kosygin and Podgorny on reform, and Brezhnev almost surely supported their election for that reason. He also rejected the plan to introduce a modified NEP. The so-called Kosygin reforms that were introduced were little more than decentralizing rhetoric to obscure the recentralization that was occurring with the re-creation of the industrial ministries.

To be sure, the East Europeans were permitted to experiment further, and Brezhnev himself refused to intervene to support the conservative Czechoslovakian party leader who was replaced by more liberal Alexander Dubček. Conceivably Brezhnev was bowing to pressure from his colleagues in approving these steps; perhaps he was really toying with the idea of substantial reform if no problems arose. However, the political liberalization in Czechoslovakia in 1968 clearly frightened him. The Soviet invasion ended not only the Dubček experiment, but also any hope of major economic reform in Russia in the Brezhnev era.

Many in the West point to the failure of the 1965 reforms as proof of the power of the bureaucracy. They argue that any step-by-step reform such as Gorbachev is proposing must also fail. But the analogy to 1965 is faulty. Today a new general secretary is proclaiming the goal of "radical" reform, while an earlier general secretary was an important factor—probably the most important factor—in the defeat of the 1965 reforms.

Still, Brezhnev knew that the Soviet economic system had real problems and that the Khrushchev solutions had failed. He did not want to show a defeatist attitude and had to do something. Importing Western technology without subjecting Soviet manufacturers to foreign competition was the conservative alternative. Maybe the Soviet leaders even thought it might work. (The Poles were allowed to carry the policy to the extreme of borrowing large sums of money to buy Western factories and semifabricates on the assumption that the debts would be repaid from the sale to the West of the products the new factories would manufacture.)[13] Maybe Brezhnev was always skeptical but thought that the appearance of a solution to Soviet economic problems was all he needed to survive in office. In any case, Westerners who saw his policy of importing technology as a substitute for reform were correct.

The interesting question is whether Brezhnev's American-centered foreign policy was also perceived as the conservative alternative at the time. Neither radical economic reform that attacked protectionism nor Brezhnev's policy of importing technology was compatible with a confrontational posture toward the outside world. Since the United States was an occupying power in Berlin and legally could block an agreement on Berlin, which was a prerequisite to a Soviet agreement with West Germany, the Soviet Union could not improve relations with Europe without dealing to some extent with the United States as well.[14]

Nevertheless, a strong case can be made that radical reform would have required a stronger foreign policy focus on Western Europe and Japan in the 1960s. The United States was increasingly involved in the Vietnam War and it was scarcely going to loosen restrictions on the export of technology, let alone equity capital, to the Soviet Union so long as its arms were killing Americans in Vietnam. A multipolar policy that really offered concessions to Europe and Japan, that really emphasized the theme of European disarmament and an end to secrecy, might have had a major impact. After all, anti-American feeling ran high in the Vietnam era, and the European young were in the streets in demonstrations and even semirevolt.

From Brezhnev's point of view, the trouble was that the semirevolutionary mood in Western Europe might spread to Eastern Europe. Indeed, the Prague Spring of 1968 must be understood in those terms. Especially when a conservative American president was elected with a mandate to wind down the Vietnam War, it was in Brezhnev's interest to work closely with him to calm the political situation in Western Europe, and, therefore, in Eastern Europe. An American-centered policy implied American dominance of Western Europe and Japan in exchange for Soviet dominance of Eastern Europe, although both halves of Europe were to be permitted some economic independence.

There were other domestic advantages to an American-centered policy for Brezhnev. His domestic economic policy produced a steadily declining growth rate, and Brezhnev needed the appearance of foreign policy success. Brezhnev stalled on a summit with President Richard M. Nixon until he was certain that he (rather than Kosygin) would meet the president and get the credit for a SALT agreement. A series of marginal arms control agreements with the United States—and any SALT II agreement that Ronald Reagan could later live with *was* marginal—could be used to reassure the Soviet elite and population that their technological backwardness was not dangerous, that American technology was being controlled. The policy was so advantageous to Brezhnev domestically that he was willing to take the extraordinary step of permitting large-scale Jewish emigration to achieve it.

Of course, the American-oriented policy bore few real fruits, and Soviet-American relations deteriorated over the next decade. Paradoxically, however, this strengthened Brezhnev's political position in one respect. The more the West talked about a Soviet threat and Soviet military superiority, the more the Soviet people and elite could be persuaded that the Soviet Union really had achieved equality with the West and had a secure defense position, despite its economic problems.

The fascinating question is whether the struggle between Brezhnev and Kosygin on economic reform also extended to the question of a bipolar versus a multipolar foreign policy. Kosygin certainly had been the Politburo member who handled relations with the non-Communist world prior to 1971. He negotiated an end to the Indian-Pakistan war of 1965–66, traveled to the United States to meet with President Lyndon B. Johnson in 1967, and was the presumed Soviet interlocutor in any summit with President Nixon until late 1970. Between 1970 and 1971 this changed, as both the Americans and Germans observed.[15] When three foreign policy specialists—Foreign Minister Andrei Gromyko, KGB chief Yurii Andropov, and Defense Minister Andrei A. Grechko—were added to the Politburo in 1973, many Westerners saw this as the reimposition of collective leadership on Brezhnev after his summit with President Nixon. In reality, all three of these new members were Brezhnev supporters, and the result of their election—and, no doubt, the purpose of it—was the complete isolation of Kosygin as a foreign policy specialist within the Politburo. Kosygin was not even allowed to attend the 1975 meeting on European security in Helsinki, Finland, although he was the Soviet head of government.

There are some signs that Kosygin was pushing a multipolar policy in the late 1960s and early 1970s, but little real evidence is available. Soviet intellectuals tend to be skeptical. Rightly or wrongly, they see Kosygin as more of an administrator than an innovative policymaker, a man with little foreign policy experience who was very much part of his generation and who was also afraid of the independence for Germany and Eastern Europe that true multipolarism would entail. My guess is that he was pushing a far more interesting policy line.

The Politics of Decline

The shattering of the illusions about détente with the United States in the mid-1970s undoubtedly led to a rethinking of the desirable foreign policy orientation for the Soviet Union. The failure to stem the decline in the Soviet economy's growth rate by importing foreign machinery raised again the question of the need for radical economic reform, and the Japanese experience suggested that integration into the world economy could produce rapid growth. The Western military buildup in the second half of the 1970s and the early 1980s caused the military to become more insistent about the need to improve military and industrial technology. It is unlikely, however, that these various problems became the subject of fundamental Politburo debate. As Brezhnev's health declined, he was surely even less likely than before to consider basic economic reform.

The political struggle centered instead on investment and social policy. While Brezhnev was "conservative" on economic reform and Kosygin was more "liberal," this had not been the only domestic issue. Kosygin seems to have been much closer to Malenkov in preferring the better-educated and the higher-income. In class terms, therefore, he was more "conservative" in the contemporary Western usage.

These questions became entangled in the rivalry between the two great factions of the Brezhnev era, one headed by Andrei Kirilenko and the other by Konstantin Chernenko.[16] In consolidating his power, Brezhnev had relied heavily on persons whom he had known in the past. He had worked long in the Ukrainian city of Dnepropetrovsk, and many of his key appointments came from that city, including Kirilenko, the longtime personnel secretary and heir apparent, and the chairman of the Council of Ministers in the 1980s, Nikolai Tikhonov. Brezhnev had also been first secretary in the republic of Moldavia, and his closest personal assistant, Chernenko, had supervised propaganda and agitation in Moldavia at that time. Brezhnev used the Dnepropetrovsk and Moldavian groups—and Kirilenko and Chernenko—as a kind of checks-and-balances system.

Brezhnev's appointments to the police were illustrative of his balancing act. The chairman of the KGB was Yurii Andropov, who had gone to school in the same provincial city as Kirilenko in the 1930s and then had worked closely with Brezhnev in implementing East European policy in the mid-1960s. One first deputy chairman of the KGB was a longtime Brezhnev associate from Dnepropetrovsk in the 1930s, another was a younger official from Dnepropetrovsk who had worked more closely with Kirilenko, and the third had worked in Moldavia with Brezhnev and Chernenko. No single subordinate, even a trusted one like Kirilenko or Chernenko, would be able to use the KGB against Brezhnev.

The KGB, with its border troops, was also counterbalanced by the Ministry of Internal Affairs (the regular police, but with mechanized armed troops) and by the troops of the Ministry of Defense. The Ministry of Internal Affairs was headed by a man who had worked closely with Brezhnev both in Dnepropetrovsk and in Moldavia. Brezhnev had been a political officer at the front during World War II, and the key control posts in the military were staffed by people who had fought on the same part of the front with him: the minister of defense until his death in 1976 (Andrei Grechko), the head of the Main Political Administration of the Armed Forces, the head of military intelligence, and the inspector general. The chief political officer in the Moscow military district, which would be crucial in case of a coup attempt, had been a close friend of Brezhnev's in Dnepropetrovsk in 1941. During the late 1950s, Brezhnev had been Central Committee secretary for the defense industry and the space program. The chief industrial administrator with whom he worked during that period, Dmitrii Ustinov, became the minister of defense when Grechko died.

When a leader plays one major lieutenant off against another, rivalry almost invariably arises between them. In the mid-1970s the personal rivalry between Kirilenko and Chernenko became associated with the battle over what to sacrifice as economic growth slowed. Kirilenko, who supervised both the economy and personnel selection, openly expressed his belief that investment must continue to receive high priority. He did not make the implications of his preference clear, but investment had to be drawn from defense or consumption or both. Whether out of expediency or more likely conviction, Chernenko encouraged Brezhnev to continue his social policy. Chernenko wrote as if he were a true believer in the privileged position of the workers and in egalitarianism and as if he were suspicious of large material incentives and the market. He wrote about important "contradictions" under socialism in a way that suggested a fear of the power of the workers as well.

In 1976 or 1977, Kirilenko was relieved of his responsibilities for personnel selection, which were given to Chernenko. Kirilenko retained supervision of the economy, but under him a Chernenko associate (Vladimir I. Dolgikh) was the Central Committee secretary for heavy industry. After 1979, Kirilenko was increasingly slighted, even in public. Just before Brezhnev's death, he was dropped from the Politburo in an unusual and degrading manner. His name simply was not included one day in a list of Politburo members.

Since little personnel selection was taking place, Chernenko was really not able to consolidate his position, but he steadily rose in power. In 1977 he became a candidate member of the Politburo, and in 1978 a full member. As Brezhnev's health declined, Chernenko became his alter ego—a second secretary who, in fact, was often the acting general secretary.

The rise of Chernenko and the fall of Kirilenko coincided with the defeat of the latter's program. As Myron Rush of Cornell University has written, "three times the Soviet leaders have been forced to choose... Each time capital investment for economic growth has been the chief victim."[17] In particular, investment was planned to grow only 24 to 26 percent in the Tenth Five-Year Plan (1976–1980), compared with 41 percent in the ninth (1971–1975).

During this period huge amounts of foreign currency were used to purchase grain instead of technology. Even in the last year of Brezhnev's life, it was decided to pump enormous sums of money into higher payments to the peasants. Chernenko was the man who publicly hailed this decision, not the Central Committee secretary for agriculture, Mikhail Gorbachev, whose branch benefited from the decision. By this time Gorbachev was looking beyond the parochial interests of agriculture to a much broader politics.

The Politics of the Successions

An incredible number of rumors about Politburo politics circulated in Moscow between 1982 and 1985. Most were totally inconsistent with one another, and few stood up to serious scrutiny. Under Andropov, Chernenko was said to speak for the party apparatus and the Brezhnevites, but Ustinov—said to be the power behind Andropov's throne—had been one of Brezhnev's closest friends on the Politburo. Moreover, many of the men whom Andropov was promoting (Geidar A. Aliev, Gorbachev, Yegor K. Ligachev, and Vitalii I. Vorotnikov) had worked for years in the party apparatus. In the first months of Chernenko's rule, Gromyko was alleged to be a Stalinist who was the architect of the harsh anti-American policy, but after he went to Washington to meet President Reagan, he was said to be the proponent of negotiations.

The most widespread and important rumor was that Andropov's succession resulted from the support of the military.[18] Throughout 1983 the chief source of information in Moscow, Roy Medvedev, was telling everyone that the military always had an especially powerful role during times of succession and that the defense minister Ustinov was the number two man in the political system.[19] Then Chernenko was elected general secretary, allegedly (and probably in fact) with Ustinov as one of his main supporters. As we have seen, Chernenko removed the head of the General Staff, Marshal Ogarkov, and Gorbachev lowered the status of the military during his first year in power. Suddenly no mention was made of any iron law about the strength of the military in times of succession.

It is too soon to sort out the nuances of the three successions between 1982 and 1985, but the nature of some of the confusion is apparent.

The first key to understanding is that there was no discreet group of Brezhnevites who could be supporting Chernenko or anyone else. In one way or another, everyone near the top was a Brezhnevite of some type or another, or he would not have survived politically. The battle after 1982 was not between Brezhnevites and non-Brezhnevites, but between different groups of Brezhnevites.

The second key is that the party apparatus was not a unified entity beholden to Chernenko and to the status quo. As indicated in chapter 4, the regional party organs are often divided among themselves and within themselves, and they agree on only one thing: they hate the ministries in Moscow. They surely are not united on how they would change the situation, but they all want a change that somehow lessens the arbitrary power the ministries have over their regions. Hence it is not surprising that Chernenko criticized the bureaucrats as strongly as Andropov did (really more strongly[20]) and that Gorbachev picked up the theme when he became leader. Whatever these contenders actually wanted to do, they knew that bureaucrat bashing was popular with the party organs.

The party apparatus was also, of course, seriously split in its loyalty to Kirilenko and Chernenko, the two senior Central Committee secretaries who had been supervising it. Far more of the regional secretaries had been selected when Kirilenko had been personnel secretary than when Chernenko was, and their prime loyalties were not likely to be to the latter. Most of the important regional secretaries were engineers with managerial experience who were likely to share Kirilenko's preference for investment and to be skeptical of Chernenko's support for worker preference.

The third key is to make a distinction between the defense

industry and the military.[21] Americans talk about a military-industrial complex in the Soviet Union, and that concept is sometimes helpful. However, the Soviet defense industry and military have important conflicts of interest. The defense industry manufacturers are judged by plan fulfillment, and they are as eager as the civilian-industry manufacturers to have an easy plan with simple goods to produce. In fact, the defense industry has not given the Soviet military weapons as sophisticated as the American military's, and it has no interest in an economic reform that would require an improvement.

The military, by contrast, have to worry about American capabilities. They have to look ahead to the end of the century, when Western conventional forces will be largely computerized, when the Strategic Defense Initiative will at a minimum have technological spin-offs, and when Chinese modernization will begin to have military payoffs. The Soviet military have to wonder whether the continuing American technological superiority will someday produce a disastrous American military breakthrough. And even if the defense industry succeeds in raising Soviet military technology to American levels, how will draftees (perhaps 40 percent of Moslem background by the year 2000) with absolutely no exposure to computers as children and teenagers be able to handle such military machines?

The minister of defense in the early 1980s was Dmitrii Ustinov, but for forty years he had been a defense industry administrator—the most important single individual in building the defense industry in the postwar period. In his articles, he wrote as if he were personally offended at the suggestion that his defense industry was not coping with its tasks, and he clearly had no desire to support a major economic reform.

The top uniformed officer in this period was Marshal Nikolai Ogarkov, the head of the General Staff. He wrote frequently in the press, and he repeatedly emphasized his concern about the technological problem. On some questions, Ogarkov and Ustinov were allied, but on the crucial question of the technological capability of the defense industry, the tension between them was palpable.[22]

The rivalry between Kirilenko and Chernenko, and between

the military and the defense industry, set the context for the rivalry between Andropov and Chernenko. As has been noted, Andropov's ties with Kirilenko went back to the 1930s. Andropov then became KGB chief when Kirilenko was in charge of personnel and organizational questions. Everything that Andropov said while general secretary indicated that he agreed with Kirilenko's position on investment and social policy. As Kirilenko's position declined, Andropov became the head of the Kirilenko machine and the leading representative of its views.

The extent to which Andropov was willing to go beyond a policy of higher investment and a tougher social policy and support radical reform remains unclear. He did, however, often speak about "unsolved problems," and in April 1982 he made a strong implicit attack on Brezhnev's policy of relying on imported technology.[23] Surely Andropov was talking about reform of some type, but once in power, he said that he had no recipes. Since he had been the Politburo's specialist on Hungary and must have supported the Soviet toleration of Hungarian economic reform, there is a strong suspicion that he was simply being cautious in laying out his domestic program because until 1986 he would have to rely on the Central Committee elected in 1981. But maybe he really was not sure what he would do.

In his foreign policy utterances, Andropov had been more urgent than any other major contender in pushing for improved international relations with the West after 1975. In 1975, when Suslov was publicly worrying about ultrareactionary forces in the West and Shcherbitsky was emphasizing that the nature of imperialism had not changed, Andropov was insisting that the "relaxation of international tension does not occur by itself...It is necessary to actively struggle for it. There cannot be any pause or breathing space since détente is a continuous process that demands constant movement forward." In 1979, he asserted that "it is impossible to underestimate the danger of a course of retarding détente," and in 1980, he was the only Politburo member to warn that détente was in serious danger.

Unlike many other Politburo members, Andropov coupled his support for peace and détente with a call for negotiations, even in 1980, in the wake of the U.S. sanctions after the Soviet invasion of Afghanistan. As early as 1976, he was quite explicit in stating that "the policy of peaceful coexistence, as is well known, presupposes negotiations and the seeking of mutually acceptable decisions, sometimes of a compromise nature." Such statements do not make clear whether Andropov was thinking of détente in bipolar or multipolar terms, but in April 1982 he emphasized "capitalist contradictions" in a way that suggested the latter.[24]

Andropov's position on the military versus the defense industry is clouded in mystery. All of the rumors had him strongly supported by Ustinov in October 1982, and well-placed Soviet citizens insist on the accuracy of those rumors. Yet, all of the esoteric evidence of 1983 (and Ogarkov's and Ustinov's fates under Chernenko) suggest that Andropov was much closer to Ogarkov's views and that he was attacking Ustinov's power and status while he was general secretary.[25] Again, as on other questions, Andropov may not have been showing his hands to insiders, and they may have been supporting him with quite contradictory expectations.

Chernenko's position on most crucial questions is easier to discern. He was truly a Brezhnevite in the sense that he favored the old Brezhnev priorities. In foreign policy he spoke fervently—if generally—in favor of détente, as even anti-Chernenko intellectuals confirmed. However, it was almost surely the more conservative Brezhnev's détente with the United States that he had in mind. Ustinov and Gromyko undoubtedly looked down on Chernenko—and this may have affected personal relations—but these two men also favored Brezhnev's priorities in their respective policy realms. Their views were fundamentally closer to Chernenko's than to Andropov's.

In the domestic sphere Chernenko clearly wanted to continue Brezhnev's social policy, and he did not favor major economic reform oriented toward the market. His year in office featured total inaction, but it is likely that he would have behaved somewhat differently if his health and political position had been stronger. When Brezhnev presented Chernenko with an award on his seventieth birthday, he praised him for being "restless" in the good sense of the term, for being a man with "a creative, daring approach." In response, Chernenko acknowledged that he sometimes made "nonstandard decisions."[26] Judging by his speeches, however, the direction of reform that he would have pushed would have been more in the direction of workers' self-management. His speeches seemed highly hostile to the bureaucracy, but his solution seemed to be to maximize the power of the workers vis-à-vis the managers rather than subject both of them to the discipline of the market.

The Interregnum

Yurii Andropov was the first (and thus far the only) man elected general secretary without serving first as Central Committee personnel secretary.[27] His coalition, no doubt, had contained a range of people—including (as we have seen in chapter 1) Mikhail Gorbachev, already an important political actor. Nevertheless, Andropov basically came to power on the back of the old Kirilenko political machine in the party apparatus, a machine of which he had been a part.

A sign of the character of Andropov's alliance was that, except for Gorbachev, almost all of his important appointments were of persons closely associated with Kirilenko. These appointments had all the appearance of payoffs for the machine's support. Yegor Ligachev (the number two man in personnel) had worked as Kirilenko's direct subordinate in personnel work in the 1960s, Nikolai I. Ryzhkov (the head of the economic department of the Central Committee) had come out of one of Kirilenko's two main bases, Sverdlovsk, and he was serving as first deputy chairman of Gosplan—an institution under Kirilenko's direct supervision at the end. (Nikolai N. Sliunkov, the new party secretary in the big republic of Belorussia, Andropov's first big appointment in the lower party apparatus, also was deputy chairman of Gosplan.) Viktor M. Chebrikov, the chairman of the KGB, worked under Kirilenko in Dnepropetrovsk. Mikhail S. Solomentsev and Vitalii Vorotnikov were chairman and first deputy chairman of the Council of Ministers of the RSFSR (another direct responsibility of Kirilenko's in the second half of the 1970s), and Andropov had them elected to the Politburo. The man who was Ligachev's first deputy for personnel (Evgenii Razumov) had been Kirilenko's personal assistant in the mid-1960s.

The policy followed by Andropov will always be a source of debate among scholars. He became general secretary in November 1982, but was seriously ill by the early summer of 1983 and disappeared from sight in August. He clearly wanted to reinvigorate the Soviet system, and he must have known that this would require major action. He did not, however, really have time to indicate what his ultimate policy would be, and perhaps he did not know himself.

In the year that he was general secretary, Andropov revealed only two policies clearly. First, he began a substantial replacement of old personnel. He immediately removed Chernenko from his responsibility for personnel and gave him the less important duties of "ideology" (relations with foreign Communists and supervision of education, culture, science, and propaganda). Gorbachev was named the senior personnel secretary and was treated by Andropov as the heir apparent. The selection of a number of new regional party secretaries allowed Gorbachev to begin building a political machine of his own.

Second, Andropov began the attack on the social policy that Brezhnev had followed and that Chernenko had supported. The code word for this change was "discipline," but the word means far more than it seems to American ears. Even on the surface, discipline meant not an unconditional right to a job, but a "right" to lose a job if a person was not productive. In addition, however, Andropov wrote about the need for prices to correspond to costs and hinted at the need to raise subsidized meat prices. He attacked excess egalitarianism, and wage decisions taken in 1983 resulted in the first increase in years in the gap between the wages of industrial workers and industrial technical personnel in 1984.

The nature of Andropov's international policy is controversial in the West, and has been characterized as everything from strongly pro-détente to Stalinist. The confusion, I think, reflected a failure to realize that Andropov was moving away from Brezhnev's American-centered policy in the direction of a multipolar one. The theme of German revanchism, the catchphrase used to defend an American-centered policy, was increasingly played

down in the press, and especially in *Izvestiia* after a longtime Andropov subordinate was made its editor. Andropov brought back
from exile in Canada one of the leading critics of the bipolar policy, Aleksandr N. Yakovlev, and named him director of the top
Soviet foreign policy institute, IMEMO. Yakovlev immediately
began writing articles that strongly attacked Gromyko's foreign
policy. (Yakovlev had been a party official in the same Yaroslavl
party organization that Andropov himself had come out of in the
1930s.)[28]

On September 29, 1983, Andropov himself issued a flat statement on the subject from his sickbed: "If anyone had illusions
about the possibility for an evolution to the better in the policy of
the present American administration, then recent events have finally shattered them."[29] Many Westerners saw the statement as a
rejection of détente with the West, but this interpretation is almost surely wrong. Andropov was talking about the United
States specifically and at length (one-third of a page), and it was
illusions about a bipolar policy that he had in mind.

Arms control in Andropov's year in office was dominated by
the question of the installation of Pershing-2 and cruise missiles in
Europe. Andropov's first action was a very forthcoming arms
control proposal on the subject—in practice, an offer to reduce
Soviet warheads facing Europe from 950 to 350 without any cor-
responding Western reduction in its existing forces balancing the
old Soviet missiles facing Europe, if only the West would not
install its new missiles. Andropov's offer contradicted the conventional Western assumption (based on years of Soviet experience)
that the Soviet Union would never trade existing missiles for potential American ones. The Reagan administration, however, rejected both Andropov's proposal and the compromise discussed
by Paul Nitze, the chief American negotiator, in the so-called
Walk in the Woods in November 1983 with the Soviet negotiator,
Yurii Kvitinsky.[30]

Although there is disagreement in the West about Andropov's
foreign policy, no one disputes his intention to attack Chernenko's
position in the Central Committee Secretariat.[31] If Andropov had
lived another six months, Chernenko's physical and political
health would have prevented him from being elected general sec-

retary. But Andropov died in February 1984 before the process of downgrading Chernenko could be completed. Even then the announcement of Chernenko's election came four days after Andropov's death, and it is not known whether the delay resulted from an intervening weekend or a real struggle for power. In the aftermath, as we have seen in chapter 1, Chernenko was made the general secretary, while Gorbachev was given control of so many levers of power that he was virtually guaranteed the succession when the ailing Chernenko died.

It is much less clear whether there was any agreement on policy. In his acceptance speech, Chernenko strongly emphasized "social justice" in a way that reversed Andropov's emphasis.[32] Andropov's subordinate who had been appointed editor of *Izvestiia* was moved to a ceremonial post in April, and the theme of German revanchism that was used to support a bipolar policy gradually returned to prominence.

In the first months, however, policy did not seem to change. A special plenary session of the Central Committee was scheduled to discuss agriculture, and someone must have thought that it would introduce significant steps. In May, Ogarkov felt that he could give his remarkable May 9 interview that implied the need for technological transformation. May and June also featured an anti-American boycott of the Olympics, apparent encouragement of visits to West Germany by East German and Bulgarian leaders, and signs of weakness in Gromyko's position. (For example, his seventy-fifth birthday was not celebrated as elaborately as it should have been in June.)

Chernenko took a long vacation in the summer, amid signs of growing illness. The impression of his political weakness was so strong that the Reagan administration could argue convincingly that the Soviet Union was too disorganized to conclude an arms control agreement. When Chernenko recovered and returned to Moscow, a major reversal of policy occurred. The Central Committee plenum on agriculture did nothing, and Ogarkov was removed from office.

At the same time, all movement toward a multipolar foreign policy disappeared. Gromyko came to Washington and his speech at the United Nations evoked memories of the wartime alliance—

one of the code words of the Americanists. The East German and Bulgarian visits to West Germany were canceled. Gromyko's stock soared, and three months after his seventy-fifth birthday it was celebrated in a virtually unprecedented way.

During this period, signs of Gorbachev's unhappiness with policy and of Chernenko's unhappiness with him grew. Gorbachev did not speak at the agricultural plenum, although he was the Politburo's agricultural specialist, and he cannot have approved the irrigation program that was enacted (merely an echo of Brezhnev's 1965 policy). In December, he was one of the few Politburo members who did not speak at the Politburo meeting that approved the draft of the Five-Year Plan, even though he was Central Committee secretary in charge of planning. (In fact, once he was in power, he explicitly criticized the draft.) In a few protocol settings, but not most, he was ranked behind Grigorii Romanov instead of in his normal spot of number two to Chernenko in the Central Committee Secretariat.

It is not clear what was going on. Some liked to paint a picture of a titanic struggle for power between Chernenko and Gorbachev, but no effort was made to build up a competing heir apparent to Gorbachev or to give one any breadth of responsibilities that would test or prepare a successor. In December, Gorbachev was the man sent to England, and no one else received such experience or such exposure abroad or on domestic television. There he acted with great self-confidence and aplomb. Moreover, unlike Andropov (or Gorbachev in his first year), Chernenko was not allowed to make any changes in the Politburo that would consolidate his position or weaken Gorbachev's. Or, maybe, Gorbachev was so strong in the Central Committee that Chernenko feared to make Politburo changes lest they actually weaken him vis-à-vis Gorbachev.

The most likely explanation for the events of 1984 is that as a condition of his election, Chernenko promised not only to make Gorbachev the heir apparent, but to continue Andropov's policies. A number of people acted as if they believed this meant a further unfolding of the pattern of reform that Andropov had begun, while Chernenko acted as if this meant only a continuation of the very minor steps that Andropov had actually taken.

When the resulting inconsistency and signs of disorder began undercutting the Soviet Union's international situation, Chernenko was allowed to impose his preferences in early September.

It is very likely, however, that the establishment of a firm policy line in September had no relevance for the agreements on the succession. Gorbachev was able to signal his displeasure with policy, but he continued his consolidation of power. As has been seen, he gave a speech in December that *The New York Times* described as "calling for a transformation of the nation as radical as the one wrought by Stalin in the brutal industrialization drive of the 1930s." The real impact of the September decision was to reinforce the right of the general secretary to impose his preferences while he was in office. It was a precedent that a man hoping to be general secretary himself fairly soon could only applaud.

7

Gorbachev's Victory

WHEN Chernenko died, the prevailing Western opinion was that Gorbachev's position would be relatively weak. He was still the youngest member of the Politburo, by five years. Half the voting members averaged seventy-five years of age, while one of the younger members (Grigorii Romanov) was his chief rival. Most Western specialists told *The New York Times* that the Politburo was a "collective body," that "general policy will be very likely still made by the collective of the Politburo," that the Soviet system featured "a very solid, firmly-in-place bureaucratic Government." We would see, the conventional interpretation suggested, "a change in the form and style of Soviet leadership rather than in substance."[1]

By early 1987 Gorbachev had convinced most Westerners that he was serious about reform, but many analysts saw him threatened with defeat in the Politburo within a relatively short period. A flood of rumors about opposition to Gorbachev surfaced in Moscow, most of which focused on his presumed inability to remove the Ukrainian party leader, Vladimir Shcherbitsky.[2] By the fall, however, people were talking instead of Yegor Ligachev as the great danger. When Boris Yeltsin was disgraced in October 1987, this was interpreted as an attack on Gorbachev's closest ally by conservatives led by Ligachev. When a page-long conservative letter signed by a Leningrad professor, Nina Andreeva, appeared in a leading Soviet newspaper in April 1988, it was seen as a virtual manifesto for counterrevolution.

Within a year, however, the concerns were precisely the opposite. Now Yeltsin was correctly recognized as Gorbachev's leading political enemy, not his ally. With the defeat of party secretaries in the March 1989 elections of the Congress of People's Deputies, with demonstrations in non-Russian republics, with strikes in Siberian and Ukrainian coal mines, many now came to believe that Gorbachev was under severe attack from the left and that party rule itself might be threatened by anarchy.

Yet, in the sudden new concern about the radical danger to Gorbachev, many have not reflected sufficiently on the thoroughness of his victory over conservatives who recently were considered almost invincible. We must give more consideration to the possibility—the probability—that a man who was so successful in crushing the conservatives may have also given a lot of thought to how he is going to deal with Boris Yeltsin, the Baltic nationalities, and striking Russian workers.

The Mechanisms of Power

One of the great problems that Americans have had in understanding Gorbachev's victory is that few give any thought to the mechanisms of power in the Soviet Union. We all know that delegates to the Democratic and Republican conventions in the United States are elected according to precise rules and that few are influenceable by the oratory of the convention. By contrast, in the Soviet Union we believe there to be a very fluid politics—a struggle between conservatives and liberals in the Politburo, with one side winning today, the other tomorrow, and the alternating outcomes deter-mined by events, by chance, by heaven knows what. It is a major mistake, for Soviet politics, too, has its rules and its levers of power, and we should try to understand them.

Thus, according to the Party Rules, the general secretary is not responsible to the Politburo at all, but he—and all the members of the Politburo—are chosen by and removable by the Central Committee. Gorbachev has been very explicit in emphasizing this accountability, and with good reason. The Central Committee is a body that had around 300 voting members in the 1980s, until the "voluntary resignation" of 74 of them in April 1989 brought the number closer to 250. It is composed largely of the leaders of the important institutions and regions of the country, although it also contains a growing number of workers and peasants—13 percent of the voting members in the summer of 1989. The Central Committee is elected at the party congress (or convention, in Amer-ican terms) that is now usually convened every five years, with its delegates elected by the various republican and regional party con-ventions held just before the congress.

Americans have been aware that the election of delegates to the party congress has been tightly controlled for decades and that the congress itself has been presented with a predetermined list of Central Committee members, which it has ratified. The Central Committee has generally met infrequently—twice a year under Brezhnev—and its sessions have usually lasted for only a day or two. When Boris Yeltsin spoke out against Gorbachev and Li-gachev at a Central Committee plenary session in October 1987, other speakers asserted that they had never heard anything like it before in the Central Committee.

As a result, analysts have had a strong tendency to see the Central Committee as a rubber stamp and to treat its election of the general secretary and Politburo members as a formality.

Virtually all Western speculation about the successions after Brezhnev's death was based on the assumption that the Politburo was the deciding body. The only exceptions were analyses that assumed that the military and the KGB had managed to stage a virtual coup d'état over the Politburo and the party apparatus.

After Gorbachev's victory, rumors suggested that the Politburo had divided 4 to 4 in the crucial vote and that Gromyko cast the deciding vote from the chair. (Viktor Grishin was said to be the opposing candidate and Vladimir Shcherbitsky, who was not in the country, is not supposed to have voted.)[3]

However, it all made little sense. The Politburo had ten voting members, listed in table 6, at the time of Gorbachev's succession. No doubt, four of them—Grishin, Kunaev, Romanov, and Tikhonov—were opposed to his election. Gromyko had had total control of foreign policy at the end of Chernenko's life, and he had to know that Gorbachev would want his own man. Moreover, when Chernenko and Ustinov were also on the Politburo in the fall of 1984, they were two more elderly voters who cannot have been enthusiastic about Gorbachev, and who might have cooperated in cutting Gorbachev down to size or building up a rival to him among the younger men. (Ustinov's position is made clear by the treatment of him after his death. Chernenko renamed the large city of Izhevsk in his honor, but Gorbachev returned the city to its former name.)[4]

The thesis that the Politburo selected Gorbachev is even more difficult to maintain if we look at the younger men on the Politburo. Under Chernenko, none—other than Gorbachev—occupied jobs in the true inner core of the Soviet system, and after his election Gorbachev did not promote a single one of them. Instead, he selected his own inner core from men who had not been Politburo members prior to his election. By 1989, all but Vorotnikov had been retired. Clearly Gorbachev did not have to make promises to the younger men to obtain their support in a Politburo battle. If the Politburo had really had the power to select, Grishin or Romanov (or even Gromyko) could easily have picked up a majority against Gorbachev by promising a big job to several of the younger members.

If there ever were any doubts, Yegor Ligachev resolved them in June 1988. He stated that the result could have been quite different in March 1985, but that Gorbachev had been elected thanks to a number of persons, including the KGB chief, Viktor Chebrikov, and "many secretaries of regional party organs." These

TABLE 6 POLITBURO VOTING MEMBERS, MARCH 15, 1985

Member	Year of Birth	Position
Geidar A. Aliev	1923	First Deputy Chairman, USSR Council of Ministers
Mikhail S. Gorbachev	1931	Secretary, Central Committee of the Communist Party
Viktor V. Grishin	1914	First Secretary, Moscow City Party Committee
Andrei A. Gromyko	1909	USSR Minister of Foreign Affairs
Dinmukhamed A. Kunaev	1912	First Secretary, Kazakhstan Republican Party Committee
Grigorii V. Romanov	1923	Secretary, Central Committee of the Communist Party
Vladimir V. Shcherbitsky	1918	First Secretary, Ukrainian Republican Party Committee
Mikhail S. Solomentsev	1913	Chairman, USSR Party Control Committee
Nikolai A. Tikhonov	1905	Chairman, USSR Council of Ministers
Vitalii I. Vorotnikov	1926	Chairman, Council of Ministers, Russian Republic

latter persons were not voting members of the Politburo, and Ligachev's statement clearly indicated that the center of power was the Central Committee.

It may be that, in fact, the selection of a general secretary is always decided before the Central Committee meets. A formal showdown in the Central Committee would destroy the image of collective leadership, and it would virtually require removal of the losers. The Politburo likes to present a unanimous recommendation to the Central Committee, for that does forestall a struggle in the Central Committee. But the Politburo knows that a dissatisfied contender can always appeal the question to the Central Committee, and it always must be aware of the balance of forces within the Central Committee in such a case. What Ligachev was saying in 1988 was that a number of Central Committee members let their preference be known to the Politburo and that the latter unwillingly recommended Gorbachev because it thought it had no other choice.

The role of the Central Committee in the selection process and the great power of a general secretary in the Central Committee are no accidents. They flow from Lenin's conception of a centralized party and the steps he took to maintain his control of it.

Lenin feared the election of provincial party officials and of delegates to the party congress as specified in the Party Rules. He wanted provincial officials to carry out central directives and knew that local elections would undercut this; he did not want the delegates to the party congress to reflect popular moods and to be able to demand a new party policy—or a new leader.

Lenin took several steps to ensure his dominance in the party congresses and to guarantee that the party would remain highly centralized. First, in 1921 he instituted a clause in the Party Rules to ban "factionalism" within the party. Differences of opinion were still tolerated, including in the press, but the clause decreed that any political analysis "must under no circumstance be submitted for preliminary discussion to groups formed on the basis of any sort of platform, etc., but must be exclusively submitted for discussion to all members of the party directly."[5] This was a complicated way of saying that no group could get together before the elections, draw up a program in opposition to the leadership, and campaign on it in the party elections.

Second, Lenin fought to establish the rule that the election of provincial party secretaries had to be "confirmed" from above. Each party committee had its list of posts, called *nomenklatura* in Russian, and personnel could not be appointed or elected to these posts or removed from them without the agreement of the specified party committee. When an official was appointed by a governmental organization, "confirmation" often was no more than that, but when officials were formally elected, confirmation came to mean appointment.

Lenin was unable or unwilling to end the power of the party congress to elect the Central Committee or the power of the Central Committee to elect Politburo members and Central Committee secretaries. One reason clearly was that without an outside body to which the Politburo was responsible, the leader would become dependent on the Politburo. Lenin's strategy was to solidify his control of the central organs by using his power and authority to gain control of the congress and, therefore, the Central Committee it elected. At the end of his life, he was toying with the proposal of electing large numbers of workers to the Central Committee, surely because he thought that they would be more certain supporters than high officials.

One of the second-echelon leaders of the Lenin era, Anastas Mikoyan, was very frank in his memoirs about how this process worked in 1922:

"The conditions in which the preparation for the Eleventh Congress is taking place," Stalin said [to me, Mikoyan, privately], "are fundamentally different from those on the eve of the Tenth Congress . . . [Now] the chief danger can come from Trotsky and his supporters, but they still are not making any noise . . . If in such circumstances relatively many former Trotskyists will be elected to the Central Committee, then this will represent a danger for the further work of the Central Committee. Then Trotsky can raise his head, provoke disagreements in the Central Committee, and, relying on his supporters, complicate the work of the Central Committee in many ways . . . For this reason," Stalin said, "we are concerned about the kind of delegates who will come to the forthcoming party congress and whether there will be many Trotskyists among them . . . In this connection Siberia worries us. There are still fairly many Trotskyists there. They enjoy a certain confidence and influence in their organizations, and for this reason there is the danger that many of them will be among the elected delegates to the congress. That is why," he said in conclusion, "Lenin entrusted me to call you in, to tell you about the situation, and if you share this view about conditions in the party, to ask you to go to Lashevich in Novoni-kolaevsk [now Novosibirsk] in order to transmit to him everything that I have told you in the name of Lenin." Without hesitation, I [Mikoyan] stated that I agree to set out for Siberia on this assignment.[6]

It was, of course, one thing to establish the principle that party secretaries should be appointed from above and the election of delegates controlled. It was something else to get the job done. Lenin was extraordinarily busy, and in declining health. How could he know about the performance of provincial party secretaries, let alone about the qualifications of the candidates to succeed them? Supervision of the provinces and of personnel selection within them was a full-time job, and under Lenin, this job became the responsibility of the Central Committee Secretariat, and, first of all, of Joseph Stalin. This was why it was Stalin whom Lenin entrusted to organize the selection of delegates from Novonikolaevsk.

Stalin's job was considered dull and relatively unimportant organizational work by his rivals, but it had its hidden charms. When Stalin selected provincial party secretaries who were loyal to Lenin, he was also careful to ensure that they were loyal to him as well. The regional party secretaries controlled the selection of the delegates to the party congresses that elected the Central Committee. After Lenin's death, these congresses rolled up huge majorities for Stalin against his rivals in the party leadership, and he was able to remove these rivals as "oppositions."

This process by which a general secretary's control of the selection of personnel in the provinces gives him control over the party congresses and then over the Central Committee that is supposed to control him—a process that Robert Daniels has called "the circular flow of power"—has remained at the heart of the structure of power in the Soviet Union ever since.[7] The general secretary is able to build a political machine in which lower officials support him because they owe their jobs to him, and because they fear punishment if they cross him. The anti-faction rule makes it extremely difficult for opposition to organize against him.

Of course, a party boss who becomes the top policymaker soon encounters a serious problem. Like Lenin, he simply does not have time for detailed supervision of the provinces and personnel selection if he is to tend to his other duties. He too needs a subordinate or subordinates who perform much of this work for him, and the cycle begins anew. This subordinate is in an ideal position when the succession occurs.

In fact, the general secretary's chief lieutenant in the Secretariat for personnel selection has done extremely well at times of succession. Nikita Khrushchev was Stalin's personnel secretary during the last three years of the latter's life. Brezhnev in turn was Khrushchev's personnel secretary when the latter was overthrown. Under Brezhnev, the situation was complicated, as we saw in the last chapter. Andrei Kirilenko had been the personnel secretary from 1966 to 1977, but then Konstantin Chernenko was given the job from 1977 to 1982. In the last five years of Brezhnev's life, however, only one-fourth of the provincial first secretaries in the Slavic republics and the republican first secretaries in non-Slavic republics were changed. As a consequence, at the time of Brezhnev's death, the strong majority of regional party secretaries had been selected while Kirilenko was the personnel secretary, not Chernenko. This is perhaps the major reason that the Central Committee in 1982 selected not the present personnel secretary, but the protégé of the former one. And it is surely the reason that Andropov drew the vast majority of his early appointments out of the old Kirilenko machine.

Under Andropov, Gorbachev was named the Central Committee secretary on the Politburo who was in charge of personnel, and Andropov not only treated him as the heir apparent, but permitted him to oversee a large amount of personnel change. When Andropov died in February 1984, however, Gorbachev had been in the personnel job for less than a year (and a voting member of the Politburo for little more than three years). The leadership chose as general secretary the man who had been personnel secretary from 1977 to 1982. None of the regional secretaries selected while Gorbachev was personnel secretary had had a chance to be elected to the Central Committee, and the old regional secretaries, a Soviet insider said, had found Chernenko comfortable to work with, even if he had not selected them.

Gorbachev remained the personnel secretary under Chernenko as he had under Andropov. Between Brezhnev's and Chernenko's deaths, party first secretaries had been elected in regions that were to elect 31 percent of the delegates to the Twenty-seventh Party Congress in early 1986. Another 32 percent of the delegates would be selected by regions whose first secretary was fifty-five or younger in 1982 and a natural Gorbachev supporter because of his hope to benefit from future personnel change.[8] The closer the party congress approached, the greater the political problem created if the leadership had not selected Gorbachev. In addition, as his first appointments showed, Gorbachev was also cutting his deals with the old supporters of Kirilenko who loathed Chernenko and his supporters.

The speed with which Gorbachev was elected after Chernenko's death certainly suggests that the process itself was not complicated at that time. Perhaps a fierce battle had been fought and won in the previous weeks while Chernenko was obviously dying. Perhaps the leadership had basically already decided on a two-stage succession when Andropov died and was simply reaffirming that decision.

In either case a Politburo, a majority of whose members must have wistfully been reflecting on the personal desirability of another outcome, basically was recognizing the reality of the balance of forces within the Central Committee. In 1957 the Central Committee had overturned the decision of a majority of the Politburo (or Presidium, as it was then called) to remove Khrushchev, while in 1964 it supported a nearly unanimous Politburo decision to remove him. No one has forgotten that in a crisis, anyone on the Politburo can appeal to the Central Committee.

As the unquestioned second secretary with an unprecedented range of responsibilities over the previous year, as a man with very strong support in the regional party apparatus, Gorbachev surely was going to challenge a Politburo decision that tried to give the mantle to another person. Even if the Politburo presented Gorbachev as a unanimously-endorsed candidate to the Central Committee, as it almost surely did, its decision was based on an awareness of the likely outcome in the Central Committee in a showdown vote. Maybe that was what Gromyko really meant when he warned the leaders against giving outsiders the chance to talk about political divisions in the Soviet Union.

Gorbachev's Political Situation

During the Brezhnev period many Western scholars explained the lack of dramatic political action and then the onset of stagnation by a long-term decline in the power of the general secretary. In the words of an American political scientist, Thane Gustafson,

> Unwritten conventions on promotion and representation have come to limit a general secretary's choices in applying the cadres weapon. The distribution of political forces has shifted: the party apparatus in the provinces matters less, while the major state institutions in Moscow have increased their presence and influence. The end result is oligarchy rather than one-man rule, a politics of accommodation instead of dictate... The long-term trend is for the power of successive general secretaries to decline.[9]

As has been seen, I do not share the view that "the cadres weapon" has lost significance. Moreover, in one key respect the position of the general secretary today is markedly better than it was in the past.

Lenin ruled from the post that is equivalent to the chairmanship of the Council of Ministers today, and Stalin, as general secretary, was only his lieutenant for personnel. Hence Lenin's official successor was the man who took over his job as head of government. Similarly, after Stalin's death, the clear leader for the first year was Georgii Malenkov, the then chairman of the Council of Ministers. In both successions the leader of the Secretariat first had to establish that he was number one.

Even when Stalin and Khrushchev unequivocably became the top leaders, the post of general secretary still was not considered fully legitimate. When Nikita Khrushchev met President Eisenhower in the first Geneva summit in 1955, his power was obviously far greater than the then chairman of the Council of Ministers, Nikolai Bulganin, but it was Bulganin who headed the delegation and acted as the Soviet leader in protocol settings. Stalin and Khrushchev both eventually took on the job of chairman of the Council of Ministers in addition to their party job.

In 1964, when Khrushchev was overthrown, it was obvious from the beginning that Brezhnev as general secretary was number one and that Aleksei Kosygin as chairman of the Council of Ministers was number two. Still Brezhnev felt uneasy about his status in the international arena, outside of Eastern Europe. It was Kosygin who traveled abroad in the late 1960s (for example, to meet President Johnson in Glassboro, New Jersey), and all of the early negotiations about a summit with President Nixon were based on the assumption that the president would be meeting Kosygin. As has been seen, Gorbachev thought as late as 1967 that Brezhnev was a transitional figure.

Only as the Twenty-fourth Party Congress approached and passed in 1971 did Brezhnev seem to feel that he could really act like the leader. He met with National Security Adviser Henry Kissinger and President Nixon alone in June 1972, and then in 1975 attended the Helsinki meeting of European heads of government as the Soviet representative. Nevertheless, in 1977 Brezhnev still had himself elected chairman of the Presidium of the Supreme Soviet, the formal head of state.

Now all of this has changed. Andropov and Chernenko met with leading foreign dignitaries at the time of their predecessor's funeral. The chairman of the Council of Ministers only met the second-ranking visitors. The same pattern was maintained by Gorbachev at Chernenko's funeral. Gorbachev did not hesitate to go to Paris to meet President François Mitterrand barely six months after his election, and then to meet President Reagan at Geneva.

The thought never even entered anyone's head that the chairman of the Council of Ministers should accompany Gorbachev to Geneva. And if anyone had suggested that the chairman should be the head of the delegation to Geneva for protocol reasons and that

Gorbachev should come along in a subordinate role, as Khrushchev had with Bulganin thirty years before, the proposal would have been seen as bizarre. Gorbachev did not even bother to take the post of chairman of the Presidium of the Supreme Soviet for himself for over three years.

The change in the status of the general secretary is a very important development, and Gorbachev may have agreed to meet President Reagan—and to insist on Geneva as the site of the summit—precisely to remind the Soviet elite of how much had changed since 1955. When Stalin and Khrushchev were selected head of the Secretariat, they were not necessarily being judged as national leaders, and they had to win authority in a basic sense. When Gorbachev was selected, the Central Committee and the Politburo knew that he was *the* leader, and unlikely to be a short-term one. This conferred an immediate authority upon him.

Still the authority of the general secretary does not extend to the ability to dismiss a cabinet officer (Politburo member) out of hand, for that power is in the hands of the Central Committee. The general secretary's ability to force through substantial policy change rests on the support of the Central Committee. In part, this is acquired through persuasion, and in part through the creation of a political machine in the Central Committee that will do his will.

As Gorbachev sought such power, he was quite fortunate in a number of respects. As we have seen, the mortality rate among members of the 1980 Politburo was high, and there were relatively few of the top officials of the Brezhnev era with whom Gorbachev had to deal. Moreover, Chernenko was a much easier man to follow than Andropov. Andropov accomplished little in his year in office, but he created the feeling that he would do something. Since he had made no compromises, his legend was larger than life, and no actual successor could match it. Chernenko, by contrast, cut such a pathetic figure that any successor would have seemed charismatic. The elite was worried about the political consequences of continuing stagnation, and there was a hunger for leadership after a decade of ill leadership.

Gorbachev was also fortunate that a party congress was scheduled within a year of his election. He had been elected by the

Central Committee of 1981, which was composed of the high officials from the end of the Brezhnev era. The retirement of a minister or a regional party boss (or even a Politburo member such as Romanov) does not mean his removal from the Central Committee until the next party congress, and hence any substantial personnel change leaves many lame ducks on the Central Committee. When Andropov was elected in November 1982, this factor may have restrained him, for he would have to deal with the 1981 Central Committee until the party congress scheduled for early 1986. Gorbachev only had to wait a year for the opportunity to reshape the body to which he was responsible.

Consolidating Power

We would have understood Gorbachev better if we had made one central assumption: namely, that he would not have advanced so rapidly unless he was very skilled politically and that he surely would not have raised expectations so unnecessarily high if he did not have a fairly clear conception of what he should and could do. With such assumptions, we would not have simply taken for granted that he would fail, but would have asked, "What is the logical sequence of steps for a skilled politician to take to overcome his opposition and achieve his goals?" If we had tried to answer that question, we would not have been surprised by the course of events.

Obviously Gorbachev's first task was to consolidate his political power, but this is not a task that should be understood in some simple manner. There is not some concrete "power" that can be consolidated. "Power" is incredibly ambiguous and varies with the issue. Khrushchev acquired the ability to force through many highly unpopular decisions, but he offended so many key figures that they united to remove him. Brezhnev managed to remain in office long after he was unfit to exercise it, to some extent because he offended no major institutional interest.

We cannot, therefore, say that Gorbachev had or had not consolidated power by a certain time. The question is—consolidated enough power to do what? If the general secretary wanted no more than a moderate or cautious economic reform, he surely already had enough power to push it through as soon as he was elected. If, by contrast, he wanted to conduct a blood purge, he probably would never have a hope of gathering enough strength to accomplish that. And if Gorbachev wanted very radical economic reform, he needed more than a majority vote on the Politburo or the Central Committee. He needed public support as well.

Gorbachev's political strategy in his first year in office was dictated by the timing of the Twenty-seventh Party Congress. The Central Committee with which he would have to deal for the next five years would be elected at the congress, and he had to get as many of his own people in place before then so that they could be put on the Central Committee. Yet, the greater the number of the 1981 Central Committee members he retired before the congress (and 38 percent of the voting members actually were retired or seriously demoted by February 1986), the more possibly disgruntled lame ducks he faced on the Central Committee that could throw him out of office in 1985.

In this situation, it made no sense for Gorbachev to launch radical policies in 1985 that might alarm the old-timers among his electorate, for his own men would be on the Central Committee in less than a year. This was particularly true in international relations, where Andrei Gromyko was the only man with foreign policy experience on the Politburo. In fact, Gorbachev even avoided substantial personnel changes at the middle levels of the foreign policy establishment as long as Gromyko could appeal to the old Central Committee.

Hence Gorbachev properly concentrated his early attention on personnel change in posts traditionally represented on the Central Committee.[10] He succeeded in an unprecedented way. In the governmental cabinet (the Council of Ministers), 38 of the 100 members were removed, and another 8 were shifted by the Twenty-seventh Party Congress. The lowest turnover (31 percent) occurred among the regional first secretaries, but Gorbachev had already consolidated very considerable support at that level before 1985.

As a result of these changes, the Central Committee elected in

March 1986 at the end of the Twenty-seventh Party Congress underwent substantial rejuvenation. At the last two congresses, over 90 percent of the living members of the Central Committee had been reelected; in 1986, only 62 percent were. Gorbachev had had majority support in the old Central Committee, and the proportion reelected was about the level of support one would have expected. At the end of the congress, 307 voting members were named, and that meant 125 new members, most of whom surely were Gorbachev supporters.

In the past, Soviet leaders could seldom change the Politburo membership significantly in their first years in office. Between March 1953 and May 1957, Nikita Khrushchev removed only one Politburo voting member (the secret police chief, Lavrentii Beriia, after a collective decision) and added only two new ones. Between October 1964 and January 1971, Leonid Brezhnev retired two Politburo voting members (who were already aging and in ceremonial posts) and replaced them with three new men—and all of the latter were subsequently removed, two of them clearly because they opposed Brezhnev on key issues. Andropov was able to name three new members in his year in office, but one of these decisions may have been made before Brezhnev's death, and no Politburo member was removed. No changes at all occurred during Chernenko's year in office.

Between March 1985 and March 1986, by contrast, three of the ten voting members of the Politburo were removed, all of them important: Nikolai Tikhonov, the chairman of the Council of Ministers, and the two credible rivals to Gorbachev as general secretary—the Central Committee secretary, Grigorii Romanov, and the Moscow party leader, Viktor Grishin. In addition, the fourth powerful member of the Politburo, foreign minister Andrei Gromyko, was moved to the ceremonial post of chairman of the Presidium of the Supreme Soviet.

At the same time, five new voting members were elected to the Politburo by March 1986, and, with one exception, they constituted the new inner core of the Politburo. (In June 1987 another three voting members—Viktor Nikonov, Nikolai Sliunkov, and Aleksandr Yakovlev—were added.) Change just as drastic or more drastic occurred at levels just below the very top. The Politburo has candidate (nonvoting) members as well as voting ones, and five of the seven candidates in March 1986 had been elected during Gorbachev's year in office. Besides Gorbachev and Ligachev, the Central Committee Secretariat included nine secretaries. Seven of them were elected while Gorbachev was general secretary. The turnover at middle levels was also extremely high.

A second part of Gorbachev's political strategy was to select personnel who had little experience in Moscow during the Brezhnev era and who had little identification with old policies. In the Catholic Church the Curia in Rome has long tended to be more conservative, while the bishops outside the country have tended to be closer to local needs and problems. For similar reasons the central Moscow apparatus—or at least the higher reaches of it—has tended to be more hidebound than the republican and regional party secretaries scattered throughout the country.

At the beginning of 1982 the central "Curia" of the Communist party was extremely ossified. If Gorbachev is excluded, the top eighteen persons in Moscow—the Central Committee secretaries and the Politburo members in Moscow—averaged seventy-two years of age. They had worked for an average of thirteen years in the same job and twenty-seven years in top posts in Moscow. Small wonder that they wanted little change.

The personnel policy of Andropov and then of Gorbachev was to disperse this central group and to bring in the "bishops." The Central Committee secretary for the defense and machinery industries (first, Grigorii Romanov and then Lev Zaikov) were brought in from Leningrad; Gorbachev's second secretary, Yegor Ligachev, had been first secretary in remote Tomsk for seventeen years in 1982; the new foreign minister, Eduard Shevardnadze, was first secretary of Georgia and had never worked for a day either in Moscow or in foreign affairs; Anatolii F. Dobrynin, the head of the international department of the Central Committee—the man responsible for the world revolution—was an urbane diplomat, who had just spent twenty-five years in Washington, D.C.; Aleksandr Yakovlev, the Central Committee secretary for domestic ideology, had been ambassador in Canada; Murakhovsky, the top agricultural official, came from Stavropol (and had been the first man to give Gorbachev a job in 1955); and Georgii Razumovsky, the Central Committee secretary for personnel, from neighboring Krasnodar.

When Gorbachev selected the inner core of his Politburo—Ligachev, Ryzhkov, Shevardnadze, Sliunkov, Yakovlev, Zaikov—he not only chose most of them from these "bishops" (even Ryzhkov had come to Moscow in 1975 from the directorship of a large plant in Sverdlovsk), but (with the exception of his friend, Shevardnadze) selected men with extremely low status at the time of Brezhnev's death. Ligachev's province of Tomsk was extremely small and unimportant; Ryzhkov was one of four first deputy chairmen of Gosplan; Zaikov was chairman of the Leningrad city soviet (the seventh or eighth ranking job in the city); Sliunkov only a deputy chairman of Gosplan and Yakovlev, as has been seen, ambassador to a relatively minor country.

There are always many explanations for developments in the Kremlin, but by far the most likely is that Gorbachev was following a deliberate strategy of selecting top lieutenants who had far less seniority than himself in 1982 and who would owe their promotion to him. When Andropov promoted Ligachev and Ryzhkov from obscurity, their first jobs were as heads of Central Committee departments, and they served directly under Gorbachev's supervision. When Zaikov had been promoted from his lowly soviet job to the important post of the Leningrad regional party leader in 1983, Gorbachev went to Leningrad to install him. And, of course, promotion into the Politburo—and into the inner core of the Politburo—for Ligachev, Ryzhkov, and Zaikov came after Chernenko's death, while Gorbachev was general secretary. In 1985 Ligachev was a sixty-five-year-old second secretary to a fifty-four-year-old general secretary, and younger regional officials were scarcely likely to think that their future careers were better served by loyalty to the older man. With each year, Ligachev looked less attractive as a leader.

A third part of Gorbachev's strategy was to move men who were even closer to him personally into key power positions. Many of his early appointments had risen under Andropov and had close connections with Kirilenko in the past, but the newer men had career ties with Gorbachev directly. Some of these were simply people with whom he developed miscellaneous connections over the years, but they primarily came from three main groups: (1) those who had worked in Stavropol and the regions contiguous to it in the Caucasus and the Transcaucasus, (2) those who like Gorbachev worked in high posts in the Young Communist League (Komsomol) in the second half of the 1950s and the early 1960s, and (3) those who, like Gorbachev, graduated from Moscow University in the 1950s.

At the same time Gorbachev continued the consolidation of his control over the party. From March 1986 to the end of 1989, 50 percent of Politburo members, 67 percent of the regional first secretaries, and 78 percent of the republican first secretaries were replaced. Some of these men were promoted, but many others were retired. By January 1990, 85 percent of the republican and regional first secretaries had been selected while Gorbachev was general secretary.

Gorbachev, however, had no intention of simply relying on the loyalty of the political machine he was building. Nikita Khrushchev had made that mistake before he was overthrown in October 1964, and Gorbachev was determined not to repeat it.

Gorbachev's first problem, paradoxically, came from the very rapidity with which he was building his machine. As has been seen, a member of the 1986 Central Committee who was retired or demoted would normally remain on the Central Committee until the next party congress, which was expected in March 1991. The rapid turnover of officials was increasing the number of lame ducks on the Central Committee very quickly: 12 percent in December 1987, 19 percent in June 1988, and 28 percent in April 1989. If no change had been made in the composition of the Central Committee, the personnel changes of the summer would have brought the figure to 43 percent by January 1990 and surely would have moved towards 50 percent or above by late 1990.

The rise in the number of lame ducks on the Central Committee created a potentially very dangerous situation, and Gorbachev solved it. In April 1989, he induced 74 voting members of the

Central Committee, one quarter of the total, to resign "voluntarily," and he promoted 24 candidate members to voting status to
replace them. As a result, the proportion of lame ducks was reduced to 4 percent of the membership. With the great personnel
turnover of the summer and early fall, the figure had risen to 19
percent by late September and was certain to increase further.
This time Gorbachev moved the party congress from 1991 to October 1990, and planned to institute a new party rule by which
up to 20 percent of Central Committee members could be replaced
by party conferences held midway between party congresses.

In addition, Gorbachev took additional steps to emancipate
himself further from the Central Committee and to solidify his political control by competitive elections. The pro forma Supreme
Soviet was replaced as the national legislature by a directly elected
Congress of People's Deputies, with 2,250 members, and by a 542-
deputy Supreme Soviet elected indirectly by the Congress. Gorbachev called for competitive elections to the Congress of People's
Deputies, and asserted that the Supreme Soviet should become a
working legislature that was in session for six to eight months a
year. Gorbachev, who had been chairman of the Presidium of the
Supreme Soviet, became chairman of the Supreme Soviet under
the new constitution.

The consequences, at least in the short run, were very favorable
for Gorbachev. A number of Politburo conservatives were humiliated in the elections, but the Congress and Supreme Soviet
which emerged seemed marginally more radical than Gorbachev
on the whole, but still under his tight control. The change from
a chairman of the Presidium of the Supreme Soviet to a chairman
of the Supreme Soviet seemed trivial on the surface, but, in reality,
was quite important: formerly the chairman could be removed
behind closed doors, but now he could only be removed by the
Congress of People's Deputies in open session.

The conservatives find themselves in a very difficult position. With
local elections coming soon, officials have to be very careful about
their public position. As the Kirgizian first secretary noted in July
1989, "Communists and leaders of party committees are afraid to
be conservatives."[11] Moreover, if conservatives in the Central Committee remove Gorbachev as general secretary, they still cannot

remove him as chairman of the Supreme Soviet unless the Congress of People's Deputies is convened and agrees. With Gorbachev and Boris Yeltsin standing together and denouncing "anti-democratic" forces in the Central Committee, millions of Soviet citizens would be in the streets of the major cities.

The Soviet Constitution now formally specifies that the chairman of the Supreme Soviet is also chairman of the Defense Council. In a conflict between Gorbachev and the Central Committee, the military would have to decide whom to support. If they stayed with the chairman of the Defense Council and the constitutional forms, the conservatives would lose. If they decided to follow party discipline, they would have to assume the task of controlling the masses in the streets. It is extremely unlikely that they would dare the latter course, especially after the Romanian experience.

But with the Congress of People's Deputies and Supreme Soviet being slightly more radical than Gorbachev, he can use them as he wishes to overcome conservative opposition in the government and the Central Committee. The chairman of the Council of Ministers, Nikolai Ryzhkov, had a difficult time in the Congress and the Supreme Soviet in June and July of 1989, with sharp questions about his own candidacy and a rejection of a number of his nominees to the cabinet. He later described the experience in chastened terms:

> Hearing all that was said about me, I caught myself thinking that in some cases I was insufficiently self-critical. . . . In this month and a half that I had to stand face to face with the people's deputies, I fully realized that this is a process of rectification. From all this I will draw fundamental conclusions about the essential improvement of the government's work and of my own work. It is difficult, of course, but in many respects I have to re-examine my views and approaches to what was done and what needs to be done. I agree that so long as we do not solve the basic economic problems, this will be reflected in the general political situation in the country. And I think that the new government which will be formed has to draw very, very serious conclusions.[12]

That was the major point of the whole "democratization" exercise.

Gaining Social Support

Ultimately, of course, any substantial reform in the Soviet Union does not depend primarily on a general secretary's consolidation of power within the Politburo and the Central Committee. He must persuade officials to work with a sense of enthusiasm and professionalism; he must persuade students and young intellectuals not to go into the streets in a large-scale and threatening way; he must persuade workers not to riot in the face of higher prices, greater discipline, and demands for other sacrifices. And now he must prevent a majority from voting for candidates to the soviets who will either sweep him away or will force the suppression of the election results as was done in Panama. He must accomplish this both with Russians and non-Russians, whose interests and demands can be quite contradictory.

One's judgment about Gorbachev's "power" and his chance of success in consolidating it, implicitly or explicitly, rests on one's judgment about his short-term and long-term skills in handling the conflicting political and social forces with which he must deal. This judgment in turn rests on one's opinion both of his own political ability and the tractability of the task he faces.

Although everyone thinks that Gorbachev is a skillful politician, scholars disagree passionately about the balance of social and political forces that Gorbachev faces and the degree of skill he needs. Some see a virtually united phalanx of opposition forces other than the intelligentsia: the bureaucrats, the party apparatus, the military, the workers, the Russians (who fear decentralization), and the non-Russians (who fear continuing central control). If this is true, then Gorbachev has a monumental and probably insuperable problem.

The picture presented in this book, however, has been very different. The very list of presumed opponents of reform is too long, for that which annoys some of them must—by that very fact—pleases others. Indeed, this book has suggested that we should not see the Soviet Union divided between supporters and opponents of reform. Instead, virtually everyone in the

Soviet Union has an excellent reason to favor reform and an excellent reason to fear it. The total level of support for an opening to the West and economic reform is very strong, even if sometimes ambivalent.

In essence, the Gorbachev revolution is a middle-class revolt— a revolt supported most strongly by the bureaucrats, the professionals, and the intelligentsia. The Western talk about bureaucratic opposition is grossly overdone. Bureaucrats over sixty may be very doubtful, but they are moving toward retirement. Younger bureaucrats have to weigh the interests of their institutions against their own personal career interests. On balance, they must strongly approve Gorbachev's social policy and the relaxation of controls on information and culture. Over time, the bureaucrats are Gorbachev's strongest supporters, for they will be most contented with political liberalization within a strong one-party system, with economic reform that remains within a socialist framework. And that is Gorbachev's program.

The workers are the strongest opponents of reform in the short run, for they must bear the brunt of the change in social policy. But they have chafed at the dull television and the restrictions on mass culture. (They, more than intellectuals, have yearned for rock and roll.) In addition, young workers are becoming much more educated and "middle class" in their values. By the 1980s, the number of students receiving a high school diploma was approximately 80 percent of those who entered first grade in the early 1970s.[13] The most ambitious workers—and, therefore, the most politically dangerous of them—will favor the chance to earn money after work and to form their own small businesses and shops in the form of cooperatives. In various ways (even the display of Stalin's portrait) they have shown that they yearn for strong leadership, and Gorbachev's decisiveness and his bureaucracy bashing, coupled with his appeals to Russian nationalism, are appealing to them. In the medium run, the workers are likely to be quite supportive of reform, particularly the workers who matter politically.

Paradoxically, the opposition that is the most dangerous for Gorbachev in the medium and long run is the group that does not yet see itself in opposition—the intellectuals. Industrialization has been very corrosive of right-wing authoritarian regimes, and Communist countries in Eastern Europe have not been immune from revolt. Although people talk about conservative opposition, that opposition is essentially broken, and Gorbachev's real political problem is to keep the surging pressure for reform under control. Already the intelligentsia have shown a repeated tendency to deny that real change is occurring. When the leadership introduced radical economic reform in the fall of 1989, Moscow intellectuals dismissed it because it was not full marketization. While they follow a Russian tradition of saying that the tsar's advisers or the bureaucracy are at fault, eventually Gorbachev will become the target as they come to understand the power of his position. He will never be able to do enough to satisfy them, and grumbling will grow.

The factor that is likely to provide the cement for the Soviet system for some years, even among the intelligentsia, is the multinational character of the country. Most Americans would find this statement very surprising. They have seen the Baltic republics demanding independence, the Armenians and the Azerbaidzhani engaged in a bloody conflict over control of the small Nagorno-Karabakh province, and nationality-based movements and incidents occuring everywhere. As a result, many have been led to believe that the Soviet Union is in danger of flying apart and that national conflict may bring Gorbachev down.

We need to ask ourselves one simple question: since Gorbachev has been so extremely cautious and skillful in his consolidation of power, how can he have been so foolish as to have deliberately unleashed uncontrollable nationalist feelings when he has full access to the reports of the KGB and other secret information?

The answer to this question is almost surely just as simple: Gorbachev would not have acted as he did unless he were convinced that the situation was completely under control. He deliberately loosened controls in what seems like a reckless way, but he is the one with all the secret information, not those who call him reckless.

Gorbachev has understood several crucial facts that we have been slow to appreciate. First, with 60 percent of the Russians having a high school diploma or better, his real problem is to keep

Russian students from demonstrating for multi-party democracy, as has happened in other dictatorships with burgeoning middle classes. Troops may well not fire on large Russian demonstrations.

Second, the non-Russians are very divided among themselves. Some of the most radical peoples (e.g., those in the Baltic republics) are very small, while several of the largest peoples (notably the Ukrainians and the Belorussians) contain substantial Russified elements. (Moreover, the land taken from Poland in the Stalin-Hitler Pact of 1939 was included in the Ukraine, Belorussia and Lithuania. The apparent movement of Poland toward independence draws the Ukrainians, the Belorussians and the Lithuanians toward the Russians as protection against some future Polish demands for a rectification of their borders.

By all indications, the vast majority of the Russians are not ready for a dissolution of the Soviet Union. Many were taken in by the Soviet propaganda about the national issue having been resolved. White southerners in the United States in the 1940s and 1950s knew that there was some problem with their black population, but most of the rest of the country thought the majority of blacks were basically contented. Many Russians had a similar attitude. The recent demonstrations have now made the situation very clear to them, and, as a consequence, they are very receptive to the argument that Yegor Ligachev is putting bluntly into words: "A multiparty system would mean the disintegration of the Soviet federation and . . . the Communist Party is the only real political force which unites and consolidates all the peoples of the country."[14] Gorbachev has been deliberately letting some of the less dangerous non-Russians express extreme positions in order to convince Russians to support the Communist Party as the country's only hope.

Yet, economic reform inevitably means a major reduction in the power of the Moscow ministries over the republics. Private trade and services inevitably will respond to local ethnic tastes and desires. Looser censorship means a greater freedom for local culture and the writing of local history. No doubt, there will have to be arrests, and the Soviet equivalent of the National Guard will sometimes have to be called out. Nevertheless, Gorbachev is betting that the non-Russians will not give up the three-quarters of a loaf offered in a futile quest for a whole loaf. It is a good bet, at least for the next ten to fifteen years, and Gorbachev will let his successors worry about a later period.

My strong sense is that the configuration of attitudes and interests in the Soviet Union is quite susceptible to intelligent political manipulation and to the building of supportive social coalitions over the next ten to fifteen years. The internal logic of economic reform—beginning with the services, agriculture, small-scale industry, and an export strategy and leaving fundamental heavy industrial reform for later—corresponds well to the political logic of reform. Gorbachev seems to have an excellent sense of how to balance the various political demands and how to undercut the opposition to reform.

Nevertheless, politics always is somewhat of a shell game in which the attention of different groups is directed to the pluses of policies for themselves and distracted from the minuses. Politics is a process in which people are persuaded to sacrifice private interests (and their money) for national defense and the common good in general. Gorbachev's balancing act is a particularly ticklish one, both because of the inherently unstable nature of dictatorship in industrial society and because of the difficulty of reform.

Certainly everyone who has met Gorbachev is impressed by him as a natural politician who instinctively seems to know how to say the right things and make the right gesture. The speed of his rise both before and after Brezhnev's death is further testimony to his skill, and an aficionado of Soviet esoteric communications and symbolism like myself is very impressed by the way he plays this part of the Soviet political game. My sense in 1985 was that Gorbachev is "a truly world-class chess player who delights in complex combinations and knows how to make them,"[15] and still the judgment seems accurate. Conceivably he is overreaching himself in the way he is changing personnel and introducing reform, but it is hard to believe that a man of his demonstrated skill in other respects is making elementary political mistakes in these areas.

It is, however, crucial that Gorbachev retain this sense. If he begins to give the impression that he is all words and that he does not know what to do, his authority will quickly decline. The radical nature of his promises creates a very high standard by which he will be judged. He will need to maintain a sense of momentum in order to retain public support, but the more he succeeds in doing this, the less the Politburo and the Central Committee will dare to stand up to them. If his health holds, the real question will come in the mid-1990s. Will he be another Deng Xiaoping who retains his dynamism into his eighties? Or, like many previous Russian tsars, will his drive begin to fade in his sixties? If so, the opposition from the liberals will grow rapidly.

8

Gorbachev's Domestic Policy

THE United States has a tradition of a vigorous presidential action in the first hundred days: a dramatic announcement of new policies and as much new action as possible in the "honeymoon" period. The Soviet Union, by contrast, has a tradition of maintaining the fiction of collective leadership. A new leader pretends that he is carrying out the policies of his predecessor or at least the last party congress, and only with subtle hints and subtle changes in ideological language does he begin to change policy. This creates enormous problems for the analyst, for, although Soviet springs have their harbingers, not all harbingers have their spring.

In the case of Mikhail Gorbachev, the general secretary actually began changing his language sooner and more substantially than usual. He repeatedly pledged new approaches, new ideas, a fundamental restructuring of the economy and society, greater openness (*glasnost*), and democratization (*demokratizatsiia*). Yet, with a few exceptions, the actual change of policy that occurred in Gorbachev's first year in office was fairly modest.

Hence we were left with the question whether Gorbachev's promises and his innovative ideological language represented his real policy or the relatively marginal first steps. Even after Gorbachev gradually began convincing even the doubters of his intention to reform the Soviet system, the question arose: did he have the will and ability to overcome opposition?

But even this question did not face up to the possible scale of the changes being undertaken. Clearly Gorbachev did not plan to introduce capitalism or Western constitutional democracy into the Soviet Union, and even those who believed that his reforms were major or even radical still saw them as taking place "within the system," and they subconsciously discounted them. Others were quite conscious in doing so.[1]

The word "system" is, however, a trap, for it includes everything from formal institutions to the subtle ways in which these institutions operate—or even to the concrete policies followed. The degree to which a "system" changes depends on how we define "system" in our own mind. If the essence of the system is the existence of a single party that is not challenged in meaningful elections, then system change of that type is not on Gorbachev's agenda unless he is fooling us all. But if the essence of the system—or at least a fundamental feature of it—has been two Iron Curtains—one against Western ideas and one against Western market forces, then we are, in my opinion, talking about the possibility of a most fundamental change in the system as it has been visualized by Americans.

Of course, Gorbachev would say that the features of the system that Americans have seen as "essential" are really the unfortunate, temporary by-products of a decision to introduce a socialist revolution in a peasant country that was culturally not ready for it and that had an enormous problem of national defense. He has a vision of socialism that he read about in school in the works of Marx and Lenin. It was a socialism whose planning creates the possibility of more technological sophistication than the West, but no unemployment. It was a political system in which the oppression of state action "withers away," in which cooperative enterprises are guided by strategic planning rather than administrative decree from monopolistic ministries and in which people are directly involved in government rather than indirectly through representatives in "parliamentarism." Americans, myself included, believe that such a vision is wildly utopian and that Gorbachev will be a disappointed, if wiser, man a decade from now. Yet, even this pessimistic prediction leaves us with a better sense of the scope of Gorbachev's domestic policy than the misleading truism that he doesn't want to abandon "the system."

If the fear of markets, the fear of Western culture, the fear of travel to the West, the fear of open discussion, were to a large extent—as suggested in this book—the product of an extremist, anti-Western, Khomeini-like revolution, then we are talking about the end of the Khomeini period in Russian history. Gorbachev is not merely returning to NEP of the 1920s, he is implicitly repudiating Lenin and returning to Marx. It took twelve years for Russia to get from 1917 to the completion of the construction of two solid Iron Curtains by 1929. It will take a similar period to move to a "normal," one-party, "authoritarian" dictatorship that we have often seen in the modern world. But if this happens, the high-school student of the late 1990s will find it very difficult even to visualize what the Russia that we have taken for granted was like.

Movement Toward Economic Reform

From his first days in office, the new general secretary was absolutely clear about the central thrust of his program. Again and again, he called for "an acceleration of social and economic development," with an emphasis on a sharp improvement in Soviet technological capability. He set the goal of bringing Soviet technology to world levels and of achieving superiority in computers and radio technology. Already by June 1985, Gorbachev was saying that the realization of this goal depended on a "deep reorganization of the system of planning and administration of the whole economic mechanism." It is necessary, he said in this speech, "to overcome dictation to the consumer by the producer, to end the shortages of capital goods and consumers' items, to make the economy dynamic, balanced, and receptive to scientific-technical progress in a maximum way, and to give all the links of the economy a vital interest in this."[2]

Everyone in the West assumed that drastic measures indeed would be required to reach such goals—and that maybe even these would not suffice. Gorbachev cautioned that the necessary steps would have to be introduced gradually and that they would have to be well thought out, but he gave every indication that he agreed with the Western assessment. He derided "the fear to make a mistake, to take decisive measures." He told the editors of *Time* magazine that "we think that we must manifest boldness and decisiveness." At the Twenty-seventh Party Congress, he spoke with contempt about "the peculiar psychology in which it was assumed that things could be improved without changing anything."[3]

But how did Gorbachev plan to improve the economy? As Seweryn Bialer, a political scientist at Columbia University, emphasized, Gorbachev had a multipronged strategy in mind.[4] He intended to use exhortation; on the old issue between Kirilenko and Chernenko over investment priorities, he was firmly on the side of growth; he used new administrative measures such as a new state inspection agency with the authority to reject low-quality items produced by the factory.

Two of Gorbachev's most frequently used words in his early days were "discipline" and "order," but they did not imply any return to Stalinism. Instead, they were really code words for a broader change in social policy. Gorbachev, of course, continued to speak of social justice, and surely to believe in it, but he moved away from the egalitarian, guaranteed job security, "coddle-the-worker" definition of Chernenko. Gorbachev specifically criticized "the underevaluation of the problem of the material base" of the social sphere, and he said that the principle "from each according to his ability, to each according to his labor" was "the essence" of social justice. He even defined fair prices not in terms of their labor input, but in terms of the consumer demand and the societal need for the goods being priced. He attacked excessive egalitarianism in wage distribution. Gorbachev was the first Soviet leader to discuss the terrible economic consequences of selling meat for two to three times less than its cost, but he did not then propose an increase in meat prices.

Gorbachev's personnel policy seemed a concerted part of economic policy. Obviously Gorbachev's primary concern in removing aging members of the Central Committee was to consolidate his political power, but this inevitably had the side effect of replacing tiring administrators with younger officials who should be more energetic. Gorbachev clearly hoped that this would contribute to growth, and he continued to humiliate ministers who had performed poorly (e.g., the minister of the automobile industry) in order to indicate to his new appointees that they could not afford to relax.

In changing ministers—and especially industrial ministers—Gorbachev continued the practice of "jumping" the generation born in the late 1910s and early 1920s that had had its college education disrupted by World War II. The age pattern of the industrial ministers at the beginning of 1976, 1982, and 1987, and in July 1989 is very revealing (see table 7).

In addition, Gorbachev began selecting industrial ministers with a different background than Brezhnev's appointees. Of the twenty-five new industrial ministers appointed from 1976 through May 1985, the vast majority had long years of work high in the ministry. Even excluding several who had headed another ministry, the new ministers averaged eight years of experience as deputy minister within their ministry. Several of the new industrial ministers appointed after May 1985 once headed other ministries (often reversing the supplier-customer relationship), but the twenty-two who became ministers between May 1985 and December 1987 averaged only three years as deputy minister within their ministry (two years if one excludes one older minister, since replaced). Thirteen of the twenty-two were never a ministerial official at all.

The same policy was followed with even greater consistency in the selection of the nonindustrial ministers and chairmen of state committees appointed in the two and a half years after May 1985. Ninety percent never worked in the ministry at all. The new minister of defense, a transitional figure in his seventies, had been a longtime employee of his ministry, and after the landing of a

TABLE 7 YEARS OF BIRTH OF INDUSTRIAL MINISTERS

Year of Birth	Number of Industrial Ministers			
	1976	1982	1987	1989
1898–1912	24	13	0	0
1913–1919	8	10	4	0
1920–1926	3	5	4	1
1927–1933	1	9	16	7
1934 & After	0	0	11	11

SOURCE: The ministers are listed in the yearbook of the *Great Soviet Encyclopedia*. The biographies of new ministers are found in *Izvestiia* immediately after their appointment and those of old ministers in the sources listed in note 2 of chapter 10.

small plane on Red Square, he was replaced by an officer who had been deputy minister for several months. Clearly Gorbachev was seeking new ministers who had not become identified with old policies and who hopefully would be responsive to a new approach.

For Americans, however, the real question was whether Gorbachev was going to follow the Hungarian and the Chinese paths, and introduce more market mechanisms and open the economy to foreign investment.

At first, Gorbachev talked cautiously. He spoke of "discipline" and did not use the word "reform" (*reforma*)—the codeword for more radical change. His first agricultural speech was very traditional, and his first major law in the services realm condemned "unearned income." As a result, many Westerners concluded that Gorbachev himself was rather conservative, and they later asserted that he had understood the need for economic reform only after the passage of some time.

In reality, this judgment underestimates Gorbachev. He had several severe problems. First, until a new Central Committee was elected at the 27th Party Congress in March 1986, it was not prudent for him to show his hand too clearly. Second, since Gorbachev was revising ideology in the most fundamental way, he had every reason to proceed step by step rather than all at once, but for the same reason he had to keep his language—his modifications of ideology—ahead of his action. Third, economic reform itself required sophisticated timing. The nature of the planning and budgetary process required that major changes be enacted at least a year before they were to be implemented, and any major reform really required a year or two of trial before being introduced in a large-scale manner. Hence the exigencies of reform themselves demanded that time be "wasted."

Gorbachev's first answer to these problems was to radicalize his language progressively. In March 1986 he spoke of "radical reform"; in September 1986 of "revolutionary transformation"; in his book, *Perestroika*, of a revolution on the scale of English revolution of 1688. In March 1986, he called for "the creative use of Lenin's ideas on the food tax" in agriculture—a subtle reference to the private agriculture of the 1920s; in June 1987 he emphasized the need for a "family contract"; in November 1987 he rehabilitated Nikolai Bukharin and spoke of the heavy costs of collectivization (while suggesting that they had been required by the times); in March 1989 he simply denounced the collectivization decision and said only that Stalin's "circle" had *claimed* that collectivization was required by the times.

Similarly, Gorbachev moved in incremental steps in actually introducing reform. He essentially began reform in the services and trade. Already at the Twenty-seventh Party Congress he had begun to speak about a Hungarian-type reform in the services. He promised outright that "the state will facilitate the development of different forms of satisfying [consumers'] demand and of providing services. It is necessary to give attentive consideration to the proposals to regularize the labor activities of individuals." He insisted that "such kinds of work should be based either on cooperative principles or on contract with socialist enterprises,"[5] but, of course, an independent franchise (such as found in McDonald's hamburgers) or an independent service station with three or four mechanics working cooperatively would easily fit this definition. Gorbachev also asserted that cooperative enterprises should be widely used in production and housing construction. He praised the small enterprise in general as one that "can more quickly and flexibly take technological innovations and changes in demand into account."

Gorbachev did not use the words "market" or "market relations" in any of his early speeches, but at the party congress he came extremely close. "It is time," he said, "to overcome the suspicion of money relations and their underestimation in the planned leadership of the economy." He demanded that prices be linked not only with production costs, but also "with consumption characteristics and with the degree of balance between the output of the product and the consumer demand and social need for it."[6]

In November 1986 the Supreme Soviet passed a law permitting people employed in the state sector to earn money privately in their spare time in a number of occupations, notably in the services. Housewives, students, and pensioners (men over sixty and women over fifty-five) could engage in such activities full-time. By the summer of 1987, many in the second economy showed a reluctance to legalize themselves because of an unwillingness to pay taxes, but it was easy to predict that the law on unearned income would eventually be applied to curtail tax-dodging.

At the same time, a new law permitted the formation of co-operatives to produce industrial goods from recycled material and scrap, and in February 1987 the Politburo endorsed a broader program of cooperatives. To the citizen, the most visible of the new private cooperatives were restaurants, but they were the forerunner of far more important ones in industry and construction. In November 1987 Gorbachev insisted that Lenin was, first of all, interested in "cooperative socialism."

The establishment of cooperatives was far more important than the law on moonlighting. Those engaged in individual labor cannot hire labor outside their own family, and even a gasoline station or restaurant needs a number of people. Someone who wants to work full-time in the private economy and requires a staff of people can create a cooperative and make the "hired labor" members of the cooperative. The word "corporation" and "cooperation" have a similar character, and in theory a Soviet cooperative could have much in common with a small American corporation, depending on how entry and withdrawal from the cooperative is handled and the ease with which one can be established.

Gorbachev kept denouncing capitalism and private property, but if examined closely, his language referred to individualistic, precorporate capitalism and to an unregulated capitalism of the type envisaged by the free-market theorist Milton Friedman. He never wavered in his basic support for cooperatives, and he defined as "cooperative" many forms of property that Americans would consider "private." For example, Americans consider General Motors to be "private," but such a company with publicly owned shares is actually collectively owned and would now be considered a cooperative in the Soviet Union. Indeed, in Moscow, private taxi owners who own their own cars belong to co-ops, but other than paying a monthly tax (eight rubles a month in one case) they have almost no contact with the co-op and engage in no profit-sharing. And despite the continual public complaints about cooperatives, their number soared. Between January 1989 and July 1989 alone, the number of operating cooperatives rose from 77,000 to 133,000, with the number of people employed in them rising from 1.4 million to 2.9 million and the gross output rising from 6 billion rubles to 12.8 rubles.[7]

The situation in agricultural reform was more peculiar than in the reform of the services. The framework for radical reform had actually been introduced during the Brezhnev years. A system of "contract brigades" was introduced within the collective farm system. Peasants were supposed to form brigades voluntarily and then to be assigned a specific segment of land (and presumably equipment) for an extended period. They would make a contract with the farm to deliver a certain amount of production, but would then be reasonably independent in farming their land. If the brigades were formed voluntarily, they normally would be based on a family or a small group of friends; if they worked independently, they would not be that different from the type of family farming within a collective farm framework that was found in Hungary and China.

In practice, the collective farm chairmen could not give the brigades independence, for the farms themselves were given very detailed plans and subjected to very strict control. (In 1984, the collective farm received six hundred plan indicators.)[8] In practice, although the statistical handbook reported a sharp increase in the number of family-size "links" inside the brigades from 1982 to 1984, the contract brigades themselves averaged twenty-four persons in the latter year, and clearly were not voluntary.[9]

Gorbachev had endorsed the small-scale link as early as 1976, and presumably was the major force behind the contract brigade.[10] At the Twenty-seventh Party Congress, he suddenly dropped a series of hints about radical reform. He spoke not only about a significant increase in the independence of the collective and state farms, but also about a reliance on "economic methods of management." He supported the wide use of a system of assigning "means of production, including land, to brigades, links, and families on a contract basis for a set period of time." Then in June 1987 Gorbachev said that it was necessary "decisively to stop" governmental interference in the work of the collective farms. He specifically endorsed the "family contract"—not just in a brief mention, but repeatedly with the citation of a number of examples.

The March 1989 plenum of the Central Committee pushed the reform even further. It was at this time that Gorbachev denounced the 1929 collectivization decision without reservation. He spoke for the first time about the possibility of people leaving the farm altogether, and he said that "sooner or later" it would be necessary to go fully to market prices in agriculture. But despite these decisions, progress was slow. Planned requisitions remained high, prices were not modified, and little changed. 1991 seemed the year toward which Gorbachev was aiming.

Industrial reform also went slowly. A number of experiments in heavy industry had been conducted in the Brezhnev period, and Andropov had introduced a major one in 1983. By all indications, the changes being introduced had minimal impact. Gorbachev himself complained in September 1986 that the officials of the ministry with the most far-reaching experiment are "parting with old habits with great difficulty . . . Conservatism is firmly entrenched in this ministry."[11]

While Gorbachev had repeatedly called for radical reform in industry during his first two years in office, he had been disappointing in his generality. It is easy to endorse decentralization of power from ministries to enterprises, but that is a meaningless cliché unless a series of parallel changes are introduced to make it possible. Gorbachev was not talking in this way. Then in his speech to the June 1987 plenum of the Central Committee, Gorbachev's language changed. He correctly pointed to the system of planning supplies as the heart of the problem, and he touched upon all the issues the reformers had been discussing: the replacement of administrative measures by economic ones, "fundamental change in the supply system—a movement from a centralized system to one based on wholesale trade in producers' goods," "a radical reform of price formation," "a radical financial-credit reform," a "cardinal" change in the functions such as Gosplan.[12]

The essence of the new system would not be allocation of supplies by a "budgetary process" within a bureaucracy, but the freedom to obtain supplies from a number of sources and an incentive system that rewarded managers for economizing on supplies and labor. Instead of producing goods in response to directives in the plan, a factory would have to seek out orders. A certain percentage would come from the state and would be obligatory, but the others would be obtained through a contract process.

The meaning of the reform would depend on the proportion of production that would be determined by state orders. As that percentage approached 100, then the old system would be preserved, but with "orders" being a different name for the old plan directives. If the only governmental orders are for the defense industry and the like, then the system could approach a Western one. Abel Aganbegyan, the chief scholarly strategist of the economic reform, told a Swedish newspaper that the percentage of state orders in an enterprise's plan would soon fall to 50–60 percent and then to 30 percent by 1990.[13] The director of the Institute of Economics, Leonid Abalkin, suggested in a post-plenum interview that the strategic planning of Japan would be the model for Gosplan in the Soviet Union.[14]

During 1987 two major laws were introduced in the industrial sphere. One was a general law on the industrial enterprise that promised (but did not deliver) real independence from the ministerial line of command. From the perspective of Russia's relationship with the West, the most important changes came in the end of the monopoly of the Ministry of Foreign Trade in the conduct of foreign trade, with some of the larger enterprises permitted to lead trade on their own and with all enterprises permitted to establish joint enterprises with foreigners (although at first with the approval of their ministries).

Soviet citizens had been told for years that capitalist managers were totally exploitative of their workers and that integration into the world economy led to dependence on foreigners. Now Gorbachev explicitly indicated that he understood the disastrous consequences of protectionism inherent in Soviet anarchy. He insisted that it was necessary "to strengthen the influence of the foreign market on the work of the branches and enterprises, on the quality of their production, and on scientific-technical progress." He emphasized that this was "particularly important."[15]

By the summer of 1987 a whole series of steps were being initiated to integrate the Soviet economy into the world economy and to bring Soviet industrialists under the sting of foreign competition. The most dramatic was the legalization in January 1987 of foreign investment inside the Soviet Union for the first time since the mid-1920s. Wholly owned foreign plants were not to be permitted, only those in which the Soviet Union had a 51 percent interest and the foreigner 49 percent. The joint ventures were not normally to be new plants in remote areas, but ventures with existing Soviet factories. A German firm, for example, took 25,000 square meters of floor space in the major Soviet Sergo Ordzhonikidze machine tool plant in Moscow, in order to produce computerized machine tools. A Japanese plant had a joint venture in timber processing in Siberia, and a Spanish plant was to produce pulp-and-paper products. Emphasis was supposed to be given to machinery, pulp-and-paper, and agricultural chemicals, but in practice many were in the services.[16]

Joint ventures were, however, only one technique by which Soviet firms were to be subjected to foreign competition. The Japanese accomplished this in part by an export strategy, and Soviet leaders put great emphasis on the need to export manufactured goods. Western firms frequently produce component parts throughout the world, and the Soviet Union began to emphasize joint production. A cement truck, for example, would be produced jointly by a Soviet and a German firm. The parts would be produced in both countries, and the assembled trucks sold in both. The Soviet firm would be under special pressure to produce parts that did not lower the reputation of the Western product, and that was precisely the pressure that Gorbachev was seeking.

As Soviet economists and Western observers watched the reforms introduced from late 1986 to mid-1987, they forgot what an incredibly radical break was being made with decades of sacred ideology, and they focussed only on the defects of the new laws—which were many. In fact, Gorbachev was following an intelligent strategy. With no market experience since the 1920s (and that often very inappropriate[17]), the wise course was to introduce ideologically radical, but practically limited, laws in industry, agriculture, and the services, and see what the problems were.

That is, although it was not officially so stated, the first round of laws on economic reform were really experiments. If the 1986–1987 laws were not radically improved, then the critics were right that the reform would be little more significant than previous ones. But if the intention was, in fact, to radically change and expand the laws after a few years, then an excellent base had been created for economic reform. While he was waiting for the experiments to work themselves out, Gorbachev diverted his attention—and that of Soviet society—to political reform.

Glasnost

At first Gorbachev talked primarily about economic acceleration, about technological improvement, and about change in economic management. Westerners concentrated even more exclusively on this aspect of his domestic program, and some treated Gorbachev as a technocrat who would tighten restrictions on culture. This, however, was a mistake. Gorbachev was also speaking about political reform ("democratization" and "*glasnost*" were his words), and in real terms he introduced more political liberalization than economic reform in his first two years of office.

"Liberalization" is a term that accurately conveys to an American audience what Gorbachev was doing. The "zation" ending correctly indicates that he is talking about a process and a trend, not the introduction of some final, perfected system, and to an American audience at least it implies looser political restrictions while "democratization" implies elections. To Soviet spokesmen or intellectuals, unfortunately, liberalization has another connotation. In Marx's and Lenin's time, "liberal" tended to denote representatives of the middle and business classes. Marx and Lenin denounced them as the class enemy, and any talk of "liberalization" carries the pejorative implication that the Soviet Union is becoming bourgeois and capitalist. But Soviet denial of "liberalization" in the Soviet Union has only confused Westerners.

Of the two words that Gorbachev used to describe his political program, *glasnost* became the watchword of the Gorbachev period. It is an old Russian word that embodied a call for a more open society without advocating (or seeming to advocate) an undercutting of the ultimate authority of the tsar. That seems to be the sense Gorbachev has in mind.

Gorbachev spoke with nearly as much urgency about *glasnost* as he did about economic acceleration. These are his words at the party congress:

> The widening of *glasnost* is a question of principle for us. The question is a political one. Without *glasnost*, there is not and cannot be democratism . . . This is the beginning point for a psychological reconstruction of our cadres. (Prolonged applause.)
>
> Sometimes when we speak about *glasnost*, we hear appeals to speak more cautiously about our defects and shortcomings, about the difficulties that are inevitable in any living work. There can be only one answer to this, the Leninist answer: Communists always, and in all circumstances, need the truth. (Prolonged applause.)[18]

Glasnost was often misinterpreted in the West. In practice, the most obvious early liberalization came in the freedom to discuss economic reform. No one could say in print that capitalism was superior to socialism, but the Soviet press continually published articles arguing whether greater private (or cooperative) enterprise should be permitted in trade and light industry or whether greater income inegalitarianism should be permitted. All of these issues could be raised in the past, at least in scholarly articles, but usually they had to be discussed cautiously. Now the articles could be quite explicit—and in mass newspapers. Both sides were represented: one person would say that private property is an abomination and will lead to price-gouging and exploitation, while another would say that small-scale private or cooperative property will lead to a more just form of socialism than that in which the services are dominated by huge ministries.

Then the disaster at Chernobyl marked a major turning point in Soviet information policy. In the first days after the accident, little information was published, but then increasingly an unprecedented flood was provided both the domestic and foreign audience.[19] A writer could publicly link "the national disaster at Chernobyl with the pernicious shortcomings in literature"; both had their roots in a system "in which hack work, incompetence, money-grubbing, servility, corruption, and cadre failings are combined."[20]

The language of this writer was not altogether temperate, but the analogy was accurate. Chernobyl showed precisely why freer information is important to rulers and not just to the people. Anyone familiar with bureaucrats around the world should have expected the Chernobyl officials to try to cover up the disaster while they thought they might control the situation. (The officials at the Three Mile Island nuclear plant in the United States were not all that forthcoming.) But if the Soviet Union had had a tradition of a freer press, some newspaper correspondent in Chernobyl would have filed a story as soon as the first explosion occurred, or some citizen would have called a friend in the media to provide a scoop. Gorbachev would not have had to wait for a report to come up the line of command. He or some assistant would have seen a news flash on the television or on the TASS wire shortly after the trouble, and he could have initiated action immediately. This case illustrates a general problem. The leadership will not have the information it needs to bring the ministries under control unless a broader public can discuss their defects and propose solutions to them.

As a result many Americans formed the opinion that *glasnost* was primarily a tactical liberalization—that the leaders were simply loosening up restrictions on the flow of advice to themselves and on criticism of lower bureaucrats. This is a mistake. Information and policy advocacy still were censored, but a wide range of ideas were permitted in almost every conceivable policy. People complained about quotas for non-Russians in universities, and they debated, pro and con, the issues raised by right-wing Russian nationalists, including anti-Semitism.[21] They talked about environmental problems more freely, and they began raising sensitive issues about personal life that formerly were taboo. A popular documentary film, *"Is It Easy to Be Young?"* examined disaffected youth, including some with punk orientations and others who were Afghanistan war veterans.[22]

Of course, *glasnost* itself was the subject of debate. The media was repeatedly criticized for being too closed or too timid. The sociologist, Tatiana Zaslavskaia, voiced a more general complaint about restrictions on certain types of information: "Publication of data from the census has become all the more skimpy. Data are not published on crime, suicide, use of alcohol and drugs, the 'environmental' situation in different cities . . . Why are data on the distribution of illness secret?"[23] Others called media criticism too extreme and "irresponsible."

Information about foreign views also increased. Television news had been extremely dull, but it now increased its coverage of foreign news substantially and made it more lively. The 9:00 P.M. program, "Vremia," carried some muckraking stories, and the talk shows became somewhat freer. The major one, "Studio 9," had foreign guests for the first time. One of them, former British Foreign Minister David Owen, was able openly to compare Soviet involvement in Afghanistan with American involvement in Nicaragua and to criticize both. His position was criticized by Soviet participants on the program, but he was given the last word. When Prime Minister Margaret Thatcher visited the Soviet Union in April 1987, Soviet television broadcast an hour-long press conference with her. Articles appeared in *Pravda* and *Izvestiia* by Americans such as George Shultz, Robert Dole, Les Aspin, and Edward Teller. The jamming of Voice of America ended.

The policy of looser controls on information in the media was applied in the cultural realm as well. The Writers' Union Congress, held in June 1986, provided a forum for a series of criticisms, many of which were published. One famous poet, Andrei Voznesensky, asserted that Soviet culture is beset by "spiritual aridity . . . [It] has become so twisted that it is running dry like the rivers." He listed the names of innovative authors who had not been elected delegates to the congress and asked, "Did the elective principle truly prevail in the Moscow Writers' Organization?" He demanded that

Boris Pasternak's dacha be turned into a museum.[24]

A dramatic prose-verse autobiography by Evgenii Evtushenko appeared in the September 1985 issue of the leading literary magazine, only shortly after a close Gorbachev adviser (Aleksandr Yakovlev) became head of the propaganda department of the Central Committee. Evtushenko referred unmistakably to Stalin's secret police chief, Lavrentii Beriia, in a way that suggested a parallel to Hitler (in the English translation he put Beriia's name in), and he included a poem that was explicit in the extreme in denouncing national borders as limitations on people.[25]

In every border post
        there's something insecure
Each one of them
        is longing for leaves and for flowers.
They say
        the greatest punishment for a tree
is to become a border post.

It was borders who invented
customs-men, passports, and other shit

Thank God, we have invisible threads and threadlets, born
of the threads of blood
        from the nails in the palms of Christ.
These threads struggle through,
        tearing apart the barbed wire

The Iron Curtain,
        unhappily squeaking her rusty brains,
probably thinks:
        "Oh, if I were not a border,
if jolly hands would pull me apart
and build from my bloody remains
        carousels, kindergartens, and schools.
In my darkest dreams I see
        my prehistoric ancestor:

he collected skulls like trophies
                    in the somber vaults of his cave

How foreign is the word *foreigner!*
I have four and a half billion leaders.

By 1987, barrier after barrier was falling. Émigré writers from
the 1920s and the 1930s were rehabilitated. Vladimir Nabokov
was published, as was Nikolai Gumilev, a poet shot by the secret
police in 1921. The highly controversial artist, Marc Chagall, was
given an exhibit in Moscow on the hundredth anniversary of his
birth.[26] Chagall had been highly sensitive in the past for four
different reasons: he was a semiabstract artist; he included religious
themes in his work; he had emigrated after the revolution; and he
was Jewish. All of this cultural liberalization raised objections, of
course, and part of *glasnost* was the freedom of both sides to de-
nounce each other.

Some of the most exciting changes occurred in the theater. A
number of theaters were given greater independence, and, particularly in Moscow and Leningrad, plays were shown that would
not have been possible a year earlier. Films that had been produced,
but then suppressed under Brezhnev, began appearing in movie
theaters and on television. The most notable, *Repentance*, featured
an attack on Stalin and the secret police, and reportedly was seen
by three million people in the Moscow area alone.[27]

One of the stranger aspects of Soviet culture—one of the signs
of the Khomeinism of the Soviet period—has been a deep suspicion
of the mass culture that has been so popular among the workers
of the West. Much of this culture has had little political content
that would subvert stability. In fact, its toleration would have only
increased the happiness of most Soviet citizens and thereby
strengthened political stability in the country. Already during the
Brezhnev period, love stories, detective stories, and the like had
become regular subjects of books and films, but they were shown
less frequently on television. The mass culture that was most popular among the youth—rock and roll—was grudgingly tolerated
at best and was not given access to official outlets.

Under Gorbachev, this acceptance of mass culture accelerated rapidly. A Soviet version of *Rambo*, with an unusual amount of violence by Soviet standards, was shown in the cinema theaters and was very popular. Television too developed a spy adventure series, as well as a game show and a larger number of variety programs. Rock and roll became legitimate, and very diverse types of rock shows—although still with almost no sex in the lyrics— were permitted. The leading underground rock-and-roll singer, Boris Grebenshchikov, was recorded by the state record company and released in mass numbers.

The acceptance of rock and roll by the authorities seemed so complete that it gave rise to a problem familiar in the West: how can rock and roll be a youth protest against adults if the adults are not offended? Grebenshchikov openly worried, "We are so official now . . . the people who were for us before are not sure of us [anymore]."[28] Fortunately for the rock and rollers, the architect of liberalization, Aleksandr Yakovlev, told a Western interviewer in 1987: "Recently, I saw a hard rock group from the United States on television. I could not accept the principle of driving the youths mad, absolutely frantic. . . . To bring the crowd to this frantic state is a crime. Such things we will never accept."[29] The Soviet singers will clearly learn how to move their hips just enough to drive their fans frantic, but not quite enough to be totally suppressed, and they will be happy again with their hard-won nonrespectability.

The great anomaly during the early stages of Gorbachev's reign was the official attitude toward history. Accidentally or not, Gorbachev scheduled the opening of the Twenty-seventh Party Congress to coincide with the thirtieth anniversary of the day when Nikita Khrushchev gave his secret speech at the Twentieth Party Congress denouncing Stalin. At the Twenty-seventh Party Congress, however, Gorbachev did not mention the Twentieth Congress or any historical issue whatsoever. He did call upon the historians as well as other social scientists "to raise new problems with initiative and in a daring manner," to develop "an atmosphere of creativity," and to avoid "scholasticism and dogmatism," but he gave far less attention to the social sciences than to the mass media and culture.[30]

Gorbachev's speech was symptomatic of what was actually occurring. The *glasnost* in the media was not, in fact, extended to history. There were a few interesting references to Stalin—and several of the most prominent came from Evtushenko—but these were extremely limited. The very names of Khrushchev, Brezhnev, Andropov, and Chernenko were almost completely taboo. The crucial questions of the Soviet past could seldom be raised in any open—and sometimes even in any covert—manner. The only real historical innovation was increasing attention to Lenin's support of the New Economic Policy in the early 1920s in order to legitimate privatization or cooperatives in the services and agriculture, but most of these were distortions of Lenin's views for polemical purposes. The leading conservative figures in the social science establishment were not replaced.

The strange dichotomy between increasing *glasnost* in discussions of current problems and policy issues and virtual silence on the historical issues of the Soviet period corresponded to an equally strange division of labor within the Central Committee Secretariat. Normally the media, culture, and the social sciences are supervised by one Central Committee secretary. However, in early 1986 the highly progressive official, Aleksandr Yakovlev was named a Central Committee secretary in charge of the media and culture, but the more conservative Mikhail Zimianin supervised education and science, including the social sciences.

A reason for this division may have been a reluctance to add another source of controversy—and a very emotional one for many older officials—to those already burdening a Soviet system facing difficult decisions on reform. Still another factor may have been severe divisions in the leadership, with the uneasy compromise being the result. The number of Politburo members who had risen precipitously during the Great Purge had declined to one by 1986—Andrei Gromyko—and only a handful of others are likely to have felt warmly about Brezhnev, but Gorbachev may have felt that it was unwise to offend them on this issue at this particular time. And perhaps most important of all, it was one thing to loosen up restrictions on early political struggles in Moscow, but something far more frightening to permit the Ukrainians to write freely about the famine in 1933–34 or the Kazakhs about the reasons for the decline in the number of Kazakhs from four million recorded in the 1926 census to just over three million in the 1939 census.[31]

Then in February 1987 Zimianin was retired as Central Committee secretary and Yakovlev was named a candidate member of the Politburo and given responsibility for the social sciences as well as culture and the media.[32] At the same time Soviet articles began the first serious criticism of Stalin as the seventieth anniversary of the Bolshevik Revolution in November 1917 approached. For the first time in over fifty years many of the leading figures of the revolution were recognized as playing a positive role in history. In *Izvestiia* in July 1987, for example, an article discussing the first Soviet cabinet in 1917 mentioned Trotsky and Stalin neutrally, describing their prerevolutionary pasts in a respectful way.[33] Even this, however, was still a long way from a free-swinging discussion of the ideas of the 1920s.

Then in June 1987, Yakovlev became a full member of the Politburo. The major policy significance of this move was probably a foreign policy one, but it meant that the chief architect of *glasnost* essentially occupied the old Suslov slot. He was now the party's ideologist, but with an ideology Suslov abhorred.

The celebration of the 70th anniversary of the Bolshevik Revolution in November 1987 provided the occasion for the rehabilitation of Stalin's opponents of the 1920s, especially Nikolai Bukharin. The discussion of the evil side of Stalin and the consequences of Stalinism became extraordinarily free—one might even say irresponsible. Those westerners whose estimates of the deaths in the 1930s had been the most extreme were published freely in Soviet sources. Khrushchev too was rehabilitated and discussed fairly freely, but criticism of Lenin remained a touchy subject and the analysis of the politics of the 1970s and 1980s was also virtually completely taboo.

In other ways too, *glasnost* remained a limited concept. For example, although a few details were published on Gorbachev's early life, descriptions of the life, personalities, or views of other Politburo members were impossible to find in any meaningful form. The more interesting question was whether some of the most extreme statements on nationality and political themes in 1989 were simply tolerated because they were useful to Gorbachev in his consolidation of power vis-a-vis the conservatives, or whether they represented the long-term development of a normal politics. In

September and October 1989, Gorbachev issued a threat against extremism in the Baltic republics and then began showing his anger about articles published in the more radical press. Clearly he was trying to induce a more sober tone in the press without engaging in direct repression, but it will be interesting to see whether the attempt will work.

Democratization and Economic Reform

The word "democratization" has long been used in the Soviet Union for so many fraudulent techniques of dictatorial control that it has little concrete meaning. Normally it tends to refer to citizen participation and electoral mechanisms, activization of the trade unions and local soviets, the creation of women's councils, and the like. However, Gorbachev often uses it to refer to a more responsive style of ruling, and one leading Soviet intellectual emphasized *glasnost* as its key component—that is, greater freedom to make suggestions in the policy process.

The February 1987 Central Committee plenum that gave Yakovlev supervision of history put its strongest emphasis upon democratization. Gorbachev spoke about electoral reform such as the election of plant managers and maybe secret ballots in party elections. He said that the Supreme Soviet and trade union elections should become more meaningful, and he called for a party conference in 1988 to further the democratization process.

At the time, the 19th Party Conference created a sensation. The election of the delegates was not a completely controlled process for the first time in decades, and radicals were able to compete in the nominating process. Some of the speeches of the delegates to the conference were unusually frank, especially for prime-time television, and one regional party secretary even called openly for the resignation of several Politburo members, including the country's president, Andrei Gromyko. Boris Yeltsin and Yegor Ligachev exchanged direct attacks on each other.

In retrospect, even the 19th Party Conference seemed quite cautious. For all the competition, the elections of delegates were quite controlled. The statements of the delegates were not as radical as those that were to be on television within a year, and the conference took no decisions that the Politburo had not already taken or could have taken.

The most important political development of 1988 was the promise of constitutional change and of competitive elections to the soviets. The constitutional changes themselves were actually retrogressive. A directly elected Supreme Soviet that was quite democratic on paper was replaced by a Congress of People's Deputies, a third of whose deputies were elected by official "public organizations." (For example, 100 were "elected" both by the Communist Party and by the official trade unions.) The Supreme Soviet itself, which was now to meet in sessions for months instead of a few days, was elected indirectly at the Congress.

It was 1989 that was the year of real political drama. Most of the elections to the Congress of People's Deputies were competitive, and a number of regional first secretaries and military commanders went down to defeat. Popular fronts which had been allowed to emerge in the Baltic republics dominated the elections there, and the Communist parties moved to the left to try to gain legitimacy. Boris Yeltsin, after being removed in disgrace as Moscow party leader, was allowed to run in a district that embraced all of Moscow, with his opponent a drab manager of the Moscow Auto Plant. Yeltsin received 89 percent of the vote. Then in June and July the Supreme Soviet rejected nine of Ryzhkov's nominees to the seventy posts on the Council of Ministers.[34]

The televised sessions of the People's Congress of Deputies featured speeches much more radical than the party conference of the previous year. Thus, the army was condemned for its bloody repression of a demonstration in Georgia; Armenians and Azerbaidzhani emotionally denounced each other over the issue of the disputed Nagorno-Karabakh region; and economic and environmental troubles were often described in the harshest terms. One economist, for example, went so far as to say that "the degree of the exploitation of the labor force in our country is the highest of all the industrial countries."[35] When, not surprisingly, such elections and speeches were followed by a major coal strike in Siberia and the Ukraine and by even more extreme acts in the Armenian-Azerbaidzhan conflict, many Americans began talking about the Soviet Union becoming ungovernable.

It was, however, a judgment that reflected the novelty of the political developments of 1989, not a sober assessment of the evidence. The great majority of party officials and military commanders were, in fact, successful in the March 1989 elections. Over 85 percent of the deputies to the new Congress of People's Deputies and Supreme Soviet were members of the Communist Party and were obligated to vote as directed by party leadership if the latter chose to enforce party discipline.

Least of all should it have been assumed that the country was about to fly apart. Americans have had little experience with ethnic unrest based on linguistic demands, and they have grossly over-reacted to what they have seen in the Soviet Union. In fact, most countries are multinational and multilingual to some extent, and their politics can be tumultuous at times. Yet, it is striking how extraordinarily rare it is for ethnic groups within the borders of a country to become independent countries unless the central power has been defeated in war. (By contrast, dominated people outside the border of a country almost always receive independence eventually.)

From a comparative perspective the Soviet Union looks like one of the more stable multinational countries. The non-Russian peoples are deeply divided among themselves. Historically, the ethnic and religious conflicts that are most explosive involve the blocking of the upward mobility of ambitious members of the minority. If individuals in the ethnic minority are able to rise and prosper, their willingness to continue fighting in the face of repression is usually short-lived. Soviet leaders have long been sensitive to the need for this mobility, and individual Lithuanians, for example, have less to gain personally from independence than does Lithuania as a collective nation.

As has been discussed in the last chapter, the turmoil of 1989 served Gorbachev well politically. A conservative or military coup d'etat became virtually impossible; the Russians were reminded that a multiparty system might well lead to the disintegration of the country, and their allegiance to the Communist Party was maintained; some of the leading conservatives on the Politburo were humiliated, and Prime Minister Nikolai Ryzhkov was left in a very difficult position in his efforts to oppose economic reform.

The turmoil also served Gorbachev well economically. As has been seen, 1987 and 1988 were years of experimentation in economic reform. If reform was to be pushed forward, the steps needed to be in place by the beginning of the new five-year plan in January 1991. Given the lead times involved, the key decisions had to be taken by January 1990, and the final details had to be in place by the fall of 1990.

From this perspective, what then did Gorbachev need in 1989? A sense of economic crisis in the country—a sense that reform must absolutely be pushed forward if the regime were to survive, political action that would frighten the conservatives into acquiescence, strong ethnic pressure for decentralization of power from Moscow ministries to the regions, and an atmosphere in which politically explosive price reform could be forced through in the name of equity among the republics and ethnic peace, and a party congress moved forward from March 1991 to the fall of 1990 to ensure that any final resistance could be smashed.

Americans have had a strong tendency to underestimate Gorbachev, to assume that he is incapable of a strategy and that events which serve his interests are simply good luck. In reality, Gorbachev is not a helpless pawn on the chessboard of Soviet politics. Instead he is a world-class chess player who has been planning moves well in advance. Obviously no chess player can predict the precise way in which the game will evolve, but Gorbachev is a player who dominates his board.

It was not a coincidence that 1989 was a year in which the number of persons working in cooperatives rose from 1.4 million to 2.9 million between January 1st and July 1st, in which radical agricultural legislation was introduced in March, in which all enterprises were given the right to export goods, and in which the Supreme Soviet in the fall passed laws on property, on the enterprise, on tax policy, on regional economic autonomy, and so forth. Economic reform will not produce instant results, but 1989 is likely to go down in Soviet history as a year of economic transformation that was as far reaching as 1929–1930.

The democratization of 1988–1989 will also have a profound effect. Decisions whose exact details were once worked out in interagency committees composed of ministerial representatives will now be worked out in legislative organs in which regional interests are more important. Regions will receive relative autonomy in tax and budget affairs, and local forces will be able to make many decisions that formerly were the province of Moscow ministries. As industrial enterprises become independent of Moscow ministries, trade unions will gain greater freedom to protect workers from managerial decisions. But those who hope that democratization means a multiparty system or the establishment of a system of rule by elected soviets to replace rule by the Communist Party are likely to be quite disappointed, at least for years.

Toward the Future

Americans had a great difficulty in understanding Gorbachev during his first two years in office. Part of the problem was a failure to understand that much of the familiar xenophobia and extreme censorship of Western ideas reflected the values of a peculiar generation born at the turn of the century rather than unchanging Russian national character or the inner laws of the Soviet system. Another part of the problem was that Brezhnev had made so many empty speeches and passed so many meaningless laws that we had become accustomed to discounting everything coming out of the Soviet Union.

Then, after Gorbachev convinced most people that he was a reformer, many went to the other extreme. Many saw him leading an heroic struggle against overwhelming conservative opposition, and any conservative note in one of his speeches or any conservative action was interpreted as a defeat for the general secretary. The unspoken—and usually unintended—implication was that Gorbachev himself was incapable of a conservative thought and was an Andrei Sakharov pushing for constitutional democracy.

In fact, while Gorbachev has been promising radical and even revolutionary reform, we should keep in mind the word "reform" as well as the words "radical" and "revolutionary." Gorbachev has committed himself to a radical reform of an existing socialist system, not to its abandonment. We should not judge his actions by the standards of a total revolution against the Soviet system. The American New Deal provides the proper analogy, although Gorbachev's reform will be more fundamental. No one judges the New Deal by what President Roosevelt had accomplished by 1934. No one says that the New Deal was meaningless because it failed to replace the country's basic political and economic institutions.

Reform in the Soviet Union is also like reform in the United States in another respect. It is not some unified package which "reformers" enthusiastically support as a whole and "conservatives" stubbornly resist. Just as some Americans are conservative on economic issues and liberal on social ones (or the reverse), so many Russians take a differentiated attitude on various aspects of reform and many are ambivalent. We cannot simply look at one question and assume that progress or the lack of it in that sphere is symptomatic of the fate of "reform" as a whole.

Indeed, reform in the Soviet Union has at least five different facets:

1) A drive against corruption, alcoholism, and the lack of discipline. This usually entails a reversal of the social policy that coddled workers in Brezhnev's last years.

2) A greater use of market mechanisms, and, more important, an evolution from state socialism toward cooperative socialism.

3) *Glasnost*—a relaxation of the censorship of the media and culture and a greater openness of Russia to Western ideas.

4) "Democratization"—greater citizen participation in decision making and, at its most extreme, the toleration of political group activity that is autonomous from the party.

5) A changed relationship to foreigners—the opening of Russia not only to Western culture, but also to Western investment and market forces.

A leader who is quite reformist on one type of issue can be more cautious on another. Indeed, a politician trying to balance various constituencies will naturally take a mixed position. Thus, Boris Yeltsin as Moscow first secretary was dedicated in his drive against corruption, privilege, and lack of discipline and seemed quite reformist on *glasnost* and democratization. However, both his speeches and the slow pace of economic reform in Moscow bespoke his lesser enthusiasm for the market. He also conducted no campaign to open Moscow to foreign newspapers or foreign restaurants. As an electoral politician, he associated himself with economic reformers, but his main appeal remained populist—that is, protection of workers from the market.

In my judgment, Gorbachev's relative enthusiasm about the different facets of reform is the reverse of Yeltsin's. He seems determined to attack the Moscow ministries and to greatly expand cooperative socialism. He is determined to open Russia to the West. But he seems much more dubious about elections and group activity that is autonomous from the party. While we cannot be certain, Ligachev seems to share most of Gorbachev's relative priorities, but is more cautious on the opening to the West.

But whatever proves to be the precise views of this or that Politburo member, we must remember that reform is divisible and that Gorbachev has a very delicate balancing act to perform. He doesn't simply face the problem of overcoming conservatives. Industrialization and increasing education levels among a population produce growing pressure for freedom and democracy. Over a ten-year perspective Gorbachev's greatest political problem will be that the broad bureaucratic, professional, and skilled worker strata—at least those under fifty—will want more radical change than he does, much as the social forces in Czechoslovakia in 1968 and Poland in the late 1970s wanted more change than the reforming Communist leaders of those countries. Gorbachev has been quite aware of this, and the denunciation and removal of Yeltsin was but one reminder that Gorbachev has no intention of being swept away by social forces he is gradually unleashing.

In short, if Gorbachev is successful, he will be introducing reform in steps, planning a number of moves ahead and considering the sequence and pace of reforms very carefully so as to avoid arousing all fears about reform simultaneously—and also so as to avoid erasing all fear of radical political action by the intellectuals. He will be successful if he is able to give his population enough exposure to the West and understanding of it to export effectively to it and enough access to computers to have them function well in an information age while he still maintains enough dictatorial control to prevent challenges to his political position from a population that is well-educated enough to want to get rid of dictatorship.

If Gorbachev is able to stand on Lenin's mausoleum in triumph to usher in the new century, Russia will look very different from what it did in 1985, but it will also be very different from the America of 1985. But as he progresses toward this goal, we must take care to keep our standards of judgment reasonable and not simply listen to the Soviet intellectuals who will never be satisfied with anything less than constitutional democracy—and probably not by that. Intellectuals are inherently critical in any country.

Least of all should we judge Gorbachev's economic reform by the standard of a totally free market. It is striking how many moderate and liberal Americans who are strongly opposed to Ronald Reagan's economic policies, let alone to the free market doctrines of economist Milton Friedman, then talk as if only ideological dogmatism prevents the Soviet leaders from introducing free markets in the Soviet Union. In fact, the free market can have devastating impacts on individuals, and the domestic politics of Western countries normally center on efforts to control the market in one way or another and provide individuals with some security. Workers want minimum wages and legalized trade unions, manufacturers (and workers) want protection against foreign (and domestic) competition, farmers want price supports, professors want tenure, a broad range of people want the government to set safety standards for medicines and to impose pollution controls on manufacturers.

Even with the most radical reform imaginable, the Soviet Union will retain strong limitations on market forces, and it will tolerate countless inefficiencies in the economy in an effort to achieve various social goals. But as we judge how far the Soviet Union is from a market economy or from perfection in economic performance, let us at least compare it to the realities of the capitalist world. Even if the Soviet Union reached the American level of economic performance, it would be far from perfect. The same week in February 1987 that the Central Committee plenum met to endorse democratization and an acceleration of reform, the cover story in *Time* magazine dealt with American services. The cover proclaimed:

"The Hapless American Consumer: Why Is Service So Bad?"[36]

Similarly, in the political sphere, the maintenance of a one-party system and the control of elections should not lead us to conclude automatically that nothing is happening. There are many gradations in freedom from the one-party system of Stalin to the one-party system of Mexico, and we should not assume that these gradations are meaningless. We should also not fall into the trap of recognizing only liberalization that is fully institutionalized. Great Britain has no institutional restraints on Parliament at all, no Bill of Rights, no Supreme Court to declare governmental actions unconstitutional. Yet, Great Britain is a free society. The process by which Great Britain evolved into the society that it is today was a long one, and many of the steps were ambiguous at the time. The protections of individual freedom that are really meaningful are those that have become deeply ingrained in the thinking of the elite—indeed, so deeply ingrained that the elite would find it personally repulsive to see them violated. All of the evidence indicates that the thinking of the Soviet elite and leaders has evolved a long way from the norms that Stalin took for granted. If the process of toleration and the legitimization of toleration continues, we should not underestimate what we are seeing.

9

Toward a
Common European Home

ULTIMATELY, the Soviet system is very different from
the American system, and its reforms are not likely to be
taken as models for the United States. We rejoice at the expansion
of political freedom anywhere, and we would react well to political
liberalization in the Soviet Union. But the continued suppression
of dissidents and the slow movement toward a multiparty system
will keep our enthusiasm low for a long time.

We are really interested in what Gorbachev and his reforms
mean for Soviet foreign policy and for Soviet-American relations.
Gorbachev piqued our curiosity on this score with his closing
statement in his interview with the editors of *Time* magazine in
August 1985:

> In conclusion, I would like to emphasize a point that has been the
> main one in our conversation. It has been rightly said that foreign
> policy is a continuation of domestic policy. If this is so, I ask you
> to ponder: if we have a grandiose program in the domestic sphere,

then what are the external conditions in which we have an interest?
I leave the answer to you.[1]

This statement was all the more remarkable because it was a
deliberate end to the interview, rather than a response to a question. While foreign policy *is* often determined by domestic factors,
few national leaders admit it. Most claim that their policy is intended to promote the national interest, the defense of the country,
and (perhaps) human rights. But we still are left with the question
that Gorbachev asked us: what *are* the foreign policy implications
of the "grandiose" domestic plans that he has in mind? Or, more
to the point, what does he think they are? If foreign policy is a
continuation of domestic policy and the latter is undergoing "grandiose" change, then it logically follows that grandiose changes in
foreign policy are in line, and we should give the deepest thought
to what those might be.

Options in Soviet Foreign Policy

We often see Soviet foreign policy in quite oversimplified terms.
Some, of course, believe that there are no issues at all in Soviet
foreign policy—that Soviet foreign policy always is and will be
expansionist. Most, however, see a conflict between pro-détente and
anti-détente forces in the Soviet Union. They believe that some
Soviets are willing to relax tension and to cooperate with the United
States on some issues, while other Soviets are determined to follow
a policy of all-out confrontation.

The basic problem with this dichotomy is that Americans have
misunderstood the word "détente." They think that it implies a
warm, cooperative relationship, but, in fact, it is far more limited
and means little more than a relaxation of tension between fairly
hostile powers. ("Entente" is the word that the French use to denote
a warm, cooperative relationship.) As a consequence, supporters
of détente in the Soviet Union occupy an intermediate position,
and they can be opposed both by those who favor confrontation
and by those who want to adopt an entente policy.

Without question, there are forces in the Soviet Union who see international relations as a fundamentally hostile struggle between two fundamentally hostile classes and two diametrically opposing ideologies and who see no alternative to confrontation. However, except for those in the military and the security apparatus, they tend to be older, and the failure of economic autarchy to produce high-technology, high-quality growth leaves them without a convincing policy argument. If the world is so hostile and dangerous, it is simply unsafe to withdraw into an autarchy that means the country falls further and further behind.

As a consequence, the real policy battles in the Soviet Union in recent decades have been between the proponents of détente and the proponents of entente. A normal Soviet conservative of the Brezhnev stripe now favors détente, or, to use the Soviet word, *razriadka*. The Russian word originally meant unloading a weapon, not discarding it, and its spirit is captured by a phrase used by Gorbachev in 1985, "smooth, correct, if you like, civilized intergovernmental relations." This view is quite consistent with a rather traditional two-camp image of the world, but simply recognizes the obvious fact that the two camps cannot afford to go to war, and have to coexist until historical forces decide their respective fates.

The entente position has gradations within it, but at its heart it goes beyond intergovernmental relations and seeks to break down the broader barriers between Russia and the West. In greater or lesser degree it favors a freer flow of ideas and far more serious integration of the Soviet Union into the world economy. Those who advocate entente speak not simply of *razriadka*, but of "cooperation" and "collaboration" in warm and broad terms. Vladimir F. Petrovsky, whom Gorbachev named a deputy minister of foreign affairs, wrote earlier that "the concept of international conflict as an eternal, root category or even essence of international relations . . . in whatever phraseology it is clothed, in practice, ignores the objective fact of the constantly widening collaboration in politics, economics, science and technology of states of different systems." Such people speak of a new "phase of development" of mankind in which there is an "increased mutual connection and mutual dependence of different countries."[2]

A second set of issues in the Soviet foreign policy process is the choice of countries or social forces with whom to cooperate in the outside world. With a very few exceptions (e.g., Israel), the Soviet Union has sought diplomatic relations—and reasonably correct diplomatic relations—with any nation that would have them. The United States has often refused such relations with new revolutionary regimes. It did not recognize the Soviet government for fifteen years or the Chinese Communist government for over twenty years. More than a quarter of a century after the Cuban Communist revolution, we not only refuse diplomatic relations, but impose an economic boycott. The Soviet Union, by contrast, not only has diplomatic relations with capitalist Turkey on its border, but provides it with large amounts of foreign aid even though it is a member of NATO.

Nevertheless, foreign policy requires choices. In the 1920s and 1930s the Soviet Union adopted a real multilateral policy, shifting its alliances from one country to another in an effort to prevent Europe from uniting against it. In 1922, it developed a special relationship with Germany, then weakened by World War I, and even had a secret military pact with it directed against France and England. Then in 1935 the Soviet Union entered into a military alliance with France against Hitler's Germany. For the next four years it sought to expand the alliance into a genuine collective security system. When this failed, the Soviet Union then signed a nonaggression pact with Germany that actually was a temporary alliance to divide Poland. And, of course, when Germany attacked in 1941, the Soviet Union was more than glad to enter into the Grand Alliance with the United States and Great Britain.

In the postwar period, this pattern of shifting alliances came to an end, at least in the industrialized world. The European countries that were allied with or subordinated to the United States and to the Soviet Union respectively, basically retained that position for forty years. In that sense the world became bipolar.

Unfortunately, however, as we thought about bipolarity, we came to define it in several contradictory ways: first, de facto cooperation between the superpowers that included grudging acknowledgment of each's control over its respective bloc, and, second, serious efforts to undermine the position of the other and to court its allies in Europe. We essentially reconciled these two definitions by seeing the cooperation as occurring only in nuclear arms control and by emphasizing the fundamentally hostile elements in the rest of the relationship.

Without any doubt, this traditional interpretation has contained substantial elements of truth, but in my opinion it has been misleading. There really wasn't much arms control in the Brezhnev era, and the rest of the relationship was not as fundamentally antagonistic as normally perceived.

A number of arms control agreements were, of course, signed in the 1970s, but American conservatives are correct when they question their meaningfulness. The number of nuclear delivery systems increased, and the situation was even more peculiar with respect to conventional armaments. By the mid- and late 1970s it was clear that no danger of war existed in Europe, and the death of Mao Tse-tung brought an end to the danger of armed clashes on the Soviet-Chinese border. Yet, Brezhnev made no real effort to reduce the appearance of a conventional Soviet military threat through a negotiated reduction of troops either in Europe or along the Soviet-Chinese border. He permitted Vietnam to invade China's satellite, Kampuchea, in 1979, ending any real hope of progress in Soviet-Chinese relations.

In the nuclear realm, Brezhnev very much would have liked an arms control agreement that really limited the American technological advantage in the development of multiple warheads and cruise missiles, but the United States would not accept any such limitation on its technology. In the face of this reluctance, Brezhnev was willing to accept relatively marginal agreements that only gave the appearance of control. Even the most significant of the treaties— the Anti-Ballistic Missile (ABM) Treaty—allowed the United States to continue vigorous research. As Pentagon SDI demonstration tests illustrate, the ABM treaty also had loopholes, and it could be abrogated in six months if the United States made a breakthrough. The SALT II treaty was so loose that President Reagan could live with it for six years and then had to strain in 1986 to exceed its limits. SALT II, because of American refusal, also didn't limit one of the fastest-growing types of missiles—the sea-launched cruise missile. Other treaties, such as the one forbidding the stationing of nuclear weapons in Antarctica, were even more symbolic.

Although these treaties did not limit the Soviet Union significantly, the lack of limitations on the United States was far more important. The United States was technologically more advanced, had made the major weapons breakthroughs in the past, and almost surely would do so in the future, as well. In addition, American presidents always used the agreements to justify other military programs. Yet, Brezhnev not only accepted these treaties, but also paid the price of large-scale emigration, which was said to be linked with trade but actually ebbed and flowed in conjunction with the fortunes of SALT.

The most important explanation, I believe, is to be found in Soviet domestic politics. The strongest argument for economic reform is that technological backwardness is dangerous for defense in the long run. Brezhnev absolutely did not want economic reform, and hence he wanted to defuse the best argument for it. Nuclear arms control that did no more than pretend to control American technology at least fooled the Soviet population into thinking that reform was not indispensable. The maintenance of large conventional forces created a sense of threat in Europe that, when conveyed back to the Soviet Union on Western foreign broadcasts, also made it hard for the reformers to say that the defense problem was not solved. This, I think, was the main reason for the combination of symbolic nuclear arms control and a threatening conventional posture.

The second problem with the usual interpretation of Brezhnev's foreign policy is that Brezhnev was not really treating the United States as his foremost enemy. When hard choices had to be made, Soviet support of anti-American forces and Soviet efforts to weaken American alliances were not his first foreign policy priority.

In the Third World, for example, the most virulent anti-American forces in the 1960s and the 1970s were not the traditional Communist parties, but the revolutionary "New Left." The Soviet Union, however, was not moved by their anti-Americanism to give them support, but instead often opposed them out of a fear that they were attracted to China or Cuba. Indeed, the Soviet

Union repeatedly acted as if China were its main enemy. Brezhnev's major Third World involvement came in Vietnam where the
competition with China was palpable. Even in Africa, the deepest
Soviet intervention (e.g., Angola) came in cases where the United
States was cooperating with China.

In the late 1970s and early 1980s, Soviet enthusiasm for the
Third World declined. Westerners saw this change as resulting
from a growing pessimism about the chance of Communist revolution there, and ultimately this is an accurate assessment. Another
crucial factor in the loss of Soviet interest, however, was the end
of active Chinese support for the Third World revolution after
Mao Tse-tung's death. Even in Afghanistan, the Soviet Union was
probably most afraid that this country would move out of its
longtime geopolitical alignment with the Soviet Union and into
the sphere of influence of China and its ally, Pakistan. Despite all
the Western speculation about Islamic fundamentalism as a factor,
Soviet Central Asia is Sunni, and the Soviet Union had been
relaxed about the spread of fundamentalism from Iran into neighboring Soviet Azerbaidzhan, which is Shiite.

Similarly, in the industrialized world, though the Soviet Union
often railed against NATO and the Japanese defense link with the
United States, it really treated Japan and Germany as the main
enemies. We laughed at Gromyko's supposed woodenness and
inflexibility, but a man who held his job for twenty-eight years was
not all that incompetent. The continuous talk about "German revanchism" and "Japanese militarism" in the Soviet press did not
reflect any real fear of Nazism in contemporary Germany or of
current Japanese policies. Rather it was a way of saying that if
Germany and Japan were to become independent, they would
increase their military spending and perhaps eventually acquire
nuclear weapons. It was a way of saying that this was not in the
Soviet interest and that American control over West Germany and
Japan should not be challenged too vigorously.[3] Gromyko's "woodenness" achieved precisely what he wanted to achieve.

Hence the foreign policy issues that Gorbachev faced in the
mid-1980s went far beyond the question of whether to favor détente or confrontation, whether or not to have arms control agreements. The choice was between a policy of confrontation, a policy

of détente, and a policy of entente. It was whether to persist in signing relatively meaningless arms control treaties or to insist on agreements that really limit arms and technology. It was whether to continue with a bipolar policy in which the American sphere was not really challenged or to move toward a multipolar policy in which the Soviet Union really was willing to risk the strategic subservience of Germany and Japan to the United States.

The Change in Personnel

Historically each general secretary in the Soviet Union (other than the short-lived Andropov and Chernenko) has been associated with very obvious changes in foreign policy. Gorbachev began talking about "a new way of thinking," a "new approach in foreign policy," and, whatever his precise plans, he surely wanted some kind of change in foreign policy. To achieve this, he certainly had to change personnel. The minister of foreign affairs, Andrei Gromyko, and the minister of foreign trade, Nikolai S. Patolichev, had held their respective jobs since 1957; the head of the international department of the Central Committee, Boris Ponomarev, had been in his post since 1955; the tenure of the head of the socialist countries department of the Central Committee, Konstantin Rusakov, essentially went back to 1968. These men averaged seventy-seven years of age in 1985, and surely they did not want any significant change in the foreign policy that they had been conducting for decades.

The key man among this group was Andrei Gromyko. He was the only voting member of the Politburo with foreign policy experience, and, therefore, a very awkward man for Gorbachev to deal with. To dismiss him and replace him with an enemy risked a political backlash because of Gorbachev's inexperience. To replace Gromyko with a younger protégé risked leaving Gromyko in de facto control of foreign policy.

Gorbachev found a brilliant and unexpected solution—the "promotion" of Gromyko to the chairmanship of the Presidium of the Supreme Soviet (essentially a ceremonial post) and his replacement by the first secretary of the Georgian party organization, Eduard

Shevardnadze, who did not have any experience at all in foreign policy. Since Shevardnadze was already a candidate member of the Politburo, he had enough stature to become a full member of the Politburo immediately and to serve as a counterweight there to his predecessor. He seems to have been friendly with Gromyko,[4] and the latter could not really object to his appointment. Yet, his very lack of experience meant that he was not committed to Gromyko's policy, and it was a subtle signal that Gorbachev did not think experience was necessary, that he was thinking of a fresh approach.

In addition, Shevardnadze's appointment served another purpose. He had been first secretary of the Komsomol in Georgia at the same time that Gorbachev had held this post in Stavropol, and the two regions had a common border. Indeed Stavropol was a major supplier of meat to Georgia. The two men thus had known each other for nearly thirty years. Their ties were strengthened in the late 1970s and early 1980s when Gorbachev, as Central Committee secretary for agriculture, selected a Georgian experiment in agriculture for introduction into the country as a whole. Shevardnadze had spoken enthusiastically about reform, and his selection as foreign minister and promotion into the Politburo, whatever it meant for foreign policy, gave Gorbachev another vote for his domestic program.

Another personnel change was more important, though formally it did not even relate to foreign policy. In July 1985, Aleksandr Yakovlev was named head of the propaganda department of the Central Committee—the man who directly oversaw the mass media. At that time Yakovlev was officially not even responsible for developing the information line about international relations, but his duties were expanded in that direction in March 1986, when the foreign information department of the Central Committee was merged into his propaganda department.

Yakovlev had been a low-level ideological official in the apparatus of the Yaroslavl provincial party committee when he was given a low-ranking post in the Central Committee apparatus in 1952— apparently in the propaganda department. While working in the Central Committee, he began a candidate's dissertation (doctoral dissertation in American terms) on the United States, and this suggested that his responsibilities had something to do with foreign propaganda. In the 1959–60 academic year, he spent eight months on the Soviet-American academic exchange at Columbia University in New York City.

Back in the Central Committee apparatus, Yakovlev continued to write on the United States and U.S. foreign policy; he was doing so as a party official. He rose to be the first deputy head of the propaganda department in 1966. In practice, he was the real head of the department, for the latter post was left vacant. As first deputy head of the propaganda department, Yakovlev was a leading liberal in the Central Committee apparatus, but he was out of step with the mood of the Brezhnev leadership. In 1973, he was named ambassador to Canada—a form of exile.

There he kept a relatively low profile, but in May 1983 Mikhail Gorbachev was sent on a tour of Canada. Officially Gorbachev was on an agricultural inspection trip, but since he cut the agricultural part short and met with Canadian members of Parliament in a lively question and answer session, he was also being tested as a future general secretary. Westerners generally view this trip as chance good luck for Yakovlev, but Andropov, like Yakovlev, had come out of the Yaroslavl party organization. Yakovlev was likely already slated to rise, and Andropov probably wanted his view on Gorbachev, or was sending Gorbachev as an emissary to him, or both.

In any case, when Andropov became general secretary, he brought Yakovlev back from Canada and made him director of the most important foreign institute, the Institute of World Economics and International Relations. Almost immediately Yakovlev began writing a series of articles and a book that were virulently anti-American. He was much more positive in his description of Western Europe and Japan (calling the latter "the most dynamic center" of world capitalism).[5] Implicitly Yakovlev was staking out a position as the leading critic of Gromyko's American-centered policy.

When Gorbachev went to England in the last months of Chernenko's life, Yakovlev was the leading foreign relations specialist taken on the trip. Then after Gorbachev became general secretary, rumors began flying that Yakovlev was an important informal adviser to Gorbachev. In July 1985, one well-connected scholar in the Soviet Union insisted that Yakovlev was Gorbachev's chief foreign policy adviser. When Gorbachev met President Reagan in Geneva in November, Yakovlev was one of his top four advisers, even though his formal post as head of the propaganda department had no relation to foreign policy. In protocol settings, Yakovlev was paired with Robert C. McFarlane, the United States national security adviser.

Other than the appointments of Shevardnadze and Yakovlev, few significant changes in foreign policy personnel were made in 1985. The seventy-eight-year-old minister of foreign trade was retired, and the deputy minister of foreign affairs for personnel was changed, but that was all. No ambassador was replaced in a country more important than Pakistan. Gorbachev surely did not want to offend Gromyko as long as the Central Committee elected in 1981 still had the ultimate power in its hands.

As the Twenty-seventh Party Congress approached and then passed, however, the old Central Committee was no longer a threat, and the turnover of foreign policy personnel accelerated rapidly. The personal assistant of the general secretary and the two Central Committee secretaries for international relations were all retired. By June, eight new deputy ministers of foreign affairs had been appointed, and an old deputy minister had been promoted to first deputy minister. (There had been a total of eight deputy ministers in October 1985, six of whom were removed by the spring of 1987.) New ambassadors were named in almost all the crucial countries—China, France, Great Britain, Japan, the United States, and West Germany.

Of the new appointments, the most interesting was that of Anatolii Dobrynin as Central Committee secretary and head of the international department. This department was responsible for relations with foreign, radical, and social-democratic parties, as well as other nongovernmental institutions. It was the successor to the old Communist International (Comintern) and never had been staffed by diplomats in its top posts. Dobrynin had been ambassador to the United States for a quarter of a century and had been an urbane partygoer in Washington's fashionable Georgetown district. In addition, Dobrynin selected another diplomat (the former first deputy minister of foreign affairs) as one of the first deputy heads of his department.

Clearly, at a minimum, Gorbachev wanted a man without previous experience who would have a fresh outlook. Most American observers also assumed that the international department's responsibilities would be broadened and that Dobrynin would become the Soviet equivalent of the American national security adviser. They assumed that he would be the architect of Gorbachev's foreign policy.

These assumptions proved to be wrong. The international department traditionally has had no responsibility for governmental relations, except with radical countries such as Afghanistan, Ethiopia, and Nicaragua. Dobrynin did begin bringing into his staff personnel who were foreign policy specialists. Nevertheless, although Dobrynin met many old American friends in his new office, he was not participating in government negotiations with the president of France or the foreign minister of Japan on their visits to Moscow. Germans visiting Moscow and having contact with the department found no specialists in German foreign policy.

Most important, despite many rumors in 1985, the socialist countries department of the Central Committee was not merged with the international department. At the same time that Dobrynin was elected a Central Committee secretary, Vadim Medvedev was named head of the socialist countries department and also made a Central Committee secretary. The socialist countries department is responsible for relations with the countries that are unquestionably Communist—China, Cuba, Eastern Europe, Mongolia, North Korea, and Vietnam—and it is difficult to imagine Dobrynin or anyone else as a meaningful Soviet "national security adviser" with no responsibility for China and Eastern Europe.

Dobrynin's role during his short, two-and-a-half years as head of the international department was a relatively minor one. A majority of Central Committee secretaries became either full or candidate members of the Politburo, but Dobrynin was never so promoted, and thus he remained directly subordinated to Aleksandr Yakovlev. If Soviet-American relations had been at the center of the agenda, Dobrynin might have had a different role. As it was, he seemed to be doing precisely what his title as "head of the international department" implied: handling (burying, really) the world revolution, dealing with the peace movements, and overseeing the resolution of the conflicts between the United States and the Soviet Union's radical Third World clients.

In September 1988 Andrei Gromyko was removed as chairman of the Presidium of the Supreme Soviet, and Dobrynin as head of the international department of the Central Committee. Aleksandr Yakovlev became chairman of a new foreign policy commission of the Central Committee, and Aleksandr Falin became his deputy as head of an international department that now handled both the Communist and non-Communist world.

The retirement of the two old-time Americanists and the rise of Falin was a major event. Falin had been the country's leading Germanist in the Brezhnev period, serving for a number of years as Soviet ambassador to Bonn. He was more anti-American and pro-German in his orientation than Yakovlev. For those who understood the orientation of Yakovlev and Falin, it was clear that the coming year would be featured by major steps in foreign policy itself. So it turned out to be.

The Course of Policy

The interpretation of Gorbachev's actual foreign policy in his first years in office was intensely controversial in the West. On the one hand, the general secretary's language was more the language of entente than détente as it was understood in the 1970s. In April 1985, he stated, "We firmly stand for a revival of the process of detente. But this does not mean a simple return to that which was achieved in the 1970s. It is indispensable to aspire to much more. From our point of view, detente is not the final goal of policy. It is a necessary, but only transitional stage."[6]

Gorbachev repeatedly spoke about a new way of thinking, a new approach to international relations. The words that he continually emphasized were "trust," "confidence," and "cooperation." He spoke again and again about a world in which military force and diplomatic advantage were no longer particularly important;

"the security of Europe," he said in Paris in October 1985, "cannot be guaranteed by military means, by military force. This is a completely new situation, which means a break with traditions, with ways of thought, and with ways of acting that have been formed over hundreds and even thousands of years."[7]

At the Twenty-seventh Party Congress in February 1986, Gorbachev returned to the theme. Because of nuclear weapons, "the guaranteeing of security all the more becomes a political problem, and it can only be solved by political means... Security, if we speak about relations between the USSR and the USA, can only be mutual, and if we speak about international relations as a whole, it can only be universal... The highest wisdom lies not in worrying exclusively about oneself."[8] When French President Mitterrand came to Moscow in July 1986, Gorbachev tried to reassure him with similar words: "We don't intend to convert you to our faith. We don't want to be victors on a diplomatic 'chess board.' We must completely deliver political thinking from the conception of Europe as a 'theater of military action.'"[9]

The Soviet Union had, of course, always proclaimed that it wanted universal peace and universal disarmament and that it posed a threat to no one. Westerners always interpreted such statements simply as attempts to get the West to lower its guard. And since the Soviet Union took few concrete steps to reduce mistrust, there was little reason to challenge this prevailing interpretation. Now, however, in discussing Soviet military doctrine Gorbachev was telling the party congress that "we intend to act in such a way that no one will have a basis for fears, even imagined ones, for their security."

At the same time Gorbachev was advancing one innovative arms control proposal after another, conceding a number of points on which the Soviet Union had been adamant in the past. He agreed to large cuts in Soviet offensive missiles, called for an end to nuclear testing (coupling it with a unilateral moratorium that lasted for a year), and embraced verification. He accepted a Reagan administration proposal for removal of all Soviet and American intermediate missiles in Europe—an offer that had originally been made because many in the Pentagon were convinced that it was sufficiently unreasonable that the Soviets would never accept it.

Yet, on the other hand, all the very warm language about cooperation with the West and a new definition of security was combined with extraordinarily harsh language about the United States, as harsh as could be found in the post-Stalin period. The United States, Gorbachev said, at the Twenty-seventh Party Congress, is marked by "monopolistic totalitarianism." The previous June, he had called statements "about the defensive character [of President Reagan's Strategic Defense Initiative] fairy tales for naive people,"[10] a theme he often repeated. At his press conference after the Geneva Conference, Gorbachev referred to "the well-known phrase of President [Lyndon] Johnson who said once that the nation that will rule in space will rule on Earth."[11]

In these statements, Gorbachev did not limit his criticism to President Reagan. It was the Soviet optimists about Soviet-American relations who focused on the president, thus implying the possibility of change after January 1989. Gorbachev, instead, described the problem in more generic terms and even suggested that President Reagan wanted an agreement at Reykjavik but that "they" would not let him.[12] He saw "the reactionary upper group in the United States" and especially the military-industrial complex as the dominant political force in the country. In June 1986 he spoke of U.S. leaders "betting on brute force, on the nuclear fist, on terrorist piracy, profusely blended with ideological intolerance and hatred."[13]

In addition, Gorbachev made it very difficult for the United States to accept any arms control agreement with the Soviet Union except for the one which would require the United States to withdraw its intermediate missiles in Europe without any reduction of the threat to the United States. All Soviet proposals for a reduction of weapons aimed at the United States were made conditional on severe restrictions on American space defense and a substantial strengthening of the ABM treaty. Unless Gorbachev was going to make a major retreat in the final stages of negotiations, any American administration would find it hard to accept his proposals on strategic weapons and space, and the Reagan administration certainly was not going to accept them.

Actual diplomatic behavior in Gorbachev's first two years was more ambiguous. Certainly Gorbachev pointedly met with President Mitterrand of France before he met with President Reagan. Instead of coming to the United States as protocol suggested, Gorbachev demanded that the summit meeting with President Reagan take place in Geneva in Europe. Afterward, he said that the meeting was useful, but he complained strongly that no concrete results had ensued. In 1986, he asserted with increasing urgency that the holding of a second summit meeting with President Reagan was dependent on major progress in arms control. He finally agreed to a second "presummit" with the president in October 1986, but again the meeting had to be in Europe—in Reykjavik, Iceland—and in retrospect the meeting had far more the appearance of a well-laid trap by Gorbachev than a serious negotiation.

In arms control, Gorbachev's insistence on the control of SDI as part of any limitation on long-range missiles, made it clear that Europe was the only place where an arms control agreement might be possible, and attention focused there. On the nuclear front, Gorbachev unexpectedly agreed to accept President Reagan's "zero option" (no American missiles in Europe and no Soviet SS-20s facing Europe). At first Gorbachev linked such an agreement with a limitation on British and French missiles, then with an SDI agreement, but in February 1987 he removed all linkages. In the summer he agreed to remove Soviet SS-20 missiles facing Asia but was able to extract an agreement that American warheads for West German rockets also be removed.

Even more interesting, Gorbachev, in June 1986, had also proposed a reduction of conventional troops in Europe—not the token reduction of 5,000 to 10,000 that had been discussed previously, but 100,000 to 200,000 on each side in the first several years and a total of 500,000 on each side by the early 1990s. NATO was slow to respond and hence Gorbachev's seriousness was not tested, but the signs multiplied that he would accept unequal reductions and change the offensive configuration of Soviet forces in central Europe.

In July, Gorbachev crossed the country to the Pacific port of Vladivostok in order to emphasize the importance of the Pacific for Soviet policy. He called for a major improvement in relations not only with Japan which Foreign Minister Shevardnadze had already visited, but also with China. Most unexpected of all, he unilaterally conceded the Chinese position on the disputed border between the Soviet Union and China formed by the Amur River. The Chinese had demanded that it follow the channel and the Soviets that it follow the Chinese shore, but in one sentence Gorbachev simply asserted that the channel was the border. By early 1987 the Soviet Union had also unilaterally reduced its forces in Mongolia by a division.[14]

Gorbachev's Third World policy had a mixed quality. Although the general secretary gave little real indication that he would abandon any of the Soviet Union's existing radical clients (including Afghanistan), Dobrynin's appointment was only one of a number of signs that the new general secretary was planning to play down relations with radicals in the Third World and concentrate on the large, moderate countries. The Soviet Union provided Libya with no support at the time of the American air strike in 1986 and spoke out strongly against terrorism. He showed little inclination to encourage new radical regimes, and was so ostentatious in supporting President Ferdinand Marcos in the Philippines against the local Communists that he did not abandon him quickly enough at the time of the Aquino revolution. The same point was made implicitly in the new Party Program and in Gorbachev's own speech to the Twenty-seventh Party Congress: both described "national liberation movements" in far more modest terms than in the past.

By contrast, when Gorbachev traveled to India, the one clearcut Soviet moderate Third World ally under Brezhnev, he explicitly pointed to Soviet-Indian relations as the perfect example of the new kind of political relationship he was emphasizing. And, again, there were subtle signals. After the Geneva Conference with President Reagan, Gorbachev damned the president for "irresponsibly" treating Third World developments in East-West terms. Any experienced Soviet knew that the prevailing interpretation of Marxism-Leninism had been doing the same thing and that the general secretary was speaking to his own ideologists as well as to the American president. The interesting innovations in Third World policy centered on moderate and even conservative Third World countries. For example, the Soviet Union agreed to transport Kuwaiti petroleum in Soviet tankers, guarding them with Soviet

ships, if necessary. In September 1987 Eduard Shevardnadze trav-
elled to Argentina and Brazil, but not Nicaragua.

Nevertheless, for all the signs of a change to a multipolar policy,
Gorbachev had not taken any really decisive steps by the fall of
1987. Although all arms control negotiations focused on Europe,
they were being conducted with the Americans. The border negotiations with China went slowly, despite the apparent concession
on the border, and the rumored Gorbachev trip to Japan to meet
Prime Minister Yasuhiro Nakasone and perhaps to offer concessions on the disputed Kirile Islands never occurred. In Europe,
he made no significant moves to break down the barriers with West
Germany although the visit of East German leader Erich Honecker
to West Germany in September seemed a powerful signal. Changes
in Third World policy remained subtle.

The Driving Forces of Soviet Policy

There were several possible explanations for the early ambiguities
in Soviet policy. One that was often advanced in the West was
that while Gorbachev probably wanted to conduct a multipolar
policy, the distribution of nuclear weapons forces the Soviet Union
to a bipolar policy focused on the United States. In this view,
Gorbachev's struggles with the inevitable, coupled with the inexperience of advisers such as Foreign Minister Shevardnadze and
conflicts among them, led to unevenness in policy.

Another possible explanation was advanced by Aleksandr Yakovlev: everything was a matter of timing, and the time was not
ripe.[15] And he had a good case. Decisive steps toward Europe and
Japan made little sense until the Soviet Union passed its joint-
venture law in February 1987. By that time Prime Minister Nakasone of Japan was in such desperate political trouble that it made
little sense to deal with him, and the imminence of the British
elections suggested delay as well. After the latter, Gorbachev
moved quickly to obtain agreement on an INF treaty that was
Europe-centered. His major objective, in this view, was not the
treaty itself so much as the stimulation of talk about Soviet conventional military superiority that would lead to an agreement on

that subject. A summit was necessary to draw the Americans into the latter negotiations, but the ambiguity prevented any euphoria at home.

It is impossible to prove conclusively any proposition about the driving forces of Gorbachev's foreign policy. If we have a clear view of Gorbachev's interests, however, we will not be surprised in a major way. Such a clear view is peculiarly important because our conceptions from the past are deeply misleading.

First, Gorbachev was right in saying that foreign policy in Russia is a continuation of domestic policy. The strongest political argument for economic reform is that technological backwardness is dangerous for defense. Brezhnev, who did not want economic reform, needed to defuse this argument. Nuclear arms control agreements that created the illusion of a control of American technology, as well as a large conventional army that led foreign radio broadcasts to tell the Soviet people that the Soviet Union was militarily superior, served this purpose.

Gorbachev, who wanted reform, had the opposite political interest. He needed to emphasize the dangerous consequences of technological backwardness. He did not need arms control treaties that pretended to limit American technology but failed to do so. An agreement that permitted SDI research but limited testing might regulate the American program to some extent, but it solved no real security problem. If the Americans were to make a research breakthrough, any treaty could easily be abrogated. But SDI was the perfect symbol of the technological danger. In worst-case analysis, it would leave Russia totally defenseless, and since the bottleneck in the American program is in the computer realm, only the computerization of the Soviet Union could counter SDI—precisely what Gorbachev wanted in any case.

Second, a determined attack on protectionism—an export strategy, the encouragement of licensing arrangements, joint production agreements with foreign firms, and large-scale foreign investment—requires an intimacy of technological contact and a level of foreign investment that are incompatible with the type of Western fear that was present even during the détente of the 1970s. Europe would not invest on a large scale in the Soviet Union if it feared the possibility of invasion, but the American determination to impose very strict technological controls created a more serious problem.

Third, Brezhnev and Gromyko were essentially correct in sensing that the USSR did not have a geostrategic interest in dividing the United States from Europe or Japan once intercontinental rockets with nuclear warheads had been produced. The only real military danger to the Soviet Union comes over the North Pole and would not be reduced by American military withdrawal from Japan and Germany. The withdrawal from Japan in particular would lead to a major increase in Japanese military spending—and perhaps eventually to acquisition of nuclear weapons.

Longer-term geostrategic interests pointed in the same direction. The great Western achievement in the postwar period was the end of four hundred years of war among the Europeans. In a real sense a common European home—an Atlantic community—was formed from the Elbe River to California, ending the century-old threat to Russia from Europe. As Russians look at the twenty-first century, they see any long-term potential threats coming from Asian countries on their border—first of all China or India. If any such threat should develop, the Russians see the Europeans, including the Americans, as natural allies, and they have no interest in shattering the Atlantic community, but think of joining it.

Fourth, the Soviet Union has discovered what the Western powers already had learned: colonies are not economically advantageous, and they are a political headache. The Soviet Union has far more profitable and comfortable relations with Austria, Finland, and even West Germany than with countries such as Poland, Hungary, and Romania. A Soviet leader might decide that liberalization in Eastern Europe might destabilize the Soviet Union, but clearly Eastern Europe is no longer necessary as a buffer zone against a nonthreatening Western Europe, and the military expenditure required to maintain the colonial status of Eastern Europe is far more than it is worth.

These various Soviet interests often come into conflict. If Gorbachev emphasizes the American danger embodied in SDI and places great pressure on the Western alliances in an effort to break the American technological blockade, he might actually introduce more instability into Europe than is in his interest. This is particularly so if he extends the decolonization of Eastern Europe to the most expensive colony of all, East Germany, and risks the reunification of Germany. Moreover, overt anti-Americanism forces America's allies to choose, and they may choose incorrectly, from the Soviet point of view.

In practice, the various Soviet interests have had a different priority at different times, and this factor helps to explain the path of actual Soviet policy in the Gorbachev period. At the beginning, Gorbachev's problem was to consolidate power and to overcome conservative resistance. At that time it was useful to emphasize SDI and the American threat, while playing down the drastic changes in Eastern Europe and the military spending that was to come.

But once the conservative resistance was broken and economic reform was beginning to reach the stage where an acceleration of foreign economic reform was possible, he could begin taking the steps necessary to reduce military expenditures and end the sense of foreign threat. In December 1987 came the first step—the signing of an agreement to remove intermediate-range missiles in Europe. This was the easiest step, because the Soviet military was happy to have the American Pershing II missiles removed from West Germany. But a year later he went to the United Nations to announce a unilateral reduction of Soviet troops in Europe. In March 1989 he carried out a promised withdrawal of all Soviet troops in Afghanistan, and he raised no objections to free elections in Poland and Hungary nor to elections in Poland that produced a Solidarity victory. In October 1989, when he visited East Germany for the fortieth anniversary of the Communist regime, he spoke deliberately of the key role East German citizens would play in deciding the future. Subsequent events followed quickly and predictably.

Most persons in the West were shocked by the events in Eastern Europe, and they assumed that Gorbachev too must be surprised. Many even assumed that he was acting in panic. It was a fundamental misreading of the situation. When Gorbachev named Aleksandr Yakovlev the chairman of the foreign policy commission of the Central Committee and replaced Anatoly Dobrynin with Valentin Falin as head of the international department of the Central

Committee, it was a clear signal of what was to come—a signal as clear as when Viacheslav Molotov replaced Maxim Litvinov as foreign minister in 1939.

And, of course, while the continuing instability within the Japanese government greatly complicated the improvement of Soviet-Japanese relations, it was scarcely a coincidence that Aleksandr Yakovlev chose to visit Japan at the same time that the Berlin Wall was coming down. Gorbachev had already announced that he planned to visit Japan in 1991, and it was highly likely that more "unexpected" events were in the offing.

We should not, however, be surprised. In fact, we would not be surprised if we understood the ultimate driving force of Gorbachev's foreign policy. The crucial factor in Soviet foreign policy had not been geostrategic considerations or even Brezhnev's domestic political interests. It had been the extraordinarily peculiar relationship of Russia to the West that had been a product of the Khomeini-like revolution that had occurred in November 1917. The truly peculiar aspect of Brezhnev's foreign relations had not been his policy in Afghanistan or Eastern Europe, let alone his arms control policy. It had been that Moscow in 1982 did not have a single French or Italian restaurant.

The essence of Gorbachev's revolution was a rejection of the Iron Curtain against western culture and against western market forces. It was expressed in his relaxed attitude to the expression of ideas—his glasnost program. It was expressed in his changed attitude to the market and foreign investment—his program of economic perestroika. It was expressed in his rejection of the values of the frightened workers of the Brezhnev generation and his espousal of the values of the middle class of the blue-jean generation. But all of these steps were foreign relations in the broader sense of the term—the most fundamental reversal of the foreign relations of the previous seventy years. The Russians really were returning home to Europe. Even such concrete foreign policy steps as the withdrawal from Afghanistan or the opening of the Berlin Wall were relatively minor in comparison, for they were inevitable parts of the broader reentry of the Russians into the common European home. Until we truly understand this, we will continue to be surprised time after time.

10

America's Relationship with Russia

WHEN we speak about America's relationship with the Soviet Union, we almost always talk in foreign policy terms. We debate the intricacies of geopolitics in the nuclear age and the danger that Soviet power will fill a vacuum in some "arc of crisis." We spin out scenarios of nuclear war that lead us to incredibly expensive nuclear programs because Soviet superiority in throw-weight supposedly makes us vulnerable to a first strike. Each new president must have his Truman Doctrine or his Carter Doctrine, or at least his new nuclear strategy: massive retaliation, flexible response, mutual-assured destruction, and now space defense against nuclear weapons. The result is often great public confusion on defense issues.

Part of this confusion is the result of a deliberate effort to confuse and frighten the population. Many remember the reluctance of the people of the West to rearm in the face of Hitler's aggressiveness. They are very cynical about public opinion and have thought that the Soviet threat must be exaggerated in order to keep defense expenditures at reasonable levels. Yet, most people have to panic themselves before they can panic others. The generation of public support for defense was not used to build a rational defense structure. Instead, increases in dollar expenditures became security blankets to assuage deep fears and uncertainties in those pushing the programs as well as in the general population.

America's actual relationship to Russia has been far more than the foreign policy response of one great power to the challenge of another. It has been a psychological response of a country that had been totally secure in its borders to the shock of world responsibilities and the possibility of nuclear annihilation. If the United States is to develop a less fearful relationship to the Soviet Union, the first step must be to recognize and attack the psychological problems.

An Insecure Nation

In recent years, we have heard much about a Vietnam syndrome—a feeling of insecurity and impotence that resulted from the country's defeat in the Vietnam War. One of the proudest claims of the Reagan administration was that it restored America's confidence in itself.

Without doubt, the Vietnam War was a trauma for the United States, and this was reinforced by the oil boycott of 1973. Nevertheless, Vietnam was more the consequence than the cause of American insecurity. Today we look wistfully back upon a time right after World War II when the United States dominated the world. It didn't look that way at the time. The Communization of Eastern Europe and then of China was such a shock that it produced McCarthyism, scarcely the response of a self-confident people.

Indeed, McCarthyism did not center on any Soviet military threat, real or exaggerated, but on allegations that America's defeats could be explained only by treason at home. Leaders of the right wing of the Republican party such as Senator Robert A. Taft and former President Herbert Hoover were strongly opposing the establishment of NATO as unnecessary and instead were calling for a "Fortress America." McCarthy was talking about internal subversion and control by American Communists of American foreign policy, the American media, and the film industry. And clearly this theme sounded a very responsive chord in an insecure American polity.

In retrospect, the Eisenhower years are seen as a period of good feelings, during which the president buried McCarthyism and restored the country's self-confidence. Yet, the press in 1960, the last year of the Eisenhower administration, was much like the press in 1980. The country believed that there was a Soviet military juggernaut and a "missile gap" and feared them. The unexpected Soviet successes with the first satellite (*Sputnik*) and then the first man (Yurii Gagarin) in space produced doubts about American technological superiority. The director of the CIA, Allen Dulles, made a rare appearance before a congressional committee in 1959 to warn of the Soviet economic-technological challenge.[1]

The dominant group of defense analysts in the late 1950s— Henry Kissinger was a leader among them—were writing that the nuclear stalemate destroyed the believability of our promise to defend Europe with nuclear weapons. (So much for the claim we first became insecure about nuclear questions in the 1970s with a loss of American nuclear superiority.) These analysts advocated a buildup of conventional weapons as the only answer, and President John F. Kennedy increased conventional military spending by 25 percent in his first year in office.

The Soviet Union was also seen on the move in the Third World during the late 1950s and early 1960s. Castro's victory in Cuba was seen as a possible—perhaps even probable—precursor to revolution throughout Latin America. Nasser was described as a proxy of the Soviet Union in its drive to take over the Middle East. While he was not regarded as being as crazy as Qaddafi is today, he was seen as far more dangerous. The reader in 1960 would be particularly amused to be told that in the late 1970s the Soviet Union would take advantage of détente to penetrate Africa for the first time. Besides close Soviet allies in Algeria and Egypt in northern Africa, the press of 1960 was emphasizing Kwame Nkrumah in Ghana, Sékou Touré in Guinea, Modibo Keita in Mali, and Patrice Lumumba in the Belgian Congo.

The American leadership did not go into Vietnam out of any naïveté about the scale of the problems there, for it remembered full well France's years of agony. Nevertheless, it thought that a Communist victory in South Vietnam would be disastrous in accelerating the leftward momentum it saw epitomized in Cuba and Egypt—and also in nearby Indonesia and Burma, where Sukarno and Ne Win respectively were following a similar path. Most of all, it feared the rise of the John Birch Society and thought that another Communist victory might be too much for the American people.

If American insecurity did not begin with Vietnam, we should not think that it ended with Ronald Reagan's presidency. The outside world remained a strange and scary place in 1986. Americans stayed away from Europe—even England—because of a handful of deaths from terrorists in order to travel on American highways where nearly 50,000 persons die a year. "International state terrorism" was often described in terms strongly reminiscent of those used in the past for "the international Communist conspiracy." The old obsession with internal subversion was still present in the fear that the Soviets were stealing our technology and may thereby catch up with us. Cuba and the phrase "90 miles off our shores" continued to produce a response far out of proportion to the danger. The Soviet Union lives comfortably with Turkey on its border even though it is a member of NATO and has 500,000 troops. Cuba has one-third the population of Turkey, is totally surrounded by water, and has achieved no great economic success that would serve as a model.

The causes of this insecurity are many. Part of the problem may be, as the most sophisticated Soviet specialist on the United States, Yurii Zamoshkin, argues, a fundamental contradiction in American values. On the one hand, American ideology has been highly individualistic. Novels and films that glorify the lone individual struggling against some larger force, often the government, enjoy enormous and continuing popularity. This ideology comes out of the actual experience of the individual farmer (unlike the peasant who lives in a village in much of the world), of the movement to the frontier, and of the immigrants who made a daring break with their past to come to this country. On the other hand, the essence of immigration is assimilation—of conformity to new values and new ways of life. Immigrants have tended to identify themselves as Americans from the first, and it has been easy to define Americanism in terms of conformity rather than individualism.

In addition, an increasing proportion of Americans work in organizations rather than for themselves, and this strengthens the strain with the individualist ideology. Zamoshkin suggests—and he may be right—that anti-Sovietism is intensified by this conflict. The Soviet Union is a huge organization writ large, the epitome of bureaucratic society, and we love to exaggerate the power of the bureaucrats vis-à-vis Gorbachev. We now project onto the Soviet Union those aspects of American society that don't fit with individualism, but that we can't avoid.[2]

Certainly it is fascinating to see how the Soviet enemy and the American bureaucratic enemy intertwine in Sylvester Stallone's popular recent movies. In *Rambo*, it is hard to tell who is worse— the Russians who stand behind the Vietnamese and actually torture Rambo or the soulless American bureaucrat who is willing to let Rambo and the American MIAs die rather than complicate his bureaucratic life. The movie ends with Rambo destroying the bureaucrat's large American computer with a machine gun. In *Rocky IV*, the Russian champion is almost a mindless robot, trained with the most sophisticated high technology. Rocky trains alone in the rugged Siberian hills, running through the snow, lifting logs, pulling sleds. And American simplicity and low technology defeats Soviet high tech.

Besides any long-term conflict between individualism and conformity in its values, the United States also continues to be haunted by its isolationist past. America had been shielded from foreign attack by geography. Americans had become accustomed to seeing European international relations as something dirty and to be avoided, except perhaps in an intervention on the side of good against evil. For a majority of Americans in the 1930s, Hitler was not a big enough evil. The United States refused to join the League of Nations after World War I, and it remained a holdout in the 1930s, even when another holdout, the Soviet Union, overcame its suspicions.

In the best of circumstances the United States would have found the transition from 1939 to 1946 very difficult. On the eve of World War II it had been a regional power with an elite that had little experience in foreign affairs. At the end of the war the United States was a superpower, nuclear weapons were changing the nature of international relations, and independence for colonies in Asia and Africa meant a rapid increase in the number of countries—and the type of problems—to be dealt with.

In the postwar period it was natural to continue to think in 1930s terms. The Soviet Union was seen as Hitler's Germany had been, and Americans pictured themselves as heroic Churchills, standing in the breach. The lesson was drawn from Munich that democracies would be taken in if they negotiate with dictators. The consequence of the vulnerability of the battleships at Pearl Harbor was an obsession with the possibility of surprise attack on vulnerable Minutemen rockets.

The sense that American participation in international relations was illegitimate was most easily overcome by defining the world as a struggle between good and evil. This was easy because the first country that the United States faced as a superpower posed an ideological and religious threat as well as a geopolitical one, and it was ruled by a leader who was incredibly secretive and hostile to Western ideas and the Western way of life. For a United States in which the church was historically the center of social life, the phrase "Godless Communism" could take on a quite emotional meaning. When President Reagan in his "evil empire" speech in Orlando, Florida, praised as a "profound truth" a father's statement that "I would rather see my little girls die now still believing in God than have them grow up under Communism and one day no longer believing in God,"[3] he provoked a deep response among many Americans.

To most Americans today, the 1930s seem a distant and forgotten time. International relations courses in college frequently do not even begin until 1945 and the start of the Cold War. Yet, the 1930s have had a continuing impact. All American presidents from 1960 to 1988, with the exception of Jimmy Carter, were born in the narrow period between 1908 and 1917. (When John Kennedy spoke in 1961 of the coming to power of "a new generation, born in this century," he was talking about Ronald Reagan, for the two men were only six years apart in age.) These men were already in their twenties or early thirties in 1941—Kennedy was twenty-four and Reagan, thirty—and their attitudes had been formed before and during the interventionist-isolationist debates of the 1930s. They found it particularly hard to shake some of the unspoken assumptions of that time precisely because a similar generation was ruling in the Soviet Union until the election of Mikhail Gorbachev.

The Kennedy-Reagan generation had to face a new and frightening world, and throughout their lives the Soviet Union came to symbolize a series of challenges to an older way of life. During the Great Depression, when they were in their twenties, the rapid growth and absence of unemployment produced by Soviet planning presented a major ideological challenge to the American economic system, which was sputtering. As America became more urban, more secular, and more bureaucratic in its government and private institutions, the Soviet Union was the symbol of the materialistic attack on religious values and of the threat of government and large organization to individualistic values.

After the war, when this generation was already in its mid-thirties, the Soviet Union became the country's first serious adversary as the United States left the cocoon of isolationism. At the same age, these persons had to face the loss of total security that the atomic bomb represented. As they entered their late forties and fifties, the mass introduction of the intercontinental rocket meant that the United States was literally thirty minutes from nearly total destruction.

The insecurities of the transition to superpower status retained special force in the 1980s not only because of the age of the president and his skills as a communicator, but also because the Reagan administration was the first in the postwar period to come out of the isolationist wing of the Republican party. President Reagan himself supported President Roosevelt in the 1930s, but he was raised in a small town in isolationist Illinois and came from Irish-American stock that generally was quite isolationist in the 1930s.[4]

Yet the problem went beyond the Soviet threat. The dominant memory of the Kennedy-Reagan generation from its youth was of another character altogether. Their world had been disrupted not by Soviet actions, but by conflicts between England, France, and Germany. The latter had not only destroyed Europe physically, but had torn at the American domestic fabric. World War I had created major tensions between the German-Americans and the English-Americans, and the Irish-Americans were also angry to be fighting on England's side at the time of the Irish uprising. The isolationist rejection of the League of Nations and the isolationist movement of the 1930s had an overwhelmingly ethnic base.

European wars inevitably had an impact on the national unity of a country of European immigrants—a fact that underlay George Washington's warning about entangling alliance. Postwar Americans were worried that their new superpower status might reignite old domestic battles. And, indeed, McCarthyism had the same ethnic base as the isolationist-interventionist debates, but with the "losers" of the 1930s exacting revenge on the "winners."

Fortunately, the Cold War with the Soviet Union created few ethnic problems in the United States, for the country contained few ethnic Russians. In fact, defense against a Soviet threat was very satisfying to the many Americans from Eastern Europe and the former Russian Empire, for all these peoples had suffered at Russian hands. Moreover, defense of Western Europe against the Soviet threat permitted the formation of a North Atlantic alliance that helped end any danger of yet another war between England, France, and Germany. The Soviet threat also permitted the American government to pursue domestic and foreign economic policies that were vital in preventing another Great Depression, and thus in defeating Communism as a doctrine.

In short, the same policy line worked to alleviate the insecurities produced by the old English-German antagonism, by the challenge of Communism as an ideology, and by the Soviet geostrategic threat. But because the Communist challenge in the West was quickly defeated and because the goals of policy within Western Europe (and Japan) could not be frankly discussed in public, we focused on the geostrategic threat in an exaggerated manner. We talked about the Soviet drive for military superiority, about Soviet war plans, about the danger of the Finlandization of Europe in ways that did not reflect reality—and that increased feelings of insecurity unnecessarily.

Small wonder that it has been so difficult to develop a sound relationship with the Soviet Union. Such a relationship has not so much involved correct decisions on deterrence theory or on the handling of Nicaragua. Rather it has involved coming to grips with our general relationship to the outside world and to the unknown. It has involved coming to grips with the possibility of the reunification of Germany and the laying to rest of the insecurities that came out of the first half of this century.

A New Generation in a New Era

For all our anxieties and insecurity, the last forty-five years have been good ones for the United States. Those who guided the United States through the postwar period had enormous achievements. In 1945 the expectation of a major postwar depression was very strong, and everyone feared that another prolonged depression would make the Communist model very attractive. Conflicts between England, France, and Germany had rocked the world twice in the first half of the century, and there was no guarantee that such conflicts would not be repeated in the second half of the century. Seldom has a generation—really two generations—been so successful in solving its major problems.

But now a new ruling generation is looming. Birthrates were low during the Depression and World War II, but then they soared beginning in 1946. The so-called Baby Boom generation of those born in the immediate postwar years is, therefore, quite large. In 1980, there were 26 million Americans who had been born between 1936 and 1945 (i.e., who were then between thirty-five and forty-four years of age), but 38 million who had been born between 1946 and 1955.

Those members of the Baby Boom generation born in the first decade after the war were also the Vietnam generation, for it was precisely a person born in 1946 who was twenty years old in 1966 and one born in 1952 who was twenty years old in 1972. This generation had a number of other interesting experiences. It was the group of schoolchildren who were subjected to tougher academic standards in grade school and high school after *Sputnik* (no wonder they rebelled against high standards in college). The big political events of its high-school years were the Cuban missile crisis in 1962 and the assassination of President Kennedy the following year. And then came eight years of Vietnam. Now the Vietnam generation is entering its forties, and by the early 1990s it will become the ruling generation.

As Arthur Schlesinger, Sr., pointed out,[5] the United States has had a cyclical politics in this century. The early 1900s, the early 1930s, and the early 1960s all featured "liberal" reform of some kind. (The trend also was observable in the early 1870s if we see the Reconstruction policies in the South in these terms.) The same thirty-year cycle is found on the conservative side as well: President Calvin Coolidge in 1925, President Eisenhower in 1955, and President Reagan in 1985 all represented similar moods within the population.

By all appearances, this thirty-year cycle has had a generational base. A country usually has a ruling generation that is more or less in its fifties. This generation in the 1960s had been the student activists of the New Deal thirty years earlier and it conducted a Great Society policy that had New Deal echoes. The college students of the 1960s were the children of these New Deal parents. Similarly, the ruling generation of the 1980s were the twenty-year-olds of the Eisenhower years. The students of the 1980s were the children of the Eisenhower generation, and they were described just as their fathers of the "beat generation" of the 1950s had been— materialistic, self-centered, uninvolved in social interests, career-oriented.

If the thirty-year cycle is to reassert itself in the early 1990s, we don't have to ask where its human base will come from. Not only will members of the Baby Boom generation be moving toward the age of fifty, but their children will be moving toward college entry.

In each of the three "liberal" cycles of the twentieth century, the central issue has been a different one, and this time, too, we should not expect a simple replay of the civil rights and Great Society years of the 1960s. The abortion issue of 1989 was only the most dramatic indication that the counterrevolution of the Moral Majority is likely to fade, for even the 1960s conservatives tended to be libertarian in the social realm as well as the economic. The economic solutions will probably remain market-oriented, but there will be much more attention to infrastructure and competitiveness.

Most of all, however, it is hard to imagine that the rise to power of the Vietnam generation and the passage of the last generation with isolationist memories of the 1920s and 1930s will not have a major impact on U.S. foreign policy. For the first time the country will be ruled by those who take atomic bombs and ICBMs for granted, and who also take for granted that the Soviet Union as now constituted is not an ideological threat.

Since the last forty-five years have been good ones, we have instinctively felt, "If it ain't broke, don't fix it." But, in fact, it is broke. The last twenty years have not been good ones for the Russians, and they are now determined to correct the situation. Economic reform *is* going ahead full speed, and the Soviet Union *is* going to integrate fully into the world economy. The new Soviet middle class wants it, and the maintainence of Russian power requires it. The Soviet Union is not going to continue to provide the threat that has helped maintain Western unity.

If the Soviet leadership continues to dismantle the Soviet military threat and to reintegrate into Europe, the Vietnam generation will surely demand that this country respond. Like the generation whose education was shaped by the challenge of *Sputnik*, it surely will demand that the United States meet the technological challenge of Japan and the EEC. Yet, it has been raised in a period in which the discussion of international relations has been seriously distorted by the inability to admit that a key function of NATO was not simply defense against the Soviet Union, but the maintenence of postwar stability in Western Europe. We need to think through our options with new-found clarity.

American Options in a New Era

As the United States faced the Gorbachev phenomenon in the late 1980s, it found it as difficult to discuss its options honestly as it had in the past. Conservatives said that the uncertainty of Gorbachev's prospects made caution necessary. Yet, if the argument were really a serious one, it would lead to very different implications. If Gorbachev is going to be overthrown, clearly the United States should negotiate a reduction of Soviet military power as quickly as possible while there is still an opportunity.

In reality, the public conservative argument is a convenient cover for several quite different—and more sophisticated—arguments:

First, the Soviet threat has been so useful in maintaining Western unity that the United States should avoid arms control and other types of agreement in hopes of maintaining the perception of a Soviet threat.

Second, Gorbachev is in such a difficult position that the United States can maximize the pressure and crack the Soviet system. It can promote the full democratization of the Soviet system if it does nothing to relieve Soviet economic conditions and if it helps to destabilize the non-Russian republics.

Third, Soviet economic perestroika eventually will improve Soviet military capability. Since this is not in America's interest, the United States should try to retard Soviet economic performance.

Of these three arguments, two of which are always unspoken, the first has essentially been destroyed by Gorbachev. The general secretary has legitimated such dramatic change in Eastern Europe, including East Germany, and has been so willing to reduce military expenditures, that nothing can prevent him from reducing the sense of Soviet threat. Once German reunification is seen as possible, a lack of American response could transform West German public opinion more dangerously than the disappearance of the Soviet threat. Henry Kissinger, who was the leading—if unacknowledged—exponent of this point of view, recognized this and began to speak of German reunification being unavoidable.

The argument that the United States should promote the democratization of the Soviet Union is a more seductive one. As Gorbachev decided that he would abandon the promotion of a world Communist revolution, the dissolution of Communist systems in Eastern Europe inevitably strengthened the hand of those most optimistic about such a course of development in the Soviet Union. The argument is seductive because it is always difficult to argue against the promotion of values one holds dear and because it is at least possible that the policy is achievable.

The greatest danger in conducting a crusade for one's own values or ideology, however, is that commitment to the values may lead easily to wishful thinking—or to the acceptance of the wishful analysis of those who hold these values abroad. It may lead to actions that are actually counterproductive. If the glue in the Soviet system is, as suggested here, the fear of the Russians that democracy will lead to the disintegration of the Soviet system, then strong American support of Soviet democrats, especially in the non-Russian republics, may discredit their cause rather than promoting ours. And since the means required to destabilize a Soviet system with a 2.8-trillion-dollar economy are surely more than the United States will expend, it is very easy to fall into the kind of policy that was followed in the Bay of Pigs or in the support of the Contras in Nicaragua: enough identification with rebels to make them appear foreign agents, but not enough support to do them any good.

Most important, concentration on the policy of world democratic revolution, especially in the Communist world, can distract us from more important goals. The most interesting argument against economic support of the Soviet Union is the one that seems the simplest: we should not help the economic rejuvenation of the Soviet Union because it will give the Soviet Union the potential for greater military power in the future.

The argument is interesting because the basic analysis is correct, but the conclusion is far more debatable. What is taken for granted but is far from certain is that it would be in America's interest for the Soviet Union to be militarily weak in the future. The Soviet Union bought a great deal of machinery from the United States between 1928 and 1932 for the great industrial projects of its First Five-Year Plan. In 1941, when the Soviet Union turned out to be an ally in the war against Hitler, these projects may have made the difference between victory and defeat. The U.S. government was very glad that it had permitted the sale of machinery a decade earlier. If the Soviet Union had been allied with Hitler in that war, the U.S. government would have regretted its earlier decision. In 1928 there was no way to know.

That is the problem that we face today. It is absolutely clear that *perestroika* will reduce the Soviet military threat over a five- to ten-year period, for the impact of a reduction in military spending will clearly be more significant than the impact of any improvement of technology on military capability.

Over the long run the United States can be no more certain whether it wants the Soviet Union to have a strong military capacity than it was in 1928. If the Soviet Union will be the main adversary in 2020 and afterward, we want it weak. If a country such as China or India has become dangerous and the Soviet Union is an ally against it, we want the Soviet Union to be strong. It seems to me far more likely that China and India will compete for the dominance of Asia in the twenty-first century and that Russia will be aligned defensively with the European powers, but there is no way to know.

Yet it is this uncertainty that is already the beginning of wisdom. In the immediate postwar period, the United States had a clear sense of the wisdom of Lord Palmerston's dictum, "England has no eternal friends and no eternal enemies, but only eternal interests." It reversed the World War II "friendships" with breathtaking speed. In the postwar period, however, we fell into the habit of seeing the Soviet Union as—to quote President Reagan—"the focus of all evil." If we thought that something helped the Soviet Union, we were inclined to oppose it. If something harmed the Soviet Union, we supported it. Weapons decisions were often justified by the amount of money the Soviet Union would have to spend to counter them, not by their intrinsic value.

Similarly, if a country was an ally of the Soviet Union, it was ipso facto our enemy. If a country was our ally against the Soviet Union, we often forgave it much. We were obsessed by insignificant defeats in Angola and Ethiopia, while we still defined Saudi Arabia and the Shah's Iran as "friends," even after the major defeat they inflicted on us in the 1973 oil boycott, simply because they were anti-Communist. In the 1980s we even provided funds to the most murderous of all Communist dictators, Pol Pot—the former ruler of Cambodia—because he was opposing the Soviet ally, Vietnam.

These tendencies were particularly strong under President Reagan. By 1980 it was clear that the Soviet Union under the half-moribund Brezhnev was, indeed, in a state of stagnation and that

Japan was a major challenge to American economic supremacy—maybe even another superpower. Yet the Reagan administration poured huge sums of money into the struggle against the Soviet Union at the expense of the United States economic position vis-a-vis Japan and the EEC.

Although the United States had often defined its goals in economic terms (President Coolidge was proud to say that the "business of America is business"), it became almost shameful for Americans to pursue their economic interests if they conflicted with noneconomic foreign policy goals, especially anti-Soviet ones. One of the most frequently used instruments of foreign policy became the economic embargo. There were exceptions (the American farmers overpowered the grain embargo on the Soviet Union), but policy toward Libya and Angola was typical. American oil companies functioned quite happily there, but the U.S. government scarcely supported them.

As we leave the postwar period, we need, first of all, to gain a sense of the multiplicity of our interests, the complexity of international relations, and the unpredictability of the future. If international relations were a game with a sixty-minute clock, if one were simply trying to score touchdowns against a single opponent with the same aim, then one could argue about which game plan to adopt. The assumption that the Soviet Union was the single enemy was precisely such an effort to simplify the game, but even in the postwar period it was an illusion.

In fact, there are many opponents with widely varying goals that change over time. And the game will never end. International relations is more like a continuously operating casino than a football game. It includes a variety of games with different rules, and the player had better know which he is playing and who the other players are. Historically, the long-term odds have been against the player. Recorded history goes back some six thousand years, and it is surprising how few countries have the same boundaries and political system that they had just two hundred years ago. And, of course, the people who represent the countries are at the table for only a very short time.

The big game at the casino is poker. The players may shift between an aggressive strategy and a defensive one from time to time, but they should know that they cannot win every pot. They will do far better if they know the odds, understand the psychology of the other players, keep cool, and bluff only judiciously. Since the stakes are the highest, they should be extraordinarily careful. The enormous danger of the game is that the individual players know that their time on earth and especially in power is very limited. Out of emotion, vanity, frustration, anger, or a desire to stay in power, they may take the most awesome and reckless chances with what is essentially other people's money.

The task of the United States is to sort out its interests and to try to develop a sense of their relative priority. Observers would vary in their ranking, but these interests clearly include (but are not limited to) the avoidance of nuclear war, the deepening of the ties among Western countries, the addition of still more countries (for example, the Pacific countries) to the "Western" community, the defense of the Western world against outside threats, the increase of the American standard of living and economic competitiveness, and the control of emerging ecological problems.

As we think about our different interests, we should remember that we need to continue to work to defend the achievements of the twentieth century. Nothing is more profoundly dangerous than the euphoric belief that we are at "the end of history," that all problems have been solved.

In 1929 we believed that economic problems had been permanently solved, that we had made the world safe for democracy, and that the Kellogg-Briand Pact had abolished war. The world soon looked very different. Indeed, if Hitler had been content with his conquests by 1941 and had not invaded the Soviet Union or challenged the Anglo-Saxon democracies directly, if he had lived as long as Andrei Gromyko and died in 1969, it is not at all certain that the system of fascist satellites he created would have collapsed by then. It is not certain that we would be speaking so confidently about the inevitability of democratic development.

In the postwar period, we have not had to face a really major, prolonged economic disaster, nor have we even proven that West-West economic relations can be smoothly managed without the unifying effect of the Soviet threat. We have never had to face a plague such as AIDS, let alone a terrorist use of atomic weapons.

We try to construct buildings to withstand earthquakes, and we should build the capability of withstanding similar economic and political shocks into the democratic system.

The looming problems in the Third World are even more visible. Even if we are on our way to a permanent end of war among the Europeans (within the North, to use more familiar language), the "South" remains much more populous and is plagued by poverty, severe ethnic conflicts, and all of the psychological problems of the transition to modernity. W. W. Rostow was right about Communism being the disease of the transition—of early stages of industrialization—but fascism seems to be a disease of middle levels of industrialization. This was certainly the case of Europe, and Iran suggests that the Third World will be no different.

It is within this framework that we need to think about our relations with the Soviet Union. Rather than debating whether we should help Gorbachev, Americans should have been asking themselves how Gorbachev could have helped us. A $200 billion deficit that produced high interest rates that hurt Latin America and that distorted flows of capital and trade did great damage to American foreign policy interests. When Gorbachev began offering major conventional arms reduction in 1986, we should have seen this as a way to solve our own problems before they distorted our economy too seriously. We did fall into cooperation with the Soviet Union in the Iran-Iraq war when both of us sent warships to protect Kuwaiti ships from Iranian attack, but we were slow to cooperate to bring the conflict in Lebanon under control. We gave no thought at all to how the Soviet Union might be developed into a counterpoint to Japan and the EEC in the economic negotiations that will characterize the international relations of 1990s.

This is not the place for a detailed discussion of the foreign policy of the 1990s. It is, however, the place to note that the insecurity of the postwar era has affected the educated moderates and liberals as much as the uneducated portion of the population. The liberals and moderates basically lost their voice in the face of the Reagan administration. At a time in the 1970s when the Soviet Union was stagnant and the desperately ill Brezhnev was leader, they never challenged Reagan's view that the Soviet Union was on the march. They did not even attempt such obvious tactics as denouncing him for selling American defenses and credibility short or for failing to recognize that the United States was winning the Third World because of the strength and attraction of its economic institutions (and we were winning for that reason, when he claimed we were in retreat). Instead they concerned themselves with saying that they were strong on defense, as if it had been them rather than the Republicans who had led the country during its loss of Vietnam.

The same response characterized the Reagan presidency. In 1984 public opinion polls showed that President Reagan was more vulnerable on foreign policy than on domestic issues. Yet the subject was almost completely ignored in the Democratic party platform and the speeches at the convention. In 1988 Michael Dukakis managed to avoid discussing Soviet-American relations almost totally in his campaign.

There was something almost bizarre in the claim that the Democrats would never regain public confidence until they showed that they were not afraid to use military force. Only a decade ago, a Republican vice-presidential candidate, Senator Robert Dole of Kansas, was repeating a much more long-standing cliché—namely that the Democrats were the party of war. Even more recently Jimmy Carter used much harsher sanctions against the Soviet Union in the wake of the Afghanistan invasion than President Reagan applied to the Soviet Union and Poland after the latter nation's imposition of martial law. The Democrats have had close ties with the very anti-Soviet trade unions and with a number of anti-Soviet ethnic groups.

Sophisticated analysts have long argued that a right-wing leader can often take actions—such as Nixon's opening to China—that a liberal cannot. One should not assume that less sophisticated persons are not listening to these assessments. The general public knows that a president may need great courage to stick to a chosen policy or to abandon it when events warrant. The public may worry—and justly so—that a moderate who is afraid to stand up to the conservatives in public debate before an election will also be afraid to stand up to them once in power.

When the United States was bogged down in Lebanon in 1983, Henry Kissinger and under secretary for political affairs Lawrence

Eagleburger of the State Department insisted that this was a crucial test of will in U.S.-Soviet relations and that the United States and Israel should take on Syria. President Reagan had the courage to disregard their advice and to retreat, and he quickly "retired" Eagleburger. (He also had the wisdom and sense of theater to cover his retreat with an invasion of Grenada.) Would President Mondale have felt able to do so? Similarly, if the Democrats had won the election, would defense spending have been limited to zero real growth in 1985, as it was, or would the final result have been some compromise between their 4-percent promise and the higher proposal of the Republicans? The likely answers to these questions may have made the public feel in 1984 that the real peace candidate was Ronald Reagan, not Walter Mondale.

Similarly the Democratic campaign in 1988 left the indelible impression that George Bush was more likely to have the courage to deal with Gorbachev than was Michael Dukakis. It was not the negative advertising about Willie Horton or the American Civil Liberties Union that decided the campaign, but the public sense that a candidate who did not know how to respond to this kind of attack would not know how to respond to conservative attacks on a reduction in military spending or meaningful agreements with the Soviet Union.

Americans wanted the sense that their president had the courage not only to stand up to the Russians when necessary, but also to retreat when necessary—and, furthermore, that he had the wisdom to know which issues warrant such response.

We are entering a new era in which new issues are on the agenda and a new generation is in power. This will not, however, change the essential demand of the population for a leader who has the vision to lead the country in uncharted international waters and the courage to stand up to ideologues committed to old dogmas or to a democratic world revolution or to those engaged in the bashing of old or new economic adversaries.

The time has come for the moderates to begin speaking about foreign relations—and to begin speaking with confidence. They should say that much of what we have taken for granted for forty years is not inevitable, but the product of a very peculiar time. The generation that has handled these past forty years is to be commended for solving the problems of 1945 and for having avoided nuclear war, and President Bush is likely to be the man who negotiates the end of the Cold War with the Russians. But what is necessary is to begin to define the relationship of the United States and the Soviet Union in a new era when the central concerns will be different from those of the postwar world. It is time for the United States to become a self-confident participant in international relations.

Acknowledgments

This book is really the summary of a lifetime of work, and the list of acknowledgments could go on for pages. Some of my deepest debts are to the theorists of totalitarianism and political development—men like Zbigniew Brzezinski, Barrington Moore, and Walter W. Rostow—from whom I learned in the 1950s. Their ideas, if taken seriously, have very different implications today when the Soviet Union is a middle-class society than they did in the 1950s.

It is impossible even for me to judge the impact on my thinking of my former wife, Sheila Fitzpatrick, or of the hundreds of Soviet officials and scholars who have been generous enough to talk with me over the years. In addition, Archie Brown gave a careful reading of an early draft, and Ivan Frolov and Marc Raeff gave detailed critiques of individual chapters.

Inge Hansen played an important role in the initiation of the project. Jane Isay and Bob Asahina improved the manuscript immeasurably with their editorial direction. I also want to acknowledge the contributions of Rhonda Johnson, assistant to Bob Asahina, and of Joe Smith and Mary Solak in Simon and Schuster's copy editing department.

Notes

INTRODUCTION

1. B. H. Sumner, *A Short History of Russia* (New York: Reynal and Hitchcock, 1943), 341.

2. *Pravda*, May 20, 1987, 3.

3. Seweryn Bialer and Joan Afferica, "Reagan and Russia," *Foreign Affairs* 61, no. 2 (Winter 1982–83): 257.

4. *Pravda*, December 11, 1984, 2.

5. *Pravda*, June 12, 1985, 1.

6. *Izvestiia*, June 1, 1985, 3.

7. See Jerry F. Hough, *The Struggle for the Third World: Soviet Debates and American Options* (Washington, D.C.: The Brookings Institution, 1986), especially chap. 4 on economic development.

8. *Pravda*, December 11, 1984, 2. Gorbachev's actual speech, which Soviet officials heard, was much more radical than the excerpts in *Pravda. Sovershenstvovanie razvitogo sotsializma i ideologicheskaia rabota partii v svete reshenii iun'skogo (1983 g.) plenuma TsK KPSS*, Materialy vsesoiuznoi nauchno-prakticheskoi konferentsii, Moscow, 10–11 dekiabria 1984 g. (Moscow: Politizdat, 1985), 7–45.

9. Sergei Schemann, "The Emergence of Gorbachev," *The New York Times Magazine*, March 3, 1985, 45.

10. *Pravda*, July 21, 1989, 3.

CHAPTER 1

1. "Rech' tovarishcha A. A. Gromyko na Plenume TsK KPSS," *Kommunist*, no. 5 (March 1985): 6–7.

2. There are two major sources for biographies of Soviet officials. One is the biographical directory of Supreme Soviet deputies, published after each Supreme Soviet election as *Deputaty Verkhovnogo Soveta SSSR* (Moscow: Izvestiia sovetov deputatov trudiashchikhsia SSSR, 1959, 1962, 1966, 1970, 1974, 1979, and 1984). The other is the biographical appendix of the yearbook of the *Great Soviet Encyclopedia* that includes all the Central Committee members selected at each party congress: *Bol'shaia sovetskaia entsiklopediia* (Moscow: Izdatel'stvo "Bol'shaia sovetskaia entsiklopediia), *Ezhegodniki* (Yearbooks) of 1962, 1966, 1971, 1977, 1981, and 1987).

3. See Sheila Fitzpatrick, "Stalin and the Making of a New Elite, 1928–1939," *The Slavic Review* 38, no. 3 (September 1979): 377–402.

4. Gregory Bienstock, Solomon Schwartz, and Aaron Yugow, *Management in Russian Industry and Agriculture* (Ithaca, N.Y.: Cornell University Press, 1948), 117.

5. Vera S. Dunham, *In Stalin's Time: Middleclass Values in Soviet Fiction* (Cambridge: Cambridge University Press, 1976).

6. Edward Crankshaw, *Khrushchev's Russia* (Baltimore: Penguin Books, 1959), 90–91. Crankshaw was incorrect in speaking of those born between 1890 and 1920, for Stalin had killed off the 1890–1900 cohort of administrators in the Great Purge. The reference to the "ages of forty and sixty" (i.e., born between 1900 and 1920) was the proper one. For evidence on the completeness with which these people dominated the Soviet political and administrative system in the 1950s, see Jerry F. Hough, *Soviet Leadership in Transition* (Washington, D.C.: Brookings Institution, 1980), 69–75.

7. The best discussions of Gorbachev's life before he became general secretary are found in Dusko Doder, *Shadows and Whispers* (New York: Random House, 1986), 281–94; Zhores A. Medvedev, *Gorbachev* (New York: Norton, 1986), 22–161; Christian Schmidt-Hauer, *Gorbachev: The Path to Power* (London: I. B. Tauris, 1986), 5–65; Martin Walker, *The Waking Giant: Gorbachev's Russia* (New York: Pantheon Books, 1986), 1–23; Ar-

chie Brown, "Gorbachev: New Man in the Kremlin," *Problems of Communism* 34, no. 3 (May–June 1985): 1–23.

8. Almost no information is available on Gorbachev's father and grandfather, and even the question of whether the former died in the war is in doubt. During collectivization, the first chairman of a farm was often an outsider, but then in the mid-1930s, as power evolved to the machine-tractor station that served the farm, the regime changed its selection policy to emphasize insiders. As a Soviet newspaper reported in 1968, "The chairman was an intelligent, not very literate peasant, who knew, however, how to count centners and rubles. [The peasants] respected him for his business sense; they invited him to weddings and christenings; they rebuked him at meetings, at the same time feeling sorry for him as they would a father burdened with great cares." (*Sovetskaia Rossiia*, February 6, 1968, 1.) After the war, the chairman became a returnee from the army and a tough disciplinarian again. It would make sense if Gorbachev's grandfather had been selected in the second wave of chairmen, but we do not know. See the discussion in Jerry F. Hough, "The Changing Nature of the Kolkhoz Chairman," in James R. Millar, *The Soviet Rural Community* (Urbana: University of Illinois Press, 1971), 103–20.

9. Yevgenii Yevtushenko, *A Precocious Autobiography* (New York: E. P. Dutton, 1963), 21–22.

10. Translated from the evening television news program, "Vremia," July 26, 1986, in Foreign Broadcast Information Service, *Daily Report—Soviet Union*, July 28, 1986, R9. A bit more formal version of the comments were printed in *Pravda*, July 27, 1986, 2.

11. Werner Hahn has called Frolov, with perhaps one aged exception, "the most controversial of reform-minded Soviet philosophers" in the 1960s and 1970s. *Postwar Soviet Politics: The Fall of Zhdanov and the Defeat of Moderation, 1946–1953* (Ithaca, N.Y.: Cornell University Press, 1982), 169–81. Also see Loren R. Graham, *Science and Philosophy in the Soviet Union* (New York: Knopf, 1972), 253–56. Frolov made his name fighting Lysenkoism in genetics, but then began emphasizing more broadly the importance of factors other than class ones in human affairs.

12. Fred M. Hechinger, *The Big Red Schoolhouse* (Garden City, N.Y.: Doubleday, 1959).

13. *Stavropol'skaia pravda*, February 6, 1979, 1.

14. For the secret speech and an analysis of it, see Bertram D. Wolfe, *Khrushchev and Stalin's Ghost* (Westport, Conn.: Greenwood Press, 1983).

15. *The New York Times*, March 10, 1986, B5.

16. This was a point emphasized by Ivan Frolov in private conversation. He cited *Mission to Moscow*, a highly propagandistic "pro-Stalin" film that whitewashed the Great Purge, as one that paradoxically undercut Stalinism in the long run. During the Cold War years, young people remembered, he said, that such a film could be made in the United States and did not believe that America was as black as it was being depicted.

17. For a sense of the festival, see *Life*, August 12, 1957, 22–57; *U.S. News & World Report*, August 9, 1957, 75–76; G. Abrams, "Talking with Russians," *The New Republic*, October 14, 1957, 13–16.

18. *Pravda*, May 20, 1987, 3.

19. *Washington Post*, November 7, 1987, A19.

20. Schmidt-Hauer, *Path to Power*, p. 49.

21. Crankshaw, *Khrushchev's Russia*, 130.

22. *La Repubblica*, January 18, 1986, 20–21. Translated in Foreign Broadcast Information Service, *Daily Report—Soviet Union*, January 29, 1986, 6.

23. At the time of the 1959 census, there were 8.4 million men in the Soviet Union who had been born between 1914 and 1923, compared with 17.5 million born between 1924 and 1933. The figures for women were 13.5 million and 19.6 million respectively. *Itogi vsesoiuznoi perepisi naseleniia 1959 goda SSSR (svodnyi tom)* (Moscow: Gosstatizdat, 1962), 50.

24. Soviet scholars often refer to this factor privately, and a *Pravda* commentator discussed it publicly in his own case. *Altaiskaia pravda*, July 30, 1977, 4.

25. Jerry F. Hough, "The Generation Gap and the Brezhnev Succession," *Problems of Communism* 28, no. 4 (July–August 1979): 12.

26. One of the strongest statements of this position was Konstantin M. Simis, "The Gorbachev Generation," *Foreign Policy*, no. 59 (Summer 1985): 3–21.

27. The chairman of the Soviet Women's Committee (a former astronaut) and several workers on the Central Committee were younger.

28. The biographies of the party officials are found in *Deputaty Verkhovnogo Soveta SSSR, Deviaty sozyv* (Moscow: Izvestiia sovetov deputatov trudiashchikhsia SSSR, 1974).

29. *Pravda*, November 28, 1978.

30. *Pravda*, September 21, 1978, 1. Zhores Medvedev claims that Andrei Kirilenko visited Stavropol in October to inspect the region and talk with Gorbachev. *Gorbachev*, 92. If this is true, the CIA found no evidence of such a visit at the time. Directorate of Intelligence, Central Intelligence Agency, *Appearances of Soviet Leaders, January–December 1978* (Springfield, Va.: National Technical Information Service, 1979), 45.

31. Gorbachev's behavior after his election strongly suggested that these men were his allies. Of twenty-eight regional first secretaries in the Russian Republic at the time of Brezhnev's death in 1982 who had been born after 1925, twenty-five were in the same job or higher at the time of the Twenty-seventh Party Congress in March 1987, and one of the others had died. This was in striking contrast to the major personnel change throughout the rest of the political and administrative system.

CHAPTER 2

1. Hans Rogger, *National Consciousness in Eighteenth-Century Russia* (Cambridge, Mass.: Harvard University Press, 1960), 4–5.

2. Suzanne Massie, *Land of the Firebird* (New York: Simon and Schuster, 1980), 213.

3. This theme has been emphasized by the Columbia historian, Marc Raeff. For example, see his *Understanding Imperial Russia* (New York: Columbia University Press, 1984).

4. Rogger, *Eighteenth-Century Russia*, 9.

5. Leonid Ilyich Brezhnev, *Memoirs* (New York: Pergamon Press, 1982), 6 and 11.

6. Oliver Radkey, *The Election to the Russian Constituent Assembly of 1917* (Cambridge, Mass.: Harvard University Press, 1957), esp. 78–80. For a general discussion of Bolshevik support before and during the revolution, see Jerry F. Hough and Merle Fainsod, *How the Soviet Union Is Governed* (Cambridge, Mass.: Harvard University Press, 1979), chaps. 1 and 2.

7. Alain Besançon, *The Rise of the Gulag: Intellectual Origins of Leninism* (New York: Continuum, 1981), 192 and 196.

8. Vladimir Il'ich Lenin, *Biograficheskaia khronika* (Moscow: Politizdat, 1975), 6:558–59.

9. Leo Pavlovsky and Harold G. Moutton, *Russian Debts and Russian Reconstruction* (New York: McGraw-Hill, 1924), 4–5, 55, 162, and 167.

10. A. O. Chubarian, *V. I. Lenin i formirovanie sovetskoi vneshnei politiki* (Moscow: Nauka, 1972), 261–81; Richard B. Day, *Leon Trotsky and the Politics of Economic Isolation* (Cambridge, England: Cambridge University Press, 1973), 73–76.

11. L. A. Fotieva, *Iz vospominaniia o V. I. Lenine (Dekiabr' 1922 g.-mart 1923 g.)* (Moscow: Politizdat, 1964), 20–22, 27–30, 33–34.

12. V. I. Lenin, "O monopolii vneshnei torgovli," in V. I. Lenin, *Polnoe sobranie sochinenii* (Moscow: Politizdat, 1978), 45:2203–23.

13. Moshe Lewin, *Lenin's Last Struggle* (New York: Pantheon, 1968); Stephen F. Cohen, *Bukharin and the Bolshevik Revolution* (New York: Knopf, 1973).

14. This statement and Lenin's evolving views on the subject are discussed in Edward H. Carr, *The Bolshevik Revolution, 1917–1923* (London: Macmillan, 1953), vol. 3. The quotation is on p. 115.

15. Robert C. Tucker, *Stalin as Revolutionary, 1879–1929* (New York: Norton, 1973), 149.

16. Ibid.

17. I. V. Stalin, *Sochineniia* (Moscow: Gospolitizdat, 1947), 5:224–25. K. P. S. Menon, *The Flying Troika* (London: Oxford University Press, 1963), 29.

18. Leon Trotsky, *The Revolution Betrayed* (Garden City, N.Y.: Doubleday, Doran, 1937), 192 and 198.

19. Nicholas S. Timasheff, *The Great Retreat* (New York: E. P. Dutton, 1946), 415.

20. George F. Kennan, *Russia and the West under Lenin and Stalin* (Boston: Little, Brown, 1961), 312 and 313.

21. For a discussion of Stalin's promotion policy during the Great Purge, see Jerry F. Hough, *Soviet Leadership in Transition* (Washington, D.C.: Brookings Institution, 1980), 79–85.

22. Ibid., 113–18.

23. Charles E. Bohlen, *Witness to History, 1929–1969* (New York: Norton, 1973), 65.

24. These debates, with the appropriate references, are summarized in Jerry F. Hough, "Debates About the Postwar World," in Susan J. Linz, *The Impact of World War II on the Soviet Union* (Totowa, N.J.: Rowman and Allanheld, 1985), 253–82.

25. Percy E. Corbett, "The Aleksandrov Story," *World Politics* 1, no. 2 (January 1949), 161–97.

26. "Diskussiia po knige E. Varga 'Izmeneniia v ekonomike kapitalizma v itoge vtoroi mirovoi voiny,' 7, 14, 21 maia 1947 g., Stenograficheskii otchet," *Mirovoe khoziaistvo i mirovaia politika*, no. 11 (November 1947), Supplement, 61.; E. Varga, *Izmeneniia v ekonomike kapitalizma v itoge vtoroi mirovoi voiny* (Moscow: Gospolitizdat, 1946), 319.

27. Petr Fedoseev, "Marksizm-Leninizm ob istokakh i kharaktere voin," *Bol'shevik*, no. 16 (August 1945): 32, 46, 51–54, 57.

28. See Vojtech Mastny, "The Cassandra in the Foreign Commissariat: Maxim Litvinov and the Cold War," *Foreign Affairs* 54, no. 2 (January 1976): 366–76.

29. *The New York Times*, June 24, 1941, 7. Arthur Krock suggested that Truman had made his proposal "not too seriously," but still found it "disturbing." Ibid., 18.

30. Milovan Djilas, *Conversations with Stalin* (New York: Harcourt, Brace, and World, 1962), 114.

31. For a description of 1945–47 as a period of détente, see William Taubman, *Stalin's American Policy* (New York: Norton, 1982).

32. Timasheff, *Great Retreat*, 404.

33. [George Kennan], "The Sources of Soviet Conduct," *Foreign Affairs* 25, no. 4 (July 1947): 510; Adam B. Ulam, *Expansion and Coexistence* (New York: Praeger, 1968), 400–404.

CHAPTER 3

1. E. Burdzhalov, "Vydaiushchiisia trud I. V. Stalina o strategii i taktike leninizma," *Kommunist*, no. 4 (March 1953): 41.

2. P. Fedoseev, "Sotsializm i patriotizm," *Kommunist*, no. 9 (June 1953): 27.

3. Nikita S. Khrushchev, *Khrushchev Remembers* (Boston: Little, Brown, 1970), 258.

4. Charles E. Bohlen, *Witness to History, 1929–1969* (New York: Norton, 1973), 370.

5. These lines were not included in the shortened version of the speech published in *Pravda*, June 12, 1985, and are found in Gorbachev's collected speeches. M. S. Gorbachev, *Izbrannye rechi i stat'i* (Moscow: Politizdat, 1985), 130.

6. N. Khrushchev, "Za tesnuiu sviaz' literatury i iskusstva s zhizn'iu naroda," *Kommunist*, no. 12 (August 1957): 17.

7. *Pravda*, June 16, 1983, 2.

8. Ibid., August 2, 1986, 1.

9. Alex Inkeles and Raymond A. Bauer, "Portrait of Soviet Russia by Russians," *The New York Times Magazine*, November 25, 1951, 28.

10. Nikita Khrushchev, *Khrushchev Remembers: The Last Testament* (Boston: Little, Brown, 1974), 78–79.

11. Berliner developed the concept of the ratchet in *Factory and Manager in the USSR* (Cambridge, Mass.: Harvard University Press, 1957), 78–79. He later discussed the difficulties of innovation at great length in his *The Innovation Decision in Soviet Industry* (Cambridge, Mass.: The MIT Press, 1976).

12. This is discussed in Edward A. Hewett, *Energy, Economics, and Foreign Policy in the Soviet Union* (Washington, D.C.: Brookings Institution, 1984), 100–143.

13. Nikolai Smeliakov, "Na vneshnem rynke," *Novyi mir*, 1986, no. 3:191–99.

CHAPTER 4

1. Mikhail Alazorov, *Front idet cherez KB* (Moscow: Znanie, 1969), 127. For a general discussion of this phenomenon, see Jerry F. Hough, "The Historical Legacy in Soviet Weapons Development," in Jiri Valenta, *Soviet Decisionmaking for National Security* (London: Allen and Unwin, 1984), 87–115.

2. M. S. Smirtiukov, *Sovetskii gosudarstvennyi apparat upravleniia*, 2d ed. (Moscow: Politizdat, 1984), 214–15.

3. "O plane podgotovki zakonodatel'skikh aktov SSSR, postanovlenii Pravitel'stva SSSR i predlozhenii po sovershenstvovaniiu zakonodatel'stva SSSR na 1986–1990," *Sobranie postanovlenii pravitel'stva Soiuza Sovetskikh Respublik*, 1986, no. 31:556. This law is invaluable both in laying out proposed legislation for five years in a way that revealed the strategy of reform and in giving the institutions that would participate in the drafting of each.

4. Smirtiukov, *Sovetskii gosudarstvennyi apparat upravleniia*, 214–15.

5. Thane Gustafson, *Reform in Soviet Politics: Lessons of Recent Policies on Land and Water* (Cambridge: Cambridge University Press, 1981), 39–52.

6. Jerry F. Hough, "Soviet Decision-Making on Defense," *Bulletin of the Atomic Scientists* 41, no. 7 (August 1985): 84–88.

7. This was first discussed in Maurice Friedberg, "Coexistence in Culture: Public Taste and the Pressure of the Ruble," in Peter H. Juviler and Henry W. Morton, *Soviet Policy-Making* (New York: Praeger, 1967), 121–33.

8. *Izvestiia*, June 1, 1985, 3.

9. Calculated from *Chislennost' i sostav naseleniia SSSR: po dannykh Vsesoiuznoi perepisi naseleniia 1979 goda* (Moscow: Finansy i statistika, 1984), 90 and 137.

10. Konstantin Simis, *USSR: The Secrets of a Corrupt Society* (New York: Simon and Schuster, 1982), 68 and 70.

11. *The New York Times*, December 19, 1985, A10.

12. Gorbachev provided the 1.5 billion estimate in *Pravda*, June 26, 1987, 3. The figure for total services is found in *Narodnoe khoziaistvo SSSR v 1985 g.*, *Statisticheskii ezhegodnik* (Moscow: Finansy i statistika, 1986), 488.

13. The statistics on the superagricultural ministry are from *The New York Times*, January 9, 1986, A8. The discussions of the reduction of production personnel are in V. Kostakov, "Odin kak semero," *Sovetskaia kul'tura*, January 4, 1986, 3; Vladimir Kostakov and Valerii Rutgaizer, "Konkurenty? Net, pomoshchiki," *Sovetskaia kul'tura*, January 8, 1987, 3. The figure of 60,000 came from early November.

14. Wolfgang Leonhard, *The Kremlin and the West* (New York: Norton, 1986), 160.

15. *Chislennost' i sostav naseleniia SSR*, 157.

16. Terese S. Zimmer, "The Politics of Regional Development in the USSR: A Case Study of Uzbekistan" (Ph.D. dissertation, Johns Hopkins University, 1983).

17. See Gail Warshofsky Lapidus, "Ethnonationalism and Political Stability: The Soviet Case," *World Politics* 36 (July 1984): 555–80.

CHAPTER 5

1. Yu. Andropov, "Uchenie Karla Marksa i nekotorye voprosy sotsialisticheskogo stroitel'stva v SSSR," *Kommunist*, no. 3 (February 1983): 9–23.

2. Friedrich Engels, "Speech at the Graveside of Karl Marx," in Robert C. Tucker, *The Marx-Engels Reader* (New York: Norton, 1972), 603.

3. For a good discussion of the Asiatic mode, including its role in debates inside Russia, see Samuel H. Baron, *Muscovite Russia: Collected Essays* (London: Variorum Reprints, 1980), chaps. 10 and 12. For Marx on Russia, see Teodor Shanin, ed., *Late Marx and the Russian Road: Marx and the Peripheries of Capitalism* (New York: Monthly Review Press, 1983).

4. *Pravda*, November 3, 1987, 2.

5. All these debates are discussed in Jerry F. Hough, *The Struggle for the Third World: Soviet Debates and American Options* (Washington, D.C.: Brookings Institution, 1986). If it had not been offensive to the scholars being analyzed, a provocative title such as *The End of Ideology* would have conveyed the book's theme better to an American audience.

6. See Alexander Yanov, *The Russian New Right* (Berkeley: Institute of International Studies, University of California, 1978), 39–61. For a more general discussion of the Russian right, see John B. Dunlop, *The Faces of Contemporary Russian Nationalism* (Princeton, N.J.: Princeton University Press, 1983).

7. See Julia Wishnevsky, "El'tsin Meets with Members of 'Pamyat," *Radio Liberty Research*, RL 191/87, May 19, 1987, and Walter Laqueur, "Glasnost's Ghosts," *The New Republic*, August 3, 1987, 13–14.

8. Dmitrii S. Likhachev, *Zametki o russkom* (Moscow: Sovetskaia Rossiia, 1984), 39–44. For the Zionist charge, see Laqueur, "Glasnost's Ghosts," p. 14, and the praise of Pasternak, see *The New York Times*, February 15, 1986, 13.

9. For a survey of Glazunov's work, including a reproduction of a remarkable painting that virtually rejects the entire Soviet period (*The Return of the Prodigal Son*), see Marina Khachaturova, "Unraveling the Mystery of the Soul," *Soviet Life*, no. 2 (February 1987): 48–53.

10. I. V. Aleshina, I. D. Ivanov, and V. L. Sheinis, eds., *Razvivaiushchiesia strany v sovremennom mire: edinstvo i mnogoobrazie* (Moscow: Nauka, 1983), 16.

11. *Krasnaia zvezda*, May 9, 1984, 2–3.

12. *Pravda*, October 2, 1987, 3.

13. *Narodnoe khoziaistvo SSSR, 1922–1982, Yubileinyi statisticheskii ezhegodnik* (Moscow: Finansy i statistika, 1982), 41; *Narodnoe khoziaistvo SSSR za 70 g.* (Moscow: Finansy i statistika, 1987), 523.

14. S. Frederick Starr, *Red and Hot: The Fate of Jazz in the Soviet Union, 1917–1980* (New York: Oxford University Press, 1983), 319–21.

15. N. N. Inozemtsev, A. G. Mileikovsky, and V. A. Martynov, eds., *Politicheskaia ekonomiia sovremennogo monopolisticheskogo kapitalizma* (Moscow: Mysl', 1971), 2:391.

16. N. Kapchenko, "Vneshniaia politika i ideologiia," *Mezhdunarodnaia zhizn'*, no. 10 (October 1970): 99.

17. Iu. Arbatov, "K voprosy o roli narodnykh mass v mezhdunarodnykh otnosheniiakh," *Mezhdunarodnaia zhizn'*, no. 9 (September 1955): 64 and 67.

18. See Jerry F. Hough, "Soviet Perspectives on European Security," *International Journal* 40, no. 1 (Winter 1984–85): 20–41.

19. V. Kobysh, in "Studio 9," Foreign Broadcast Information Service, *Daily Report—Soviet Union*, December 27, 1983, CC10.

20. *Pravda*, October 2, 1985, 1.

CHAPTER 6

1. The best summary of the Politburo rumors of 1980–85, with some second thoughts about them, is provided in Dusko Doder, *Shadows and Whispers* (New York: Random House, 1986).

2. The best presentation of such an interpretation is found in Stephen F. Cohen, "The Friends and Foes of Change: Reformism and Conservatism in the Soviet Union," *Slavic Review* 38, no. 2 (June 1979): 187–220, and his reply to critics, "What Is Fundamental? A Reply," ibid., 220–23. An undated version of the article is printed in Stephen F. Cohen, *Rethinking the Soviet Experience: Politics and History Since 1917* (New York: Oxford University Press, 1985), 128–57.

3. The classic study with this point of view is Michel Tatu, *Power in the Kremlin* (New York: Viking Press, 1969).

4. Nikita S. Khrushchev, *Khrushchev Remembers* (Boston: Little, Brown, 1970), 200–205.

5. Charles E. Bohlen, *Witness to History, 1929–1969* (New York: Norton, 1973), 370.

6. Edward Crankshaw, *Khrushchev's Russia* (Baltimore: Penguin Books, 1959), 54.

7. William Hayter, *The Kremlin and the Embassy* (London: Hodder and Stoughton, 1966), 38.

8. "Khrushchev on Modern Art," *Encounter* 20, no. 4 (April 1963): 102–3.

9. *Pravda*, September 21, 1958, 2–3. Translated in the *Current Digest of the Soviet Press* 10, no. 38 (October 29, 1958): 4.

10. N. Khrushchev, "Za tesnuiu sviaz' literatury i iskusstva s zhizn'iu naroda," *Kommunist*, no. 12 (August 1957): 17.

11. See the series of articles by F. Burlatsky and V. Gerasimov, in *Pravda*, June 5, 1966, June 20, 1966, and June 27, 1966.

12. Washington Post, November 7, 1987, A19.

13. See Jerry F. Hough, *The Polish Crisis—American Policy Options* (Washington, D.C.: Brookings Institution, 1982), 11–15.

14. Henry Kissinger, *White House Years* (Boston: Little, Brown, 1979), 553, 706, and 837.

15. Ibid., 837. For the German perception, see Archie Brown, "The Power of the General Secretary of the CPSU," in T. H. Rigby, Archie Brown, and Peter Reddaway, *Authority, Power and Policy in the USSR* (London: Macmillan, 1980), 149.

16. The evidence for Kremlinological conclusions is very esoteric, being based on subtle status indicators, nuances in speeches, career patterns, and bits of information (hopefully not misinformation and disinformation) from conversations with knowledgeable Soviet citizens. The centrality of the Chernenko-Kirilenko conflict and of Andropov's connection with Kirilenko has not been part of the conventional interpretation, but I feel very deeply convinced of it. The reason that it has not been emphasized, I think, is that we began to rely too much on rumors and not enough on other indicators, and the rumors were flowing out of the Andropov camp. Andropov did not like his connection with the old Brezhnevite, Kirilenko, discussed, nor did he like to see Chernenko treated as a major factional leader who was associated with a proworker policy. Rather the purveyors of the rumors found it useful to emphasize bureaucratic privilege as the Brezhnev (and Chernenko) policy precisely at the same time that Andropov moved toward a more inegalitarian wage policy that reversed their actual policy of excessive privilege for the worker.

17. Myron Rush, "Guns over Growth in Soviet Policy," *International Security* 7, no. 3 (Winter 1982–83), 167–68.

18. Medvedev was the pervasive source of an enormous amount of misinformation that shaped our view of Soviet politics in the first half of the 1980s—the main conduit of rumors from the Andropov camp—but he mainly talked with reporters and diplomats off the record. However,

some of his views are found on the record in Joseph Kraft, "Letter from Moscow," *The New Yorker* 58 (January 31, 1983): 104–8.

19. Others emphasized the role of the police, see Myron Rush, "Succeeding Brezhnev," *Problems of Communism* 32, no. 1 (January–February 1983): 3.

20. Marc D. Zlotnik, "Chernenko's Platform," *Problems of Communism* 31, no. 6 (November–December 1982): 70–75.

21. This is discussed at more length in Jerry F. Hough, "Soviet Decision-Making on Defense," *Bulletin of the Atomic Scientists* 41, no. 7 (August 1985): 84–88.

22. George Weickhardt, "Ustinov vs. Ogarkov," *Problems of Communism* 34, no. 1 (January–February 1985): 77–82, and Mary C. FitzGerald, "Marshal Ogarkov and the New Revolution in Soviet Military Affairs," *Defense Analysis* 3, no. 1 (March 1987): 3–19.

23. *Pravda*, April 23, 1982, 2.

24. For the sources of these various quotations, see Jerry F. Hough, "Soviet Succession: Issues and Personalities," *Problems of Communism* 31, no. 5 (September–October 1982): 33–34.

25. For the esoteric evidence on this point, see Jerry F. Hough, "Andropov's First Year," *Problems of Communism* 33, no. 6 (November–December 1984): 52–54.

26. *Pravda*, September 25, 1981, 1.

27. By far the best information on Andropov, the man, is provided in Doder, *Shadows and Whispers*, 118–63.

28. Jerry F. Hough, *The Struggle for the Third World: Soviet Debates and American Options* (Washington, D.C.: Brookings Institution, 1986), 223–25.

29. *Pravda*, September 29, 1983, 1.

30. Strobe Talbot, *Deadly Gambits* (New York: Random House, 1984), 116–51.

31. Marc D. Zlotnik, "Chernenko Succeeds," *Problems of Communism* 33, 2 (March–April 1984): 17–31.

32. *Pravda*, February 14, 1984, 2.

CHAPTER 7

1. *The New York Times*, March 12, 1985, A18. There were exceptions, one of the most notable being Archie Brown of Oxford University. See his

"Gorbachev: New Man in the Kremlin," *Problems of Communism* 34, no. 3 (May–June 1985): 1–23.

2. *The New York Times*, March 22, 1987, 1.

3. The writer, Mikhail Shatrov, brought these rumors out into the open. See his interview in the Finnish weekly, *Suomen Kuvalehti*, discussed in Foreign Broadcast Information Service, *Daily Report—Soviet Union*, March 13, 1987, R1. He also subtly presented the thesis of a serious contest with Grishin in a Soviet journal. "1917–1918: neobratimost' peremen," *Ogonek*, no. 4 (January 1987): 5.

4. *Pravda*, January 5, 1985, 1, and June 20, 1987, 1.

5. See Merle Fainsod, *How Russia Is Ruled* (Cambridge, Mass.: Harvard University Press, 1953), 131–38.

6. A. I. Mikoyan, *V nachale dvadtsatykh* (Moscow: Politizdat, 1975), 140–41.

7. Robert V. Daniels, "Soviet Politics Since Khrushchev," in John W. Strong, ed., *The Soviet Union under Brezhnev and Kosygin* (New York: Van Nostrand-Reinhold, 1971), 20.

8. The changes of regional first secretaries are reported in *Pravda* as they occur. The stenographic reports of the party congress proceedings contain a list of the delegates, together with the name of the party organization they represent. Through the painstaking effort of counting the number of times each organization is represented among the five thousand delegates, one can determine the size of its delegation.

9. Thane Gustafson and Dawn Mann, "Gorbachev's First Year: Building Power and Authority," *Problems of Communism* 35, no. 3 (May–June 1986): 1–2. For a different view, see Jerry F. Hough and Merle Fainsod, *How the Soviet Union Is Governed* (Cambridge, Mass.: Harvard University Press, 1979), 263–64, 473–78. William Hyland wrote in 1982 that "the story of Soviet politics over the last five years is largely a narrative of Brezhnev's accumulation of ever greater power." "Kto Kogo in the Kremlin," *Problems of Communism* 31, no. 1 (January–February 1982):19.

10. Some of the details about personnel are found in Jerry F. Hough, "Gorbachev Consolidating Power," *Problems of Communism* 36, no. 4. (July–August 1987): 21–43.

11. *Pravda*, July 21, 1989, 2.

12. *Pravda*, July 21, 1989, 3.

13. *Narodnoe Khoziaistvo SSSR za 70 let* (Moscow: Finansy i statiska, 1987), 528, 534.

14. *Pravda*, July 21, 1989, 3.

15. Jerry F. Hough, "Gorbachev's Strategy," *Foreign Affairs* 64, no. 1, 33–55.

CHAPTER 8

1. There are, of course, a range of interpretations of what is happening in the Soviet Union. Some think that little is changing, except, perhaps, in the "tone" of Soviet politics. (Adam Ulam, Alain Besançon, and Françoise Thom, in "What's Happening in Moscow?" *The National Interest*, no. 8 [Summer 1987]: 11–13 and 27–30.) Others see change in the political realm—usually reversible change—but little meaningful change in the economic reform. (Marshall I. Goldman, *Gorbachev's Challenge* [New York: Norton, 1987].) Seweryn Bialer, the leading Establishment political scientist, sees "much potential for change [but] it is much too early to speak about major change." (*Dissent*, Spring 1987, 188.) The best book presenting the case for "moderate reform" is Timothy J. Colton, *The Dilemma of Reform in the Soviet Union*, rev. ed. (New York: Knopf, 1986). The scholars closest to the position of this book are Archie Brown (in a number of articles, but in brief form in "What's Happening in Moscow?" 6–10) and Peter Hauslohner, "Gorbachev's Social Contract," *Soviet Economy* 3, no. 1 (January–March 1987): 54–84.

2. *Pravda*, June 12, 1985, 2.

3. Ibid., February 26, 1986, 2.

4. Seweryn Bialer, *The Soviet Paradox: External Expansion, Internal Decline* (New York: Knopf, 1986), 150–53.

5. Ibid., February 26, 1986, 5.

6. Ibid., 4.

7. *Pravitel'stvenny*, no. 19 (September 1989) p. 10.

8. *Khoziaistvo i pravo*, 1984, no. 10:23.

9. *Narodnoe khoziaistvo SSSR v 1984 g.*, *Statisticheskii ezhegodnik* (Moscow: Finansy i statistika, 1984), 327.

10. See V. P. Gagnon, Jr., "Gorbachev and the Collective Contract Brigade," *Soviet Studies* 34, no. 1 (January 1987): 1–23.

11. Ibid., September 20, 1986, 2.

12. Ibid., June 26, 1987, 3.

13. *Dageng Nyheter* (Stockholm), June 28, 1987, translated in Foreign Broadcast Information Service, *Daily Report–Soviet Union*, July 13, 1987, R16.

14. Interview in *Der Spiegel*, July 6, 1987, translated in Foreign Broadcast Information Service, *Soviet Union—Daily Report*, July 10, 1987, S1 and S4.

15. *Pravda*, June 26, 1987, 4.

16. For a detailed discussion of the changes in Soviet foreign economic policy and the implications for American business, see Jerry F. Hough, *Opening Up the Soviet Economy* (Washington, D.C.: The Brookings Institution, 1988).

17. For example, when the law on stock companies was first drafted, the Ministry of Justice based it on the law of the 1920s. However, these laws had been based on German laws of the prewar period, which emphasized various types of partnership and did not reflect modern corporate practice. The law had to be redone and was based to a large extent on the law of Delaware.

18. *Pravda*, February 26, 1986, 7.

19. For a comparison of the handling of this crisis with the earlier KAL 007 one, see Gail Warshofsky Lapidus, "KAL 007 and Chernobyl: The Soviet Management of Crises," *Survival* 29 (May–June 1987): 215–23.

20. *Literaturnaia gazeta*, July 2, 1986, 9.

21. Julia Wishnevsky, "Glasnost' on Anti-Semitism in the Soviet Union," *Radio Liberty Research*, RL 254/87, July 6, 1987.

22. *The New York Times*, February 16, 1987, 6.

23. *Pravda*, February 6, 1987, 2–3.

24. *Literaturnaia gazeta*, July 2, 1986, 9.

25. Evg. Evtushenko, "Fuku," *Novyi mir*, 1985, no. 9:3–58. The piece is translated in Yevgeny Yevtushenko, *Almost at the End* (New York: Henry Holt, 1986). The poem and citation are from pp. 40–42 and 51 of the latter.

26. *The New York Times*, August 15, 1987, 1. In this article, Philip Taubman has a long and illuminating interview with Andrei Voznesensky, the man pushing for a recognition of Chagall in 1987, in which Voznesensky discusses the difficulties—especially in getting a museum opened for Chagall in his birthplace of Vitebsk, Belorussia.

27. *Los Angeles Times*, April 5, 1987, pt. 5, p. 1.

28. *The New York Times*, April 9, 1987, 1.

29. "We Will Astonish You," interview with Aleksandr Yakovlev, conducted by Nathan Gardels, *New Perspectives Quarterly*, Spring 1987, 37.

30. *Pravda*, February 26, 1986, 9.

31. Robert A. Lewis, Richard H. Rowland, and Ralph S. Clem, *Nationality and Population Change in Russia and the USSR: An Evaluation of Census Data, 1897–1970* (New York: Praeger, 1976), 233.

32. The new policy on the social studies was signaled by an article by Yakovlev in, "Dostizhenie kachestvenno novogo sostoianiia sovetskogo obshchestva i obshchestvennye navki," *Kommunist*, no. 8 (May) 1987, 3–22.

33. *Izvestiia*, July 12, 1987, 3.

34. See the discussion in Jerry F. Hough, "The Politics of Successful Economic Reform," *Soviet Economy*, no. 1, 1989, 14–36.

35. *Izvestiia*, June 9, 1989, 9.

36. *Time*, February 2, 1987.

CHAPTER 9

1. *Time* magazine, September 9, 1985, 29. The version of the interview published in the Soviet press differed in small respects from the version in *Time*. This is my translation from the Soviet version, the most important difference being the inclusion of "rightly" (*spravedlivo*) in the Russian-language version. *Pravda*, September 2, 1985, 2.

2. V. Petrovsky, "Dogmy konfrontatsii (Ob amerikanskikh konseptsiiakh 'global'nogo konflikta')," *Mirovaia ekonomika i mezhdunarodnye otnosheniia*, no. 2 (February 1980): 21–22.

3. This is discussed in Jerry F. Hough, "Soviet Perspectives on International Security," *International Journal*, no. 1 (Winter 1984–85): 20–41.

4. When Gromyko met with Secretary of State Schultz in Geneva in January 1985, the response of Shevardnadze's Georgian paper, *Zaria Vostoka* was very forthcoming. Besides the official communiqué, it published 208 column lines about the meeting. *Zaria vostoka*, January 10, 1985. The newspaper of the Ukrainian Central Committee (headed by Vladimir Shcherbitsky), by contrast, gave only 27 column lines to the meeting in addition to the communiqué, and on the same page had a large article

on European weather that likely had a political meaning: "Western Europe: In the Grip of Snow and Frost."

5. *Izvestiia*, October 7, 1983, 5; *Komsomol'skaia pravda*, December 25, 1983, 1 and 3; *Pravda*, March 23, 1984, 3–4. The book was *Ot Trumena do Reigana* (Moscow: Molodaia gvardiia, 1984).

6. *Pravda*, April 24, 1985, 2.

7. Ibid., October 4, 1985, 2.

8. Ibid., February 26, 1986, 7.

9. Ibid., July 8, 1986, 2.

10. Ibid., June 27, 1985, 2.

11. Ibid., November 22, 1985, 2.

12. Ibid., November 24, 1986, 1.

13. Ibid., June 17, 1986, 4.

14. *Pravda*, July 29, 1986, 2, and April 11, 1987, 4.

15. "We Will Astonish You," interview with Aleksandr Yakovlev, conducted by Nathan Gardels, *New Perspectives Quarterly*, Spring 1987, 34.

CHAPTER 10

1. After his testimony on November 13, *The New York Times* editorialized, "With all the authority conferred upon him both by his position and the vast intelligence resources at his command, he demolished every essential position of those who have urged complacency upon us in the face of the Soviet economic challenge." *The New York Times*, November 16, 1959, 30. In April, the secretary of defense, Neal McElroy, had expressed the worry that the United States might "lose the economic competition." Ibid., April 24, 1959, 12.

2. Yurii A. Zamoshkin, *Lichnost' v sovremennoi Amerike* (Moscow: Mysl', 1980).

3. *The New York Times*, March 9, 1985, A18.

4. See Anne Edwards, *Early Reagan: The Rise to Power* (New York: William Morrow, 1987), 24, 47–75.

5. For a discussion of his father's evolving views on the subject, see Arthur M. Schlesinger, Jr., *The Cycles of American History* (Boston: Houghton-Mifflin, 1986), 23–48.

Index

275